Greenhill
Books

Hitler's Ardennes Offensive

Hitler's Ardennes Offensive

The German View of
the Battle of the Bulge

Edited by
Danny S. Parker

Greenhill Books, London
MBI Publishing, St Paul

Hitler's Ardennes Offensive
The German View of the Battle of the Bulge

This edition published in 2006 by Greenhill Books/Lionel Leventhal Ltd
Park House, 1 Russell Gardens, London NW11 9NN
and
MBI Publishing Co.
Galtier Plaza, Suite 200, 380 Jackson Street, St Paul, MN 55101-3885, USA

British Library Cataloguing-in Publication Data

Hitler's Ardennes offensive : the German view of the Battle of the Bulge
1. Germany. Heer – Officers – Interviews 2. Ardennes, Battle of the, 1944–1945 I. Parker, Danny S.
940.5′421

ISBN-13: 978-1-85367-683-3
ISBN-10: 1-85367-683-7

Library of Congress Cataloging-in Publication Data available

For more information on our books, please visit www.greenhillbooks.com, email sales@greenhillbooks.com, or telephone us within the UK on 020 8458 6314. You can also write to us at the above London address.

Printed and bound in Great Britain by
Creative Print and Design (Wales), Ebbw Vale

Contents

List of Illustrations and Maps

Acknowledgements

The editor wishes to express appreciation to the individuals who helped with this modest volume. At the National Archives this includes John E. Taylor and Robin E. Cookson. At the Library of Congress, Roland E. Cogan assisted with the hunt for specific portions of the John Toland Collection and Dr. Richard Sommers at the U.S. Military History Institute dealt with several last-minute questions. For special perspective on the senior commanders involved, I am further indebted to my German friends, Hans Dieter Bechtold and Ralf Tiemann. At Greenhill Books, Kate Ryle and Ian Heath accepted the challenge of deciphering the poor original typescripts with which we had to contend – no small task.

The photographs in the book are all attributed to the U.S. Army Signal Corps photographers from the period. The exceptions are the photographs of Generals Brandenberger and Blumentritt which are courtesy of Michael Wenger and his personal archives. Many thanks to all.

Danny Parker, 1997

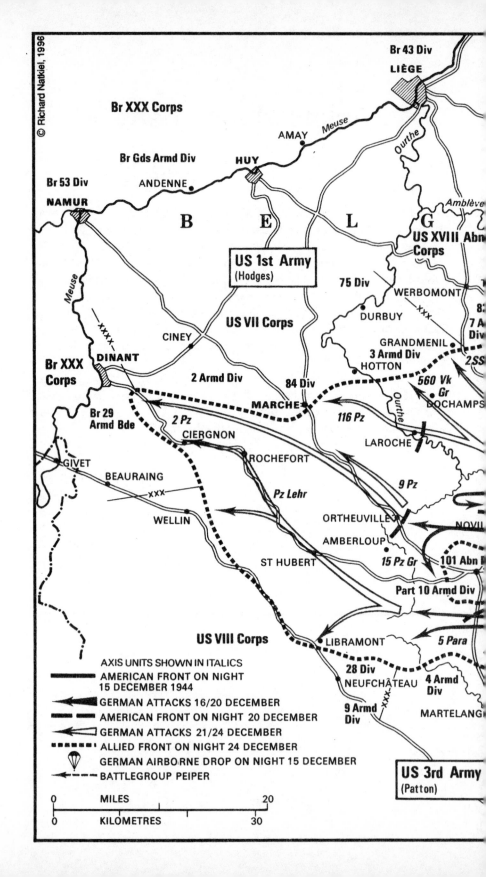

© Richard Natkiel, 1996

Br 43 Div
LIÈGE

Br XXX Corps

AMAY   Meuse

Ourthe

Br Gds Armd Div   HUY

Br 53 Div   ANDENNE

NAMUR

Amblève

B   E   L   G

US XVIII Abn Corps

Meuse

US 1st Army
(Hodges)

75 Div   WERBOMONT

US VII Corps   DURBUY   ×××   7 A Div

CINEY   GRANDMENIL   2 SS

Br XXX
Corps   DINANT   3 Armd Div
HOTTON

2 Armd Div   84 Div   560 Vk
Gr   BOCHAMPS

MARCHE

Br 29
Armd Bde   2 Pz   116 Pz   Ourthe

CIERGNON   LAROCHE

GIVET   ROCHEFORT   9 Pz

BEAURAING   ×××

Pz Lehr   ORTHEUVILLE   NOVI

WELLIN   AMBERLOUP

15 Pz Gr   101 Abn

ST HUBERT   Part 10 Armd Div

US VIII Corps   LIBRAMONT   5 Para

28 Div
NEUFCHÂTEAU   4 Armd
Div

9 Armd
Div   ×××   MARTELANG

AXIS UNITS SHOWN IN ITALICS
━━━ AMERICAN FRONT ON NIGHT
      15 DECEMBER 1944
◀━━ GERMAN ATTACKS 16/20 DECEMBER
━ ━ AMERICAN FRONT ON NIGHT 20 DECEMBER
◁━━ GERMAN ATTACKS 21/24 DECEMBER
■■■ ALLIED FRONT ON NIGHT 24 DECEMBER
      GERMAN AIRBORNE DROP ON NIGHT 15 DECEMBER
◀─ ─ BATTLEGROUP PEIPER

0   MILES   20

0   KILOMETRES   30

US 3rd Army
(Patton)

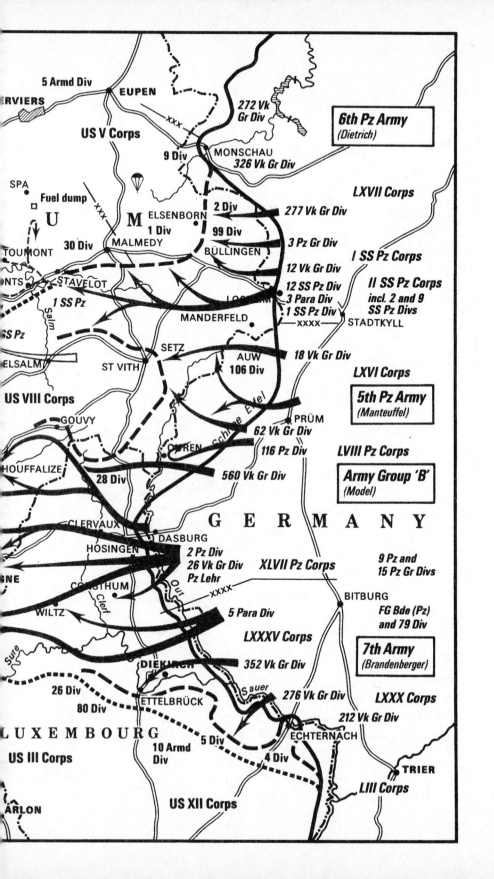

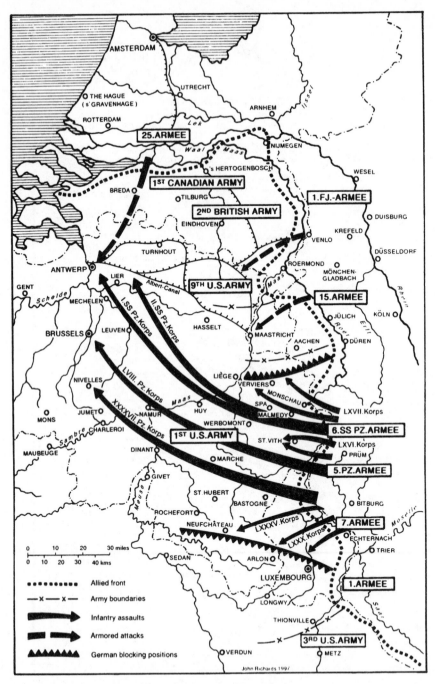

The German operational plan

Preface

BY DANNY S. PARKER

Immediately after the cessation of hostilities in Europe following the Second World War, U.S. Army military historians seized upon a fleeting opportunity. As victors, they had the ability to interview prominent enemy commanders being then held prisoner in various locations within Germany. The European Theater of Operations (ETO) Historical Section saw this as a remarkable opportunity to provide historical data of great importance for future documentation of the great conflict. The project was first initiated by Colonel William A. Ganoe, but the use of interviews with German participants in the Ardennes operations was begun by Colonel S.L.A. Marshall and Captain Kenneth W. Hechler. Colonel Harold Potter turned the operation into a fully-fledged program with the assistance of a group of able young officers. During 1945–9, this was performed with great enthusiasm and dozens of interviews and written accounts were composed on a variety of campaigns. However, no conflict elicited as much in the way of interviews, commentary and analysis as the Ardennes Offensive – known to the Allies as the Battle of the Bulge.*

The reason for this interest in the Ardennes was simple: in no other campaign had the enemy so dramatically embarrassed the Allies with their cunning and sheer ferocity as in this final great desperate gamble in December of 1944. Some confident American G-2s went from predicting impending collapse of the German war machine to pondering whether the enemy might somehow have developed some new weapon of unprecedented destructive power. Top secret espionage missions were again repeated to ensure that no further German progress had been made in the area of atomic research. Of course, all of this was untrue, but after the war the Allies were understandably curious about the nature of the German attack. Much of the collected data was instrumental in providing information for the U.S. Army green books – the official histories of the various campaigns. Until now, however, this material has largely been available only to military historians with a budget to see or reproduce the source documents. I have always seen this as unfortunate, given the insightful quality

---

* The codename for the secret German offensive was *Wacht am Rhein* (Watch on the Rhine). The source was a German patriotic poem of 1840 by Max Schneckenburger, set to music by Karl Wilhelm. With a defensive sounding name, *Wacht am Rhein* lent itself admirably for use as the cover name of the greatest German attack in the West since 1940.

of many of the manuscripts which I have had occasion to review over the years. Since many of these were composed by the German commanders without access to their official records, or maps, there are inevitable errors associated with memory. Yet this series of manuscripts, composed so soon after the end of the war, provides a compelling snapshot of the German view of the Battle of the Bulge.

While space precludes the inclusion of the majority of even the high-level material from army groups and armies, I have nevertheless made an attempt to select the best and to point out relevant documents that are not reproduced within these pages. Most of the original source documents are available at the National Archives Modern Military Branch in College Park, Maryland, in Record Group 338. Many are also available at the U.S. Army Military History Institute at Carlisle, Pennsylvania. Other documents, prepared specifically for U.S. Army historians as part of the R-series, are maintained on file at the Office of the Chief of Military History (OCMH) in Washington D.C. The editor is indebted to the assistance he has received over the years at these institutions. At the National Archives: George Wagner, John Taylor and Robin Cookson; at Carlisle: Dr. Richard Sommers and Michael Keogh; and at OCMH: Ms. Hannah Zeidlick.

This initial volume examines the German perspective of the battle from the point of view of the field-army commanders. The available resource material paints a remarkable portrait of German intentions and operations within those desperate days of late 1944. As much as possible, the editor has left the original record intact. However, in some instances, translation, grammar or brevity has dictated alteration. In other cases, the editor has taken the liberty of correcting the flawed phonetic spelling of the American interviewers. And, of course, there are factual errors in the German testimony. In cases where the editor has information conclusively showing entries to be untrue, these are noted for correction or explanation.

1

Sixth Panzer Army in the Ardennes Offensive

Interviews with SS-Oberstgruppenführer Josef 'Sepp' Dietrich

Introduction

The two interviews which are linked below provide perspectives on the Ardennes Operations from the head of the Sixth Panzer Army, Oberst-gruppenführer und General der Waffen SS, Josef 'Sepp' Dietrich. As the most powerful army in the German counteroffensive, special importance was attached to the progress of Dietrich's forces. The first interview was conducted by an unknown officer on 10 July 1945; the second was conducted by First Lieutenant Robert E. Merraim on 8–9 August 1945 at the U.S. Interrogation Center in Oberursel, Germany. Merraim commented that 'General Dietrich is regarded with low esteem by his fellow officers. He did not seem to have a grasp of the operations of his army in the Ardennes and was unable to present a comprehensive picture of the happenings.'[1] The first interviewer provided another point of view:

> General Dietrich has been described as a crude, loquacious, hard-bitten, tough man whose statements are often inaccurate – yet as a man having a great deal of common sense. His fellow officers, the more class-conscious, were often shocked at his language and behavior and attribute his meteoric rise in the Army to his party connections.

Dietrich himself was a burly Bavarian and a personal friend of Hitler from the early beer-hall days of National Socialism. 'He is a mixture of cunning, ruthlessness and toughness,' Hitler once characterized.[2] Although later confessing that the duty made him 'sick', Dietrich never denied that he presided over the execution of Erich Röhm and the other SA leaders at Stadelheim Prison on the 'Night of the Long Knives'. But beyond this and other dark incidents, Dietrich has been frequently maligned in historical accounts as a dense alcoholic who had little practical command ability, and had only ascended to his rank by virtue of his friendship with Hitler. While it is true that Dietrich was fond of cognac and had lost much of his fire by late 1944, he was also a very effective front-line commander. A father to his troops, Dietrich was extremely devoted to those under his command, and during the course of the conflict he led the men of the Waffen SS through some of the harshest fighting in the history of warfare.[3] Not being a member of the regular army, nor schooled by the General Staff, the rough-edged SS general was held in considerable contempt by many of the Prussian officers. But Dietrich was a direct and no-nonsense commander, and one of the few who dared tell Hitler, at their briefing on 12 December, that he did not believe the Ardennes operation was feasible.

I grew so big with these plans . . . I had merely to cross a river, capture Brussels and then go on and take the port of Antwerp. And all this in the worst months of the year, December and January, and through the countryside where snow was waist-deep and there wasn't room to deploy four tanks abreast, let alone six panzer divisions; when it didn't get light until eight in the morning and was dark again at four in the afternoon; with divisions that had just been reformed and contained chiefly raw, untried recruits; and all this at Christmas time.[4]

And it is a matter of record that only the day before, Hitler had overruled Dietrich's desire to use the 1st SS Panzer Division to personally lead an initial breakout attempt with a dawn tank-assault.[5] One senses, however, from the following interview material, that Dietrich did leave the operational aspects of battle to his subordinates. Certainly, his candid views show the disdain typical of SS men who, having experienced the savagry of the far-flung battle in Russia, held in contempt all those without front-line experience. Major Hechler described the scene prior to the interview at Oberursel:

Dietrich scuffed into the interrogation room, looking very much like the chauffeur that he once was. M/Sgt. Edward L. Kropf, the interpreter who had been assigned, pointedly kept his seat while Merraim and I rose to give Dietrich a smiling greeting. Sgt. Kropf looked at me as if to say, 'Why are you getting up for that SS bastard?' Merraim shot most of the questions at Dietrich, and only now and then would I interrupt . . . I now remember only one question I wanted answered, and that was concerning the belief of the members of the Ardennes section that Dietrich's Army had been aiming to encircle Liège. Just to pin this one down once and for all, and in the secret desire to see Jodl's insistence that this was not the case supported, I asked Dietrich: 'We have a captured map of the Liège area showing two pincer movements around the city. To what were these referring if you had no intentions of moving around Liège?' Dietrich's answer was direct: 'I wasn't interested in the least in Liège because I didn't have enough troops to take it or even to surround it. The town is on low ground and it is hard to get into it . . . This could have been a Fifteenth Army map made in anticipation of their later move forward on our flank.'[6] Although Dietrich was a pretty thick-skulled character and his answers were somewhat fuzzy, I could see that Merraim had been bitten by the bug of interviewing . . .[7]

Danny S. Parker

Interview 1

I. Organization and Training

1. Q: When was Sixth Pz Army formed?

A: The Army was formed in Sep and Oct 44 in Westphalia with 1, 2, 9, and 12 SS Pz Divs. Later, 12 Volks Gren Div, 3 FJ [Fallschirmjäger] Div, and another infantry division were added.

At the time of the Ardennes, Sixth Army was not an SS Army, but was a regular army unit. Headquarters in Berlin would not allow my Army to become an SS Army until Apr 45, when we were in Hungary, because I had both SS and Wehrmacht troops under my command. In Hungary, there was another Sixth Army and, to distinguish between the two, my Army was designated Sixth SS Pz Army. At that time, I had only SS troops with me.

All of these panzer divisions in the army had taken a bad beating on the Western Front, and it was very difficult to get replacements for them.

2. Q: Did the High Command always have in mind the use of your Army in a counterattacking role?

A: At first, the Army was just a reserve force; later, however, with all of its panzer divisions, it was an attack unit.

3. Q: Did you have much difficulty in getting tank replacements for your battered units?

A: The entire Army received about 250 tanks for the period Oct–Dec 44. Very few new vehicles were received; primarily, old vehicles were kept in good running condition.

4. Q: Did your troops have any special training in Westphalia? What was the status of their training?

A: Status of their training was medium, as 60% of the combat elements had less than six to eight weeks of training. An armored division has 17–18,000 men, of which 9–10,000 are service elements. Replacements, for the most part, were from the air force, navy, and other army units. Most of them were young men from 18 to 25 years of age. As unit training was carried up through battalion, but no higher, they were given only general training. The main trouble was a lack of gasoline.

5. Q: It was noted that numerous times your units attacked in the dark in the Ardennes. Did your Army have any special night training during its training period?

A: Very little night training was given because of the lack of gasoline; however, most of the tank drivers were experienced hands. The Army allotted sufficient gas for five hours' driving for each driver.

6. Q: Were your divisions up to strength at the start of the Ardennes Offensive?

A: One can say that, in general, they were up to strength. Each of the panzer divisions had about 17,000 men, of which 9–10,000 were rear echelon or service troops and the rest actual combat men.

7. Q: What extra tank units were with your Army?

A: One battalion of 45 Mk VI tanks was with 1 SS Pz Div. In addition, we had two mixed battalions of Mk V and Mk IV tanks, totalling 40 tanks, alternating between I and II SS Pz Corps and LXVII Inf Corps. Some 500 tanks in all were available to the Army, of which 100 were not in use at the start of the attack. These 100 tanks had been deadlined because of minor mechanical difficulties incurred during the three-day march. (Interviewer's Note: When I expressed surprise at the fact that 20% of the tanks would be deadlined in a three-day trip, Gen Dietrich expressed surprise at my surprise and said that this was normal for such a trip. He added that they were mostly minor deficiencies which were reparable in two to three days at the most, and sometimes within two to three hours.)

8. Q: Did your Army use searchlights in this attack?

A: No. Their use had been demonstrated to all commanders and we had one company experiment with them. However, we did not use them because of the lack of time for training with them. I also thought that the weather would not favor their use. Two main ideas with the searchlights are to provide markers for giving direction of attack, and to blind the enemy.

II. Movement To The West

9. Q: When did your Army move to the West?

A: About 15 Nov 44, the I SS Pz Corps began its move to the area north of Cologne, where it was sent because of the American–English attack aimed at Düsseldorf. The mission of the Corps was to guard against a breakthrough into the Ruhr. About ten days later, II SS Pz Corps began its move into the area southwest of Cologne to protect that city.

10. Q: Did you think the American forces could move across the Roer River toward Cologne?

A: You came very close to breaking through our line. My Army saved the situation as the other units were in very bad shape. During Nov 44, your threat was great, but the bad weather kept you from getting through.

11. Q: Were your units committed as an Army?

A: Three of the divisions – 12 Volks Gren Div, 3 FJ Div, and 162 Inf Div [sic] – were committed into the line, but as reinforcements rather than with an Army front.

12. Q: Just where were your Corps before 12 Dec 44?

A: One Corps was in the Bonn area and the other was in the general Cologne area. They had moved to these areas at the end of Nov 44 after the Ninth US Army attack had been stopped. Their mission was to be a reserve.

They were moved south because the area to the north was too crowded with troops.

13. Q: Did you have a mission, a potential employment with plans for certain possible actions?

A: The only mission in the first part of Dec 44 was training. Since armored units are for the attack, we were training for an attack but with no specific mission in mind. Panzer corps usually are employed only as attack forces, unless they are 60–70% destroyed, at which time they may be used in the defense.

III. Planning the Offensive

14. Q: When was the first time you heard of the plans for an offensive in the Ardennes?

A: On 12 Dec 44, the Führer addressed us at a meeting and said that a winter offensive would be launched. He gave a long speech, and said that they had to do something. At that time, however, Hitler did not give the time of the attack. He just said that they would have enough planes and tanks. I told Hitler that I wasn't ready to attack with my Army and that we didn't have the ammunition or fuel to carry it through successfully. The generals were all in a line waiting to speak to Hitler and I had only a minute to tell him this before the line moved on. He said that I would have all I needed.

15. Q: Weren't you able to talk to him longer, in view of your long acquaintance with him?

A: During the last eight years, I had gotten further and further away from him and hadn't seen much of him because I was constantly in the field with my army work.

16. Q: Weren't you at a meeting on 23 Nov 44, when plans were discussed for the Ardennes Offensive?

A: Yes, I now remember a meeting on that date; however, we only discussed the possibility of committing Sixth Pz Army and whether it would be ready for commitment if needed. Model said it would be, but I said it would not be ready in Dec 44. We talked only in terms of a general winter offensive and did not specify date or time or place. (Interviewer's Note: When questioned again on this, Dietrich reaffirmed his statement on this meeting. He said he wasn't there the entire time, and that it is possible that details were discussed while he was gone. He remembers that Model, Jodl, Hitler, and Keitel were there.) About 4 or 6 Dec 44, Model told me something was coming, but he was very secretive and said Hitler had not yet decided the time or place.

17. Q: Then you made no plans for the attack prior to 12 Dec 44?

A: Plans for the attack were made by Model at Army Group. About 13 or 14 Dec 44, I made corps assignments and decided on I SS Pz Corps to lead the attack.

18. Q: Is it possible that Gen von Manteuffel (Fifth Pz Army) knew of the attack before you?

A: It is possible because he might have heard through friends or unofficially. Manteuffel had a lot of good connections.

19. Q: When did you know the date was definitely 16 Dec 44?

A: On 13 or 14 Dec 44, I was told the attack would be 15 Dec 44. I said I couldn't get my troops there in two days, so the attack was postponed one day. At that, my units had to start the attack right from a march.

20. Q: Could you give us any ideas as to why you were not consulted prior to the 12 Dec 44 Meeting?

A: Army commanders are not consulted very much. All of the higher leaders in the Army knew that I needed more time to get my Army in shape for an attack. The method in the German Army is for plans to come from above, based on reports from below. I knew about the attack too late and couldn't give my best advice to my division commanders. After we knew of the attack, no one dared talk about it for fear of reprisal.

IV. Army Attack Plan

21. Q: Would you state your general plan of attack in the Ardennes?

A: The general order of attack was for I SS Pz Corps to be the attacking Corps and move toward Stavelot–Stoumont in the general direction of Liège–Huy. I instructed the commanders to secure a bridgehead any place between those two points along the Meuse. They were then to move in the direction St Trond–Hasselt–Antwerp. It was wishful thinking to hope that we could cut the British Armies off from the south. Our boundary was south of Liège because roads and terrain were such that our units could not move to the north.

22. Q: We have a captured map of the Liège area showing two pincer movements around the city. To what were these referring if you had no intentions of moving around Liège?

A: This could have been a Fifteenth Army map made in anticipation of their later move forward on our northern flank. I wasn't interested the least in Liege because I didn't have enough troops to take it, or even surround it. The town is on low ground and it is hard to get into it. I didn't care about taking Huy either.

23. Q: What was your plan for the attack of I SS Pz Corps?

A: I SS Pz Corps was to be the attack Corps with 12 SS Pz Div on the right in the area Krinkelt–Rocherath–Wirtzfeld, 1 SS Pz Div in the center, and 12 Volks Gren Div on the left.[8] The attack of 12 Volks Gren Div remained in the vicinity of Holzheim–Honsfeld– Heppenbach–Medendorf.

24. Q: Was the infantry to make the first attack?

A: Yes, but not to a great extent. The divisions that were in position in the line before the attack should have helped with the attack, but they didn't because these Fifteenth Army units had been in the line for a long time. They were supposed to go to the Elsenborn Ridge, but they didn't get there. On 15 Dec 44, the Fifteenth Army's southern Corps (LXVII Inf Corps) was given to me.

25. Q: What plans had you made for the use of II SS Pz Corps?

A: This corps was to be kept in reserve in case Ninth US Army should counterattack from the north, in which case they would be committed to protect the flank and push them back. They were to have been able to do this at any time until I reached the Meuse River. An alternative use for this Corps was to carry the attack should I SS Pz Corps fail. They were then to move on a line St Vith–Vielsalm and continue on to the objective, the Meuse. This Corps remained in the same assembly area, which was only 40–50 km from the starting point, until it was finally committed.

26. Q: What were the plans for the use of von der Heydte's paratroops?

A: They were under the command of Model. They originally were to have been used on 16 Dec 44, but, because of the weather (or perhaps the lack of fuel), they were not used at that time. I believe Model wanted to show that the Luftwaffe had something to do with the attack. I wanted them to jump in the vicinity of Elsenborn, but I was not consulted on their use. I didn't know exactly what their mission was, and, as an army commander, I had nothing to say about what they were to do. Their liaison officer was with Model, not at my headquarters.

27. Q: When von der Heydte was captured, he was very angry because the panzer units had not contacted him as promised. Were there plans for 12 SS Pz Div to move north to contact these units?

A: As far as I know, the attacking corps had no order to contact the paratroopers.[9] I thought they might be able to do it, but they couldn't succeed in widening the salient. They would have succeeded had they captured the Elsenborn Ridge, which was vital territory.

28. Q: What was the planned use of LXVII Inf Corps?

A: The Fifteenth Army Corps (LXVII) was to move from Monschau down toward Malmédy to cut off the Elsenborn Ridge and make a junction with 12 SS Pz Div on the south. They did not have communication with the paratroops and, because of that, could not tell them where they were. Because they lacked good communications, they thought that the paratroopers had all been captured.

29. Q: When did you hope to reach the Meuse River?

A: According to the original plan, I was to reach the Meuse on the second or third day. (Interviewer's Note: When told that Gen Jodl had said it was expected that reconnaissance troops would reach the river the first day, Dietrich said Jodl had waged war only on maps and that he had never had a field command. He added that Model also was always over-optimistic.)

30. Q: What were the plans for using Operation 'Greif'?

A: I had nothing to do with the planning of this operation and can't tell you much about it. I could not give them any orders. Skorzeny, who was running this operation, had special orders. He was supposed to get to the rear areas by Huy and Liège and cause trouble in general. The units were put in with I SS Pz Corps, but I didn't get any orders. Part of the operation was to destroy radio and telephone communications in the rear areas, give false orders, find fuel dumps, and capture bridges intact.

31. Q: What about the special tank units equipped in part with American tanks and equipment?

A: These units may have used the same roads as mine, but they were not under my control and were not used in the initial attack. On the morning of 16 Dec 44, they had not arrived, but it is possible that they had arrived by noon of that day. The I SS Pz Corps did not get any special communication from the Operation 'Greif' people. On 20 Dec 44, the Corps Commander asked me to take the 'Greif' people out of his Corps because they were making false statements and hindering the operation of the Corps by driving between vehicles and doing exactly as they pleased. It was interfering with the control of the Corps.

32. Q: Do you know of any successes these special groups had?

A: No, I don't know of any. I heard that in one case a regiment was directed in the wrong way. Is this true? (Interviewer's Note: Gen Dietrich laughed when I told him it was probable that one of these men had posed as an MP and misdirected part of 84 Inf Div (US) as it moved south into the Ardennes area.)

33. Q: Did you hear anything about a plot to take high personages?

A: No, but it is possible that they may have been after some of the division or corps commanders. I have never captured one in the ten years I have been fighting.

34. Q: The personage referred to was Gen Eisenhower. Do you know anything about that?

A: Always plans, plans, plans. It would be very difficult to locate a personage that high.

35. Q: Would you go into more detail regarding your plan of attack?

A: As 1 SS and 12 SS Pz Divs moved out, the flank was to be covered by 12 Volks Gren and 3 FJ Divs. The 12 Volks Gren Div had been with I SS Pz Corps at the start of the attack, and 3 FJ Div was given to the Corps on 18 Dec 44.

36. Q: Just what was Fifteenth Army expected to do?

A: When I had reached the Meuse, Fifteenth Army was to start an attack of its own from the east, moving north of Aachen. This attack was not to be directed at Aachen, as Fifteenth Army had been too weakened by the Nov

44 battles and did not have enough troops to take the city. Nor was the attack to come south from the Geilenkirchen area. Fifteenth Army, however, was absolutely worthless as an attack army.

37. Q: Are the routes as shown on captured maps – the five routes of 1 and 12 SS Pz Divs – accurate? (Interviewer's Note: This map showed five routes which, from north to south, were: (a) from Hollerath to Rocherath, west to Camp d'Elsenborn, and then to Polleur; (b) to Rocherath, Wirtzfeld, then west to Sart; (c) Losheim, Malmédy, to Spa; (d) south of Losheim to Stavelot; (e) Krewinkel west to Trois Ponts.)

A: Yes. These were the original routes that we planned to use and whichever division got there first, could have taken Malmédy. On 15 Dec 44, it was planned that the attack would move toward Liège, but on 16 Dec 44, this was changed to move the attack farther south as it already was apparent that the northern half of the attack was not progressing. If the original plan had not bogged down, we would have gone north and south of Liège. I gave the corps commanders freedom to decide whether to go north or south of the city; in fact, wherever they could go in that general area to get across the river. Later, however, after the attack had started, I changed this and ordered that they should cross only between Liège and Huy, both exclusive. At no time did we contemplate taking Liège. It was always planned to bypass the city and cut it off. These five routes were in the initial plans. (Interviewer's Note: Gen Dietrich was not exactly certain which divisions were to use which routes, but thought that 12 Volks Gren Div was to use the southern one. It was apparent that he could not remember accurately enough to vouch for the statement, so the subject was dropped. He was sure that 1 SS Pz Div was on the southern routes and 12 SS Pz Div on the northern routes.)

38. Q: How did you plan to use 3 FJ Div and 3 Pz Gren Div?

A: I do not remember 3 Pz Gren Div being in this area at all. The 3 FJ Div was to move to the flank of the Army as one of the screening divisions.

39. Q: Were your troops told to rely on our gas to complete your attack?

A: Why, sure, if they could find the dumps; however, they didn't know the exact locations of them. We didn't get one liter of your gasoline.[10] (Interviewer's Note: When told that one of his reconnaissance units had been 300 yards from the largest gas dump on the Continent – 2,200,000 gallons – Gen Dietrich made a wry face, and then said that he had had no idea of that, but that our troops probably would have burned the gas before he could have gotten to it.)

40. Q: How much did you know of our dispositions at the time of the attack?

A: We knew you were weak in the area we were attacking and we knew also that you had some green units there. I don't remember the numbers of the units.

41. Q: What did you know of the American corps attack toward the Roer dams?

A: I had not heard of your corps attack, but our attacks must have met head-on. The terrain held by your 99 Inf Div was very poor for tanks.

42. Q: How did you expect to cover your flanks all the way to the Meuse, according to your original plan of attack?

A: The flanks were weak, but, in addition to being covered by the infantry and paratroop divisions and one of the divisions from LXVII Inf Corps, the two panzer divisions of II SS Pz Corps were to move to the flank. The latter two divisions would be relieved of this mission when we got to the Meuse as the Fifteenth Army attack would then start and the pressure would be eased.

V. The Attack

43. Q: Would you go into detail about the start of your attack?

A: The infantry started the attack after a considerable artillery preparation and the tanks started moving about 1000 or 1100 hours. They didn't meet very strong opposition except at Losheim, where there were many tank traps. Also, the Krinkelt–Wirtzfeld–Büllingen triangle was heavily defended for three days. The 12 SS Pz Div bogged down right away.

44. Q: To what do you attribute the failure of the Elsenborn Ridge attack?

A: The attacking forces were to move from the north and south and, because they couldn't break out of the triangle they were in, they could not get to Malmédy.

The 12 SS Pz Div was attacking in swampy land, and it only had one part (100 liters) per tank. We thought this would be good for 50–60 km, but, in the swampy terrain, low gear had to be used quite a bit, and the gas didn't last. The division remained clogged up in this area for three days and couldn't get started. Also, your troops had many tank defenses in the area, including tank traps, etc.

45. Q: Was 1 SS Pz Div told to stay out of Malmédy?

A: No, they had a flexible route. (Interviewer's Note: Gen Dietrich then was told of the day 1 SS Pz Div approached Malmédy and turned south without even sending reconnaissance toward the town. He was told that the town, at that time, was held only by a company of engineers. He threw up his hands in disgust, and said that the fault was in the reconnaissance units and that had he had good reconnaissance, it would never have happened. He went on to explain that all of his good officers and men had been lost in the Normandy fighting and that they were very hard to replace. He emphasized again that they were not inflexible in their routes. When he was told this incident occurred 17 Dec 44, Gen Dietrich then remarked that another reason for the apparent oversight was that on 17 Dec 44, 1 SS Pz Div did not yet know that 12 SS Pz

Div was bogged down. He concluded however, that a good reconnaissance unit still would have found out that Malmédy was held so lightly.)

46. Q: Why do you think 1 SS Pz Div got trapped in the Stoumont–La Gleize area?

A: The Division didn't have the gas it needed. It waited for fuel from 17 Dec to 19 Dec, but it didn't get any. By that time, the forces had been cut off.

47. Q: Do you know why the forces which captured Stavelot moved on and left it held so very lightly?

A: I do not know. It was probably because they didn't have much to leave, probably no more than a battalion.

48. Q: What did you have in the vicinity of Stoumont?

A: We had a panzer regiment, a panzer grenadier regiment, and five artillery batteries.

49. Q: How much did you know of our troop movements into the Ardennes area?

A: I remember when word came that the 7 Armd Div (US) was moving into the Ardennes. Other than that, I don't remember specifically the numbers of the divisions. I do remember, though, that the pressure from the flank began to get heavier and heavier.

50. Q: When did you decide to use II SS Pz Corps?

A: I decided to use II SS Pz Corps when it became apparent that 12 SS Pz Div was stopped and 1 SS Pz Div was bottled up. This was about 21 Dec 44. The 9 SS Pz Div was to move to the Recht–Poteau–Petit Thier–Grand Halleux area, and 2 SS Pz Div was to move to the Schönberg–St Vith– Beho area. The II SS Pz Corps was then to continue the attack according to plan.

51. Q: Why was 9 SS Pz Div sent into the area designated above?

A: The Führer Begleit Brig (about 11,000 men) was having trouble, and 9 SS Pz Div was sent over to help them. They met around Vielsalm. At this time, Fifth Pz and Sixth Pz Armies began to get all mixed up. This, of course, was not according to plan, but the roads didn't permit the troops to follow the routes planned for them and they had to search for roads on which they could get through. Thus, not only the divisions, but also the army boundaries, got all mixed up.

52. Q: You mentioned once that 2 SS Pz Div was taken away from you for a short time. Would you relate this incident?

A: The 2 SS Pz Div was with Fifth Pz Army from about 18 Dec to 21 Dec. On 22 Dec 44, it came back to me. I don't know exactly what it did during that time. It was given to Fifth Pz Army because the Führer Begleit Brig was too weak and didn't get ahead. (Interviewer's Note: Gen Dietrich then remarked that he was sorry he could not give more specific information, but he was no longer a field soldier and that, as an army commander, he was a watch-dog and could not follow the individual movements as much.)

53. Q: Would you go into more detail on the employment of II SS Pz Corps?

A: The plan was to keep on going with this Corps after the other corps had bogged down. (Interviewer's Note: Gen Dietrich did not seem to be able to give a good explanation of the use of II SS Pz Corps.)

54. Q: Was 9 SS Pz Div under II SS Pz Corps at Poteau on 21 Dec 44 when 2 SS Pz Div was under Fifth Pz Army?

A: Yes.

55. Q: What was your evaluation of our withdrawal in the area Trois Ponts–Manhay on the night of 24/25 Dec 44?

A: I thought your withdrawal just meant you were pulling back to prevent being cut off by an attack by me from the Trois Ponts area across the base of your salient. Although I had thought about it, I couldn't make such an attack because your pressure in the Stavelot–Malmédy–Waimes area was getting stronger every day. I had my hands full trying to put reserves on the flank so that I myself wouldn't be cut off.

56. Q: On 25 Dec 44, when II SS Pz Corps launched an attack on Manhay–Grandmenil, did you think you had a good chance of breaking through toward the Meuse River?

A: Originally, when the attack started, I thought we had a good chance. I wanted Erezee and the roads north to Durbuy and just east of there as these were the best routes to the Meuse. We didn't get as far as Erezee, however, and after that I didn't think it was possible to get through. As far as I was concerned, the offensive then was completely stalled. Erezee was a key position.

57. Q: At the time of your breakthrough to Manhay, our forces were temporarily quite disorganized and we often wondered why you did not attempt to break north toward Werbomont and Liège?

A: The attack was never directed toward Liège. After the failure of the original plan, the direction of the attack was always northwest. (Interviewer's Note: Gen Dietrich then modified this statement to say that they had very heavy casualties in the Manhay fighting and that, if they hadn't had such heavy casualties, they would have gone north.)

58. Q: Were you afraid of an attack in the Malmédy–St Vith area to cut off your spearhead?

A: Yes. I thought and believed that this would happen. You were building up strong artillery on that flank and I thought you were bringing in new troops on the flank, possibly for just such an attack.

59. Q: Did you do anything about this threat?

A: On 26–27 Dec 44, I wanted to attack again in the Eisenborn area with an infantry corps, but I dropped this plan because the Corps (LXVII) had such high casualties in the earlier fighting that they wouldn't have been able to carry out an attack at that time.

60. Q: Did you know the disposition of the British units around Liège?

A: We heard that there were two British divisions near Liège.

61. Q: Could you recall anything of 3 Pz Gren Div in your sector?

A: The 3 Pz Gren Div was brought in to reinforce LXVII Inf Corps in the Monschau area. I was afraid of a possible breakthrough by your troops at that point.

62. Q: When did you move 12 SS Pz Div to the west?

A: On 28 Dec 44.

63. Q: Did you have any plans for a new general attack?

A: No. The attack on Sadzot must have been ordered by the Corps Commander. My orders after 25 Dec 44 were to continue to hold in place. We no longer were in position to attack because of the lack of ammunition.

VI. Defense and Withdrawal

64. Q: When did your divisions move toward Bastogne?

A: The 1 SS Pz Div moved south on 28 Dec 44, with 12 and 9 SS Pz Divs following shortly thereafter. With them went I SS Pz Corps. The 1 SS Pz Div moved in east of Bastogne and made some progress. The 12 SS Pz Div moved in west of the town. Model ordered Fifth Pz Army to take Bastogne, and because, of that, I had to give my divisions to the attacking Fifth Pz Army.

65. Q: Why do you think so much importance was attached to Bastogne so late in the fight?

A: Model wanted to get it at all cost. I'm not sure exactly why. He was to order a coordinated, all-out attack, but it never came. On 3 Jan 45, he changed his mind.

66. Q: What troops did you have under your command late in Dec 44?

A: I still had my II SS Pz Corps, and, in addition, had been given LXVI Inf Corps with 18 and 62 Volks Gren Divs. These divisions took the place of those I sent to Bastogne. The Fifteenth Army Corps was lost to me from about 25 Dec 44 until 10 Jan 45, when it again came under my command.

67. Q: What did you know of our attack plans in Jan 45?

A: All I knew was that your pressure kept mounting daily and that finally you launched a triple attack from the areas Trois Ponts–Manhay, Hotton–Erezee, and on the west end of the Bulge.

68. Q: What did your Army do in the defensive?

A: We first held the Trois Ponts–Vielsalm line, and then the line to the west of St Vith. The I SS Pz Corps came back to us about 10 Jan 45, and it was used on the flanks and wherever additional strength was needed. By this time casualties had been very high and the division sectors were very narrow.

69. Q: When did you receive orders to move to the East?

A: These orders came through about the end of Jan 45. We marched back over the Rhine on foot in 12 days. Because we were waiting for more gas, the tanks moved very slowly to conserve fuel and many vehicles were towed by tractors. We went to an area south of Budapest; on the way, I left over a thousand vehicles for repairs. I received some new vehicles and about 22,000 new men, most of them replacements. We left the Rhineland area by train between 5 Feb and 17 Feb, and the main body arrived in Hungary on 1–2 Mar 45. One corps attacked on 4 Mar 45, and by 6 Mar 45, we launched an Army attack on Lake Balaton. We were known as an engineer army so we would not be identified by the Russians.

VII. Review Of The Offensive

70. Q: When did you think the attack was lost?

A: On the third or fourth day.

71. Q: What would you list as the most important reasons for the failure of the Ardennes Offensive?

A: I would say it was mainly bad preparation. Also important were lack of fuel, lack of supplies, lack of training, and the time of the year, in that order. In addition, an important factor was the fast regrouping of the American forces. I had believed you could do it, however, because of all your vehicles. In 14 days, your regrouping was an accomplished fact.

72. Q: Do you know what your casualties were for the entire operation?

A: For the entire operation, I lost 37,000 men killed, wounded, and frozen, and from 350–400 tanks. (Interviewer's Note: This does not include LXVII Inf Corps, which had about 20% casualties.)

73. Q: Did you get any replacements of men or tanks while you were in the Ardennes?

A: None at all, and very little gas. The whole attack was a big mistake. To use those two armies at that time of the year was the biggest mistake they made in the War. In May 45, the attack might have gone better, but I agree the air might have raised the devil with us.[11] Normandy, in Jul and Aug 44, was the worst time I have spent in my fighting years. I had five complete corps shot out from under me. It used to take me six hours to move the ten km from my headquarters to the front. And the worst is that those planes don't distinguish between generals and anyone else. It was terrible. I told Göring his Luftwaffe wasn't worth a penny. (Interviewer's Note: Gen Dietrich then made some remarks about the general situation in the Ardennes to the effect that they had very poor weather, the roads were bad, it was a poor time of the year for tank movement, and they had a very short day in which to conduct operations. He went on to remark that he had two Volks artillery corps, but that they had only enough ammunition for two battalions, and many of the guns stayed back in the reserve areas because they didn't have enough gas to bring them into the Bulge.)

74. Q: How much communication did you have with von Manteuffel during the attack?

A: I had very little communication with him because I was out in the field much of the time, as he was. Our staffs, however, were in constant communication.

75. Q: How can you explain that von Manteuffel was consulted so much on the plans for the Offensive?

A: Manteuffel had better liaison with Hitler because he had been in command of the Grossdeutschland Pz Div and knew many of the men around the Führer's headquarters. I should have been given four weeks of planning instead of four days. I knew that the Offensive would start, but not where. I was not in the area even once before the attack, and I couldn't look at the terrain. I didn't have time to prepare my thoughts and ideas in the way they really should have been prepared. Because of that, it is hard to give a detailed description. I am one of the oldest tank men in the Army, having been in tanks in 1916–17. If I had been asked, I would have been against that terrain with swampy territory and few roads. I would have gone by Aachen or Metz. The Ardennes was the worst terrain imaginable for a thousand tanks. Only four to five of them could fight at one time because there was no place to deploy. A big tank attack in this terrain is impossible. West of Aachen, one can see from five to ten km in places and we could have gone to town. In the Ardennes, we could develop nothing.

76. Q: But at Aachen or Metz, you would have bumped into our strongest forces. Wouldn't this have been a deciding factor in locating the attack?

A: The initial fight would have been harder, but we could have broken through.

77. Q: What happened to 10 SS Pz Div?

A: It should have come to use, but I don't know what happened to it. I think it was sent to Strassbourg, although I received word I was to get it. As far as I know, it didn't come into the sector at all.

78. Q: Did our air power do much damage to you in the Ardennes?

A: Yes. Many ammunition and gas-carrying vehicles were destroyed. I lost about 25–30% of all such vehicles I had. The worst attacks were on 23 Dec 44, when the weather first became good. During good weather after that, we could move only at night.

79. Q: Did the raids on St Vith slow traffic through the town?

A: The raids completely destroyed the town and made us route transportation another way. This town was in my Army zone after it was taken. I was there during the big raid of 26 Dec 44. It was terrible.

80. Q: Did the attack on your spearheads on 18 Dec 44 in the Stoumont area do much damage?[12]

A: These attacks weren't so bad.

81. Q: Would you rate Fifth Pz Army or Sixth Pz Army the better?

A: The Fifth was probably better because it had had more experience, and its troops were better trained. The fuel situation at the time we were training was very bad. The Supreme Command apparently was holding back gas for the offensive; but, even so, we never did get enough for the attack.

82. Q: The Führer is supposed to have said at the 12 Dec 444 meeting announcing the attack that tank production was at 2,500 per month. Does this sound right to you?

A: Production was nearer 1,000 a month. It is possible that the tank experts said the rate was 2,500, but it wasn't. Just about that time, the largest tank-producing towns, Kassel and Magdeburg, were both bombed.

83. Q: What did you know about the shooting of 150 American soldiers near Malmedy?

A: I didn't know a thing about it. The first I heard was when Model asked me if we had done any such thing in our Army. I had my Chief of Staff make an investigation, and he reported that no such incident had occurred. I talked with Peiper [1 SS Pz Div Kampfgruppe leader] about eight days after the incident occurred, and he didn't mention a thing about it to me. He should have known about it. It is quite possible that the division commander didn't know about it, either. (Interviewer's Note: Gen Dietrich asked several questions about the nature of the incident.)

Interview 2

I. Organization And Training Of Sixth Pz Army

1. Between 20 and 25 Sep 44, I received orders from the Planning Division of FHQ (Führerhauptquartier) to activate Sixth Pz Army. I activated the staff in Bad Salzuflen. At that time, I had ten officers at my disposal. Within four weeks, the staff of Sixth Pz Army was filled with officers and was ready for operation. Not until the beginning of Oct 44, however, were any troops assigned to the staff. At that time, 1 and 12 SS Pz Divs, which formed I SS Pz Corps, and 2 and 9 SS Pz Divs and Pz Lehr Div, which formed II SS Pz Corps, were brought under command of Sixth Pz Army.

2. During Oct, Nov, and the beginning of Dec 44, these divisions were organized, brought up to strength, and trained. It should be mentioned that, during this time, emphasis was placed on infantry and armor commitment. The entire training was to have been completed by Dec 44, which offered insufficient time to prepare the troops for battle. At the beginning of Dec 44, I SS Pz Corps, at the urgent request of Genfldm Model, was shipped to the area north of Cologne and ordered to prevent a possible enemy breakthrough into the Ruhr.

3. In regard to Gen Strong's question whether a tactical exercise by Sixth Pz Army in preparation for the Ardennes Offensive had taken place at HQ, C-in-C

West, my answer must be 'no' as far as the divisions under my command are concerned. Also, there had been no large-scale preparations within Sixth Pz Army for the Ardennes Offensive during the three months of Oct to Dec 44. Time was needed too badly for the training in attack and defense of units up to battalion strength and for the assembly of material. During this time, Sixth Pz Army was not under OB West, but was under FHQ. On 12 Dec 44, at the conference in Bad Nauheim, the planned Ardennes Offensive was ordered by Hitler, but no exact date was given. I personally knew that a winter offensive was being planned by the Operations Division, but I did not know when and where.

II. Conference At Bad Nauheim And Orientation

4. At 1500 on 12 Dec 44, a conference of general officers took place at FHQ in Bad Nauheim. All the commanding generals of Fifth Pz and Sixth Pz Armies, as well as von Rundstedt, Model, Keitel, Jodl, and Hitler, were present. Hitler declared at this conference that he had decided on a winter offensive because the Army's continuous setbacks could be tolerated no longer. The Army must gain a victory. He said that all preparations had been made and that thousands of tanks were at their disposal. Hitler continued at great length and referred to former campaigns. 'The German people can no longer endure the heavy bombing attacks,' he said, and 'The German people are entitled to action from me.' No one else made a speech. We were not asked. At the end of the conference, the generals were introduced to Hitler and each had an opportunity to talk to him for a few minutes. Hitler asked me, 'Is your Army ready?' I answered, 'Not for an offensive.' To this, Hitler replied, 'You are never satisfied.' With that my minute was up. The answers of the commanding generals were similar – 'not fully prepared for commitment.' After the conference, the generals who had been present met for a birthday celebration at von Rundstedt's house. No one dared speak about the Offensive. The death penalty hovered over the secret, and it would have been to no avail to discuss it anyway. By midnight all generals were on the way back to their units.

5. On the morning of 13 Dec 44, I was ordered to Model's Headquarters for an orientation. On the same afternoon, I had a conference with my two corps commanders in order to make preparations for the planned offensive. The I SS Pz Corps was designated as the attack Corps, and II SS Pz Corps was to be held as Sixth Pz Army reserve. During the nights of 13, 14, and 15 Dec 44, the divisions moved out to take up their positions. They covered an average of 100 km per night. Even on 15 Dec 44, Model and I were of the opinion that the attack was premature, and we requested an extension of at least two days. FHQ refused. This winter offensive, in my opinion, was the worst prepared German offensive of this War.

Notes

1. 'All his former officers whom I have interviewed,' noted Oberstleutnant Hans-Dieter Bech-told, a German officer who knew many of the personalities associated with Dietrich, 'confessed that commanding an army was too much for him. Dietrich must have known this himself for when he got the message at the end of August 1944 that an army was to come under his command, he is reported to have grumbled, "What good is that? I have never been trained to command an army. What they need is a person like Gause who knows a lot more about it than myself." '

2. Heinrich Heim, *Adolf Hitler: Monologue im Führerhauptquartier*, Hamburg, 1980; taken from a speech of 3–4 January 1942.

3. See Charles Messenger, *Hitler's Gladiator*, Brassey's, London, 1988; also a new German account more sympathetic to the former SS leader, *Sepp Dietrich: Kommandeur der Leibstandarte SS Adolf Hitler und seine Männer*, Deutsche Verlagsgesellschaft, Rosenheim. Dietrich's soldiers trusted him a great deal and regarded him as a good comrade. According to officers who knew him, his orders often ended with the admonition: 'Now go on, but be careful with your soldiers', aiming to avoid unnecessary casualties. True to form, Dietrich was often seen at the front after Christmas.

4. Milton Shulman, *Defeat in the West*, E.P. Dutton, New York, 1948. Major Shulman served in the intelligence section of the First Canadian Army, carrying out interrogations of important German commanders in September 1945.

5. *OB West KTB*, Order from OKW to OB West, dated 11 December 1944, Microfilm Roll T-311, Roll 18, Frame 702583-85.

6. See General der Infanterie Gustav von Zangen, 'Fifteenth Army: Defensive Battles at the Roer and Rhine, 22 Nov 44–9 Mar 45', B-812, Neustadt, 15 November 1947. Major Hechler also pinned down Generaloberst Jodl regarding the map showing Liège encircled: 'If mobile forces of Sepp Dietrich were aimed at Liège,' he surmised, 'then Dietrich would be shot for disobeying orders.' In reality the map merely showed the German panzer Rollbahnen circuiting around Liège to advance further west, rather than a plan for encirclement and siege.

7. Major Kenneth W. Hechler, 'The Enemy Side of the Hill: The 1945 Background on the interrogation of German Commanders', Historical Section, Washington D.C., 30 July 1949. On file at the U.S. Army Military History Institute, Carlisle, PA.

8. Actually, 12 Volks Gren Div was to break through the initial Allied line; 1 SS Pz Div was the main formation on the right.

9. 12 SS Pz Div had specific orders to contact von der Heydte. A radio communication officer of the Hitler Jugend division jumped with the paratroopers to provide intelligence and artillery fire. Unfortunately, his radio was damaged in the drop.

10. This is incorrect. 1 SS Pz Div took on approximately 50,000 gallons of captured fuel from the US 2nd Quartermaster Company in Büllingen on 17 December.

11. A very strange presumption on the part of Dietrich, that German forces could have held the Westwall until May of 1945!

12. Air attacks were actually on 1 SS Pz Div between Lodomez–Cheneux–Neufmoulin rather than Stoumont.

2

Operations of the Sixth Panzer Army

BY GENERALMAJOR FRITZ KRÄMER

Introduction

Within the Ardennes Offensive operations, Fritz Ludwig Carl Krämer is a strange figure. Krämer was a fully-fledged regular German staff officer, having graduated from the Berlin War Academy in 1934 and served on the staff of the 13th Panzer Division until 1942 in Russia. Krämer was brought into the SS Sixth Panzer Army to provide an experienced staff officer for operational matters relative to that organization. General Dietrich, the Army commander, had previously commanded the I SS Panzer Corps in Normandy, but with his promotion it was necessary to bring someone in to fill his shoes. Krämer was the man. He had already been working effectively with I SS Panzer Corps on troublesome logistical matters in Normandy, although other Waffen SS officers deeply resented this encroachment. There was a deep rivalry between the regular Army and the Waffen SS, and Krämer was not originally an SS officer. Regardless of this, Krämer was assigned as Chief of Staff for the Army on Hitler's personal orders on 27 October, having received good reports regarding his efficacy in Normandy. Krämer took over his new post on 16 November, just one month before the beginning of the attack. According to his own description, he immediately made an extensive study of the terrain and composed the battlegroups and their suggested march routes.

> Prior to the attack, I made an extensive study of the road net in our zone, because I knew it would be one of our most difficult problems. As a result of this map study and my personal knowledge of the terrain, I selected the five routes you have on the map ... These roads were to be directional only. If division commanders wanted to take others, they were at liberty to do so ...[1]

The attack plan for Sixth Panzer Army was developed by Krämer in some detail. Although the Fifth Panzer Army's von Manteuffel later accused the Sixth of attacking on too narrow a front, Krämer insisted that this was dictated by the terrain, the lack of roads for full deployment and the need for a rapid breakthrough. He anticipated an echeloned assault where mobile units were to attack at many points in columns, hoping to break out in several places and speed forward in road formation:

> The principle was to hold the reins loose and let the armies race. The main point was to reach the Meuse regardless of the flanks. This was the same principle we used in the French campaign of 1940. My division in Russia used the same

principle, and we advanced beyond Stalingrad. I never worry about my flanks . . .
I believe, as Clausewitz, 'The point must form the fist.' Our general zone was
Monschau–Losheim. The initial attack was to be made by two infantry corps.
The LXVII Infantry Corps, with the 246th and 326th VG Divisions, was to
attack in the vicinity of Monschau, move northwest and block the roads from
Eupen to Monschau, and block the north against any enemy thrust in that
direction. The I SS Pz Corps was to attack with elements of the 277 VG, 3 FS
and 12 VG Divisions from both sides of Udenbreth and cut the three roads from
Verviers to Malmédy. After the tanks had passed through [the lines] 12 VG
Division was to swing north to the vicinity of Verviers . . . By noon, when we
calculated the roads from the north would be blocked, the tanks were to move
out, and the entire [infantry] line was to swing northwest so that the blocking
line would run Eupen-Herve-Liège. The panzers were to attack in the direction
of Liège and Huy to secure crossings of the river. We calculated that by noon of
the 17th of December, we could reach the Hohes Venn mountains, which run
northwest from Monschau to Stavelot. By 19 December, the panzer spearheads
were to reach the Meuse . . .

The main worry for Krämer before the attack was the lack of recent
reconnaissance of the enemy front. To protect the secret of 'Wacht Am Rhein',
patrol activity had been sharply curtailed since early December. This left him
believing that only a single infantry division opposed them between Monschau
and Losheim, with another in reserve. 'Our infantry did not progress as I had
anticipated, due to several factors, including the rain and fog, a destroyed
bridge just north of Losheim, and your very strong defensive sector in the
Elsenborn–Butgenbach area.'

When he later learned that the veteran U.S. 2nd Infantry Division was
attacking through the 99th Division, he acknowledged that this had severely
thrown off their plans. But if Sixth Panzer Army was considerably derided
among staff officers for its lack of experience, this view was certainly not held by
Krämer. Said his interviewers: 'He obviously has a comprehensive understanding of this operation, and his account should be considered very reliable.'
Jochen Peiper, the controversial commander of the German panzer spearhead,
admitted that Dietrich had limitations as a commander. However, he said
Dietrich performed satisfactorily if he had a good chief of staff, which Peiper
certainly believed true of Krämer.[2] The Historical Section officers who interviewed Krämer were also impressed:

I believe that far and away the most important interview which Merraim had
was with General Fritz Krämer. This tight-lipped, straight thinking, regular
Army officer, who was sent off to pound some sense into Sepp Dietrich's SS head
as the latter's Chief of Staff, immediately impressed Merraim with his deep
powers of analysis and grasp of tactical and strategic principles.[3]

Against this plaudatory evaluation, however, must stand a number of important failings in Krämer's command. Firstly, he should have known that the chosen panzer Rollbahnen for his Army were woefully inadequate for the allotted motorized troops – Rollbahn A was not even paved for the first ten kilometres. Several of the others were similarly inadequate: Jochen Peiper, in charge of the prime armored spearhead of the 1st SS Panzer Division, said after the war that the narrow and circuitous Rollbahn D 'was suitable not for tanks but for bicycles.' And yet Krämer did nothing to get these routes changed. Secondly, Krämer did nothing to attempt to alter several key tactical issues in the assault which he must have known were in error. He should at least have attempted to cancel the preparatory artillery bombardments, as von Manteuffel in the Fifth Panzer Army had done, and to change the initial assault from the poorly-trained infantry divisions to the more experienced panzer troops. The thirty-minute artillery bombardment did little more than consume irreplaceable ammunition and alert the American forces in the area that an attack was in the offing. And leading the attack with the parachute units and poorly-trained Volksgrenadiers wasted valuable time, during which the experienced panzer troops may have been able to effect a rapid breakthrough and race across Belgium to the Meuse. But Krämer never asked for either of these concessions which von Manteuffel used to his advantage.

Although Dietrich would later shoulder the blame for each of these oversights, there is no evidence that Krämer attempted to get him to change Hitler's mind on either of these flaws (the reality is that Dietrich had wanted to make the breakthrough in the Losheim Gap with the tanks of the Leibstandarte Adolf Hitler leading the assault – a plan that was overruled by OKW on 11 December). In hindsight, this has to be seen as the greatest of oversights – possibly one that, having been addressed, might have taken the Sixth Panzer Army to the Meuse River by the end of the second day of the attack.

Despite ingratiating himself to interrogators, the problems for Krämer after the war stemmed from his very involvement with the Sixth Panzer Army. As most know, during the Ardennes Operation the 'Malmédy Massacre' incident took place on Krämer's watch, and the sentiment in the American public was that SS heads should roll. During the Malmédy Trial at Dachau, the U.S. prosecution went to great lengths to implicate Dietrich and Krämer, saying that both had been involved with issuing orders that no prisoners were to be taken – an order for which no physical evidence was ever produced, and which most Germans involved denounced as untrue. Indeed, Krämer told of having first learned of the 'massacre' from Radio Calais on the 20th of December – a fact that seems true. But regardless of guilt, Krämer was convicted in the trial along with Dietrich and the others. He wept openly when his sentence of ten years imprisonment was pronounced; he would not be paroled until 1951.

Danny S. Parker

Operations of Sixth Panzer Army (1944–45)

I. Events Prior to the Ardennes Offensive

The Staff of the Sixth Panzer Army was formed in October 1944 at Bad Sal-zuflan, Westphalia. The personnel consisted of about 2/3 Officers and enlisted men of the Regular Army, and about 1/3 Officers and enlisted men of the Waffen SS. Two-thirds of the strength of the Signal Communications Regiment consisted of members of the Luftwaffe.

This Army was often called the Sixth SS Panzer Army. Its correct designation however, is the Sixth Panzer Army, according to a written directive of the German High Command issued in the beginning of December, 1944.

Commanding General: General of the Waffen SS Dietrich.

Chief of Staff: Lt Gen Gause. As of 18 Nov 1944, Major General of the Waffen SS Krämer.

TROOPS

I SS Panzer Corps with the 1 and 12 SS Panzer Divisions.

II SS Panzer Corps with the 2 and 9 SS Panzer Divisions, and the Panzer Lehr Division of the Regular Army

COMMANDERS

I SS Panzer Corps: Lt Gen of the Waffen SS Fries.

Chief of Staff: SS Lt Colonel Lehmann.

1st SS Panzer Div: SS Brig Gen Mohnke.

12th SS Panzer Div: Maj Gen of the Waffen SS Krämer: as of 15 Nov 44, SS Brig Gen Kraas.*

II SS Panzer Corps: General of the Waffen SS Bittrich.

Chief of Staff: SS Lt Colonel Keller.

2nd SS Panzer Div: Major Gen of the Waffen SS Lammerding.

9th SS Panzer Div: SS Brig Gen Stadler.

Panzer Lehr Division: Lt Gen Bayerlein.

These divisions, which were badly defeated during the Invasion and the retreat towards the Westwall, were still employed at the Front in the beginning of October 1944. They were deployed as follows:

  1st SS Panzer Division: Special units of which were employed to the northwest of Prüm and Daleiden.

---

* Maj Gen of the Waffen SS Krämer assigned Chief of Staff, 6 Pz Army, 16 Nov 44.

2nd SS Panzer Division, majority of which were employed on both sides of Prüm.

9th SS Panzer Division: at Arnhem.

12th SS Panzer Division: part of this division northwest of Prüm.

Panzer Lehr Division: part of this division at Neuerburg.

Remnants of the divisions which were broken to pieces, re-assembled in the sector around Heilbronn; towards the end of October they were shifted to the sector around Minden.

The Commanding Staffs were not immediately relieved from the Front; that of the 1st SS Panzer Division arrived on the 22 Oct 44, and of the 2nd SS Panzer Division in the middle of November. The extrication of all the Divisions with all of their component units was completed towards the end of October. At this time the majority of these units were assembled as follows:

1st SS Panzer Division in the sector SW of Minden.

12th SS Panzer Division in the sector North of Minden.

2nd SS Panzer Division in the sector of Arnsberg.

9th SS Panzer Division in the sector of Hamm, Westphalia.

The Panzer Lehr Division was not attached at this time.

The Divisions were commanded to reorganize, to retrain and to be ready to resist enemy air landings in their billeting sectors. The retraining, instruction and reorganization of the forces suffered serious delay through interruptions and rerouting of the supply and equipment trains from the interior of Germany because of a succession of enemy air attacks.

The divisions endeavoured to reorganize their units as soon as possible and strove to accomplish this with the greatest speed. Special importance was given to instruction in night fighting and combined operations of the various units. Officers and enlisted men who knew no battle assaults since the Invasion, again had to study the characteristic employment of Panzer Divisions as an assault arm. The training of drivers, who, in the past, had been used as infantrymen and had suffered serious casualties, was handicapped by a serious shortage of motor fuels. This lack of training was to prove costly to the Ardennes Offensive because of the bad network of roads. However, the attitude and morale of the troops was very good.

On 9 Nov 1944, the Divisions received the order for movement by rail. The destination and the sector were unknown. The requests of the Divisional Commanders to wait 14 days to three weeks for shipping, in order to complete the retraining, was not granted by the Army. The train transportation – 60 trains to each division – operated almost without breakdown and reached their destination despite air attacks. The movement was completed on the 20 Nov 44; fresh troops and equipment – tanks, motor vehicles, etc – continued to arrive until the beginning of December, at which time the organization of the Panzer Divisions was completed.

Towards the end of November, the units which were reserves of the OKW – High Command of the Armed Forces – were located as follows:

Army Staff and Army Troops in Quadrath, west of Köln, and in Bruehl.

I SS Panzer Corps in Frechen, west of Köln.

1st SS Panzer Division southwest of Köln.

12th SS Panzer Division northwest of Köln.

II SS Panzer Corps, west of Bonn.

2nd SS Panzer Division south of München-Gladbach.

9th SS Panzer Division in the region of Euskirchen.

Army Supply Troops west of the Rhine between Köln and Bonn.

The Corps received the order to continue the training – particularly night training – and to prepare themselves to repulse Allied air landings. Mobile reserve units were to be held in readiness. The troops were of the opinion that they were to act as reinforcements in the battle of Aachen. That was also the general opinion of the population. Vehicles were camouflaged against air observation, and motor movements were only executed at night. All members of the Army and even individuals were forbidden to cross to the west of the highway Neuss–Grevenbroich–Liblar–Euskirchen.

The dominating theme of the Officer map exercises and sand table training was: 'Attacks against the flanks and the rear of a motorized enemy who had made a penetration in depth to the main defensive area and even into the interior of the country.' The troops did not know that they were assembled for a large-scale offensive.

II. Preparation for Operations

1. Tactical: The advance preparations for the operations were carried on in the greatest secrecy. On 16 Nov 1944, on order of the Führer, General Krämer became Chief of Staff of the 6 Pz Army and received instructions about the intended Ardennes Offensive by his predecessor Lt Gen Gause and the Commander in Chief of the Army. Other officers were not advised, written orders not being left with the Army.

The Plan of Operations in general was:

Attack with two Panzer Armies on both sides of the Schnee-Eifel across the Maas (Meuse).

At the same time:

    a. Screening of flanks with Infantry Divisions.

    b. Exploiting of a bad weather period in order to eliminate air offensives.

    c. Heaviest artillery and support through air cover.

Details over the assignment of other forces were still unknown. The moment of the Operation was given as the beginning of December. Through a discussion on November 18th with the Chief of Army Group B, General of the

Infantry Krebs, it was again expressed that with the precise moment of this attack (and its secrecy) hung the success or failure of this operation. The introduction of other officers to this plan could only be done through the approval of the Army Group. There were two proven possibilities of this operation and they were:

(1) Frontal attack on both sides of Aachen and attack with the right wing along the Maas at Maastricht, in order to defeat the forces (especially British) concentrated near Aachen.

(2) Thrust across the Maas from the sector of the Schnee-Eifel to rip apart the front of the Allies and thrust to Antwerp and Brussels, to cut off the supply routes.

The Führer had ordered the second plan. As they intended with the 6 Panzer Army on the right and the 5 Panzer Army on the left under the advantage of a bad weather period, to thrust on both sides of the Schnee-Eifel over the Maas between Lüttich (bypassing this) and Namur. Bad roads had to be figured on. The moment of the commencement of the operations was about 10 December. The right flank of the 6 Panzer Army was to be backed up by 15 Army, supplying an infantry corps which was to be attached to 6 Panzer Army. The left flank of 5 Panzer Army would be protected by an advance of the 7 Army in direction southwest. It was further intended to relieve the right flank of 6 Panzer Army by an attack of 15 Army with two Panzer divisions and the corresponding infantry divisions with the right wing along the Maas toward Maastricht, and to contain the enemy forces that would eventually be committed for a thrust into the deep flank of the Army.

The Army informed the Army group that:

a. The training of the division not being accomplished, the beginning of the operations should be postponed.

b. Two Panzer Divisions should be committed side by side of the Hohes Venn and Schnee-Eifel, in order to:

(1) form a strong breakthrough wedge,

(2) exploit the favorable terrain southwest of Prüm, and to bypass the terrain of the Hohes Venn, difficult for the tanks.

The difficulty of the terrain was well known because of the withdrawal battles toward the Westwall. The Army knew that a strong demand would have to be made on the efficiency of the troops, and in particular on the drivers. The training and the reorganization of the Army was watched over during the days that followed and the Officer Corps received further training in map studies. To mask their true nature, the training courses were based on the idea that motorized enemy forces that had broken through were to be attacked in the flank. That was obvious to all the participants, as the Allied effort was being shown in their thrusts through to the Rhine. Army Group B had map exercises similar to that of the Army.

Terrain reconnaissance west of the line Grevenbroich–Euskirchen was forbidden. However, the Army received information about the enemy by the Ic of the Army Group. Close contact was kept between the group of Manteuffel (5 Panzer Army) committed as first advancing group, and the 7 Army. We knew that comparatively weak enemy forces were situated in the sector Krewinkel–Gemünd. It was supposed that three divisions were assembled in the area of Elsenborn for an attack on the dam of the Urft-valley. Between the front line and the Maas, the enemy forces seemed relatively weak. An armored division was supposed to be situated north of Spa, which would be the first combined group to make an attack against the right flank of the Army. In front of the left wing of our 7 Army strong radio activity could be observed, therefore we concluded that strong enemy forces were concentrated there.

The 6 Panzer Army never received any details on this subject. All in all, we had to expect, that only on the 3rd day of our breakthrough attack (if launched immediately), countermeasures of combined enemy units would be started, and that the combined divisions would only be committed on the other side of the Maas against the Army. The enemy main resistance line did not consist of a continuous line, but of different strongpoints (especially near roads and forest trails), and had a depth of about 4–5 km. Tanks and tank emplacements, that were employed as reserves for counterattacks, backed up the strongpoint. A decrease of the combat strength, due to the cold weather and the insufficient winter equipment, was expected. Close contact was kept between the Group of Manteuffel and the 7 Army. Even for those, who were not informed about the offensive, this seemed to be necessary, because the Army (for those who did not know) was assembled there as reserve for the fighting near Aachen.

About 20 November 1944, a written order went to the Army for the intended offensive. They dared not work on it other than the C-I-C, the Chief of Staff, and the first General staff officer – the latter also all had to write the plan themselves, and nothing concerning the plans was to be made known to the troops. The message was as follows:

The 6 Panzer Army, with the attached infantry divisions, on X-day, after heavy artillery preparation, will break through the enemy defensive front in the sector of Monschau–Krewinkel, then – regardless of their flanks – push with their armored units across the Maas, south of Lüttich (Liège), then – screening their right flank on the Albert-Canal – push toward Antwerp. Specially organized advance detachments under the command of particularly energetic officers, were to take the bridges across the Maas, south of Lüttich, undamaged. The LXVII Army Corps is to be committed in the general line Monschau–Verviers–Lüttich for the formation of a solid defensive front. After having crossed the Maas, the Corps will be reattached to the 15 Army. Boundary line to 5 Panzer Army: Prüm–St Vith–Huy. 10 December was again anticipated as X-day.

With the beginning of the strategic concentration of troops for action, the Army was organized as follows: (See organization of the 6 Panzer Army on 15 December 1944.)

The orders of the Army, that were worked out by the Chief of Staff and the Ia officer were very detailed and complete. The Army Group received a copy of the orders. It was pointed out that it would be better to postpone the start of the operation, in order to accomplish the re-equipment of the troops. The train transports with the material arrived only with great interruptions, because of the air raids. Since various arms and spare-parts did not always come from the same ordnance service, it sometimes happened, that parts were missing and had to be requested again. On 1 December, the artillery Commander of the Army, Lt Gen of the Waffen SS Staudinger and an artillery expert, Lt Gen Kruse (sent from the German High Command) received instructions. During a map exercise on 2 December, at Bruehl (south of Köln), the Commanding Generals and their Chiefs, and the Commanders of the Panzer Divisions were instructed. All steps had to be as before, with the view in mind of the defensive battles that were to be carried through. In this map exercise, in the presence of the C-I-C and under the guidance of the substituted CO, General of the Waffen SS Bittrich, the Commanding Generals, their Chiefs and the Commanders of the Panzer Division took part in the discussion of all the plans of the Army.

The army had to be entirely clear, on which places and on what time of the day the attack was to be started. The assigned Infantry divisions came in part from defensive combats and were not complete. Their reorganization followed a very short delay and their fighting qualities were not of the best. The best division was the 12 VGD that had an especially skilled Commander and had fought excellently in the Battle of Aachen. The 3 Para Div had no battle experience, and besides their Commander had very little understanding about infantry matters. The time of attack was scheduled for the early morning hours, because it was hoped, that the infantry would succeed in taking advantage of the early morning mist and succeed in breaking through the first positions. It was hoped that by midday they would win 5–8 km of ground. For a night attack, the troops were not sufficiently trained to take advantage of the most favorable time. The troops had lost themselves in the fields, the military security of the enemy was on the alert, and the Panzers in the gray of the morning had a foe held in readiness, standing opposite them.

About 200 searchlights were available of the III Flak Corps, that had worked together with the Army. Repeated attempts would be made to break through with searchlights. But it proved that the searchlights were not mobile enough and their maximum range was too limited to follow the troops.

Also important was the choice of the sector of the attack. There had to be favorable departure positions for the infantry and ones had to be especially sought out for the Panzers. The [Ardennes] country – extremely difficult for the combined attack of the Panzers – was above all especially unfavourable in the sector of the 6 Panzer Army. Open country for the operation of Panzers was first found after having passed the Hohes Venn. Until there the Panzers, in general, could not move off the road. The Army after careful consideration of the existing roads, and specific evaluation of the terrain, designated five roads, of these the four southern ones were designated as the so-called Panzer rolling roads. This was not an ideal situation, but the best selection had to be made. It was especially important for the Army to take the necessary measures, so that sufficient infantry strength could be brought up from the right side, in order to protect the right flank of the advance. The difficulty lay not only in regrouping these forces in time after the breakthrough, but to make sure that there would be sufficient room for the combat zone, and that supplies would not be cut off through a blocking of the roads by the Armored divisions. For the Army, this was not a pleasant solution, that they had to take over the protection of their flanks with infantry divisions.

By this order, they were bound on their right flank and as the proverb says: 'horses and mules were tethered together.' In no case were the Panzer Divisions to turn too early [to the north], because they were too weak for that task. Though all the available roads were to be exploited, it was the intention of the Army to reserve the northern tank track for a reinforced armored reconnaissance detachment. Afterwards, this road was to be reserved for infantry divisions. The request of the Army to give the task of the flank protection to the 15 Army was refused. Presuming that three enemy divisions (forces for an attack on the dam of the Urft and replacements) were situated in the area of Elsenborn, the Army decided on the commitment of three infantry divisions in that sector. However Army Group B altered that plan and committed only two divisions. It was also important to decide whether the Panzer Corps were to be distributed in depth or in line. The Army should have preferred disposition in line, which would have permitted the commitment of a greater number of tanks. However, the terrain was so difficult that the traffic would have been tied-up. Moreover the Army needed tank reserves for commitment, in case the situation of the right flank became critical or the infantry could not be brought up as rapidly as expected. Further, under this arrangement, the Army had the possibility to commit fresh forces, after the first wave of the attack was consumed. Therefore disposition in depth was ordered and approved by the Army Group.

The traffic control was of particular importance. Therefore a Military Police Regiment (300 men) was put at disposal of the Army in addition to the already existing MP forces (for each Panzer Corps and each Panzer Division one company of MP).

On or by 10 December all the Corps received the detailed orders of the Army. On 8 December the Army took over the command of the supply services of the sector, and on 10 December the staff shifted their Command Post to

Münstereifel. On 11 December the Army took the tactical command of the sector Monschau–Schnee Eifel. With regard to the weather, the still uncompleted reorganization of all divisions, and disposition of the artillery, the beginning of the attack was first postponed to 13, then to 16 December.

On 12 and 13 December, a meeting of all the commanding Generals and division commanders took place at the Command Post of the OB West, where Hitler explained reasons and necessity of the Offensive and insisted upon the necessity of employing all the forces, in order to obtain the final success. The general lines of the detailed order of the Army were as follows:

6 Panzer Army, on X-day, after heavy artillery preparation breaks through the enemy front in the sector on both sides of Hollerath and pushes – regardless of their flanks – without stop, across the Maas toward Antwerp.

I SS Panzer Corps, on X-day, assembles at 0600 hours, breaks through the enemy positions into the sector of Monschau–Udenbreth and Losheim, then with 12 SS Panzer Division on the right and 1 SS Panzer Division on the left, pushes across the Maas into the sector of Lüttich–Huy. Then, according to the development of the situation, it is the task of the Corps, either to continue without interruption to Antwerp or to be ready for the protection of the right flank on the Albert-Canal.

By a rapid assault, carried out by specially organized advance detachments, under the command of particularly energetic officers, the bridges, situated in the Maas sector are to be captured undamaged.

The following units are attached: 277 Volks Grenadier Division, 12 Volks Grenadier Division, and 3 Para Division. The 3 Para Division and the 12 Volks Grenadier Division after accomplished breakthrough of the enemy main zone of resistance, will return under the command of the Army.

The II SS Panzer Corps will be situated close behind the I SS Panzer Corps, in order to follow them immediately. The II SS Panzer Corps has the mission either: to cooperate with the I SS Panzer Corps to push toward the Maas; or: immediately after having crossed the Maas – regardless of their flanks threatened by the enemy – to push toward Antwerp. Permanent contact with the I SS Panzer Corps has to be maintained. Motorized advance detachments are to follow the last fighting parts of the I SS Panzer Corps. Therefore the Corps is responsible that the approach routes behind the I SS Panzer Corps be free.

LXVII Army Corps, on X-day, with the 326 and 246 Volks Grenadier Divisions breaks through the enemy positions on both sides of Monschau – after having crossed the road Mützenich–Elsenborn turning north and west – and establishes a fixed defensive front approximately in the line Simmerath–Eupen–Limburg–Lüttich.

The 12 Volks Grenadier Division and the 3 Para Division are to be committed west of Limburg for the prolongation of the defensive front. Along the highways and the communication roads running from north to south, temporary holding positions are to be established toward north, backed up by tank groups in extended formation to the rear and the flanks. The elevated terrain around Elsenborn is to be secured.

A special order was given to the artillery, scheduling preparation, support of the attack, further activity and subordination of the artillery during the development of the combat. Besides the artillery belonging to the Army, 3 Volksartillery Corps, 2 Volkswerfer brigades and 3 detachments of heavy artillery were attached to the Army. The artillery of the Panzer Corps took part in the preparation.

The observation batteries of the I and II SS Panzer Corps were employed from 28 November for reconnaissance of the enemy artillery. This measure proved very useful, but almost provoked a catastrophe. Approximately on 1 December, a strong American reconnaissance detachment penetrated an observation post of the I SS Panzer Corps. Two of this detachment were missing. Evidently they were killed, or did not give any information, when they were captured. Anyway, the Army never found out whether the Americans obtained information on the planned offensive.

At a meeting of the Commanders in Chief and the Army Chiefs in late November, Obersturmbannführer Skorzeny was present. That day the Army was informed that a combat team under the code-name 'Operation Greif' equipped with American uniforms and vehicles should take part in the offensive, advancing in front of the armored spearheads, taking the bridges undamaged and re-routing American march columns. Assembly of this combat team (code-name '150 Panzer Brigade') was conducted in Grafenwöhr (Bavaria).

They were brought up by train to Münster–Eifel. The brigade could not accomplish their preparations, and arrived with only 10 Sherman tanks ready to be committed and 80 American or British vehicles. A special order was issued for the commitment of this brigade. A copy of the offensive fell into the hands of the enemy on the third day. However this did not affect the commitment of the brigade, because it had no more been possible to send parts of this brigade ahead of the armored points.

Beginning 1 December, no more reconnaissance activity of the advanced units was allowed. This should prevent our men, if they were made prisoners, from betraying anything concerning the approach of the artillery that could not be kept hidden from the advanced units. This security measure had to be taken, in spite of the insufficient information we could obtain regarding the enemy at that time.

In order to feign the concentration of stronger forces, on order of Army Group B, the assembly of 25th Army (which in reality did not exist) took part in the area München-Gladbach–Köln– Dusseldorf. This Army was composed of smaller operations staffs equipped with radio deception. Whether this deception was very successful, the Army never knew. The population believed that these billets were for a great number of forces.

On 10 December the Army was informed that also parachute troops would participate in the operation. A parachute detachment of about 250 men [sic; there were approximately 1,000 men in the operation] under the command of Lt Col von der Heydte would jump on the day of the offensive in front of the armored points, in order to:

    a. either open the road for the tanks in the area Hohes Venn, or:

    b. prevent the American advance between Eupen and Verviers, before a defensive front was established.

The Army requested the commitment of the parachute troops in the area of Monte Rigi (12 km southeast of Verviers), because this area seemed the most favorable for the operation. The team brought many dummies with them, in order to feign a bigger jump-operation.

Because the reinforcements (artillery etc.) and the supplies for the re-equipment did not arrive in time the beginning of the offensive had to be postponed to 14, and later to 16 December.

The code-word for the postponement was known only to the Chiefs of the Staffs of the Armies and Corps. On 11 December the Army took the command of the sector of Monschau–Ormont and shifted the Command Post to Münstereifel.

2. Supplies: As with the tactical preparations, all of the preparations for supply to be carried out from the viewpoint of the greatest secrecy. All participating organizations were not advised until the last hour of the goal of all of their preparations. They were led to believe that the supplying of all types of materials and supplies were needed for defensive battles.

The supply task was divided into two parts:

    a. Transports for the retraining of troops. It had been explained to all participating commands that the Panzer Divisions had to be brought up to their former strength. Moreover in a defense battle, it was an everyday event to bring up new forces and new material to burned out divisions.

    b. Transports for the Operation: On account of the serious air attacks on the interior of Germany, the OKW ordered that the mass of the supplies be stocked on the east bank of the Rhine. The preparation for the stocking of supplies on the west bank of the Rhine was taken over by the Armies and Corps situated there. About 11 December, there was a conference held in Münstereifel over the question of the supply during the Operations, in which the Quartermaster General Major Toppe took part. The Army took over from 10 December the forwarding of supplies for all the troops in their assigned sector pretending that the supply services of the 7 Army were not sufficient for the sector and that the Chief Quartermaster Division of the 6 Army had to take over part of the work.

Up to 12 December were prepared:

(1) Gasoline supplies providing for 300–400 km of travel, 60% of which were in the hands of the Army respectively of the attached Corps (would go about half as far in the Eifel terrain).

It was ordered that 1 consumption unit (vs = 100 km of fuel) be brought up daily. Assuming a normal bringing up of the supply, and reasonable economy of the participating divisions, it must be possible to secure the necessary daily gasoline without having to count upon captured supplies.

(2) Munitions: three issues:

(a) as expenditure for artillery fire

(b) for tactical use during the battle

(c) to be distributed in dumps, situated in the rear areas.

(d) Rations food supplies. Separate steps were not necessary since these were received in permanent ration depots.

The new supply troops of the Army were located along the west bank of the Rhine, the Chief Quartermaster in Bruehl. As far as necessary, the supply troops committed until now in the sector, were taken over by 7 Army. The commitment of new supply troops would follow immediately upon the beginning of operations. All preparations in this sector were carried through with the greatest care.

(3) Organization of the Army on 15 December 1944 (Encl. 1).

III. Strategic Concentration

The strategic concentration was carried through under the camouflage (code name) of ('ABWEHR') 'Defense'. Not until 14 December was the name disclosed and passed along to the Regimental Commanders. With this event arose the possibility of deserters or captured prisoners of war giving away the codename.

In order to preserve all the motor fuels, all troops and all types of materials needed for the operation were forwarded by train transport. In spite of enemy air superiority, and with but few exceptions, the loaded trains arrived at their destinations intact. As a result of the continuous air attacks, the troops were exceptionally well trained in camouflage. There were more trains operating for this operation than there were for the 1940 Western campaign. Even though troops often had to proceed by foot marches to their destination, the transports were brought up according to plan with only little delay.

All routes of the cross-country march, both motorized and foot, were only traveled by night. An especially difficult problem was the bringing into position and the installation of the reinforcement artillery. The fire-plan was known to the artillery commander and specific members of the Staff, under the code name 'ABWEHR' ('Defense'). The movement forward was not to begin until 8 December and only by night. In the often impassable forest country, and in the dark, misty night hours these operations were not easy. It was often extremely difficult to find the right roads since the gun positions were not permitted to be marked. The guns could not be brought into a direct line until 10 December and altogether they lay 6 km behind the Front Line. As it was not always possible to avoid rattling noises and cursing during the quiet hours of the night, the guns were brought to the fire positions by horses and personnel trains. The wheeled vehicles rolled over straw-covered road. Fires were not permitted and no talking was allowed. When one stops to think of these operations at the present time, and that normally all of these movements were only accomplished with loud noises, cursing and abuse, then it must be said that the troops really accomplished a wonderful performance. Just as difficult as the bringing of the guns into position and installing them was the bringing up of the munitions. Also we dared not bring up the munitions to the present gun positions, but rather kept them on a separate line situated about 8 km from our advanced positions. The munitions had to be hand carried over the last stretch of road. This was indeed a very troublesome and laborious work, but the soldiers carried it out willingly. By 13 December, all of the heaviest artillery was in position and well-camouflaged.

From 14 December, the Infantry Divisions were brought up in night marches and assembled. The retraining of the Infantry Divisions was not as advanced as the Army had anticipated. Additional personnel and equipment was added to the Divisions on 15 December. The 3 Para Division on account of a hard battle in the sector of Jülich–Düren was committed there and their releasing took a longer time than expected, so that the Division, with only two regiments which were ready for battle could fall in on the morning of 16 December.[4] On the whole, the assembling of troops for action on 15 December by midnight was accomplished according to plan. It would have been much better, if the troops had had two or three days more time in which to become acquainted with the country in which they found themselves and in which they were preparing to attack. However, such suggestions of the Army were refused by the Army Group, who had received very strict orders from the High Command.

The Panzer Divisions were gathered together in their assembly positions after two night marches which began on 12 December. The marches were carried out under cover of darkness, so that all of the motor vehicles, which had not arrived in their assembly areas by the early gray hours of the morning, had to remain where they were. For the orderly execution of these movements it was necessary to set up an extensive system of traffic control – MPs – to effect a repair and recovery service for the motor vehicles which had fallen behind in order to prevent them being seen by day.

The sheltering areas of the Panzer Corps were so selected by the army, so that their assembly area could only be reached without difficulty. The many wooded areas and forests in this sector greatly facilitated the work of assembling the troops, the munitions and the motor fuels. The morale of the troops was very good.

In the end, all preparations had been carried through so that the breakthrough at least to the Meuse had to be successful. The German High Command expected that the Maas would be reached within two days time.

The Army had to set up the following calculations:

One day to break through to the enemy positions.

One day to go over the Hohes Venn with the Panzer Divisions.

Two days to cross over the Maas – altogether four days.

The air force and the III Flak-Corps the Army was obliged to co-operate with, were closely instructed in the intentions of the Army; with the Army were some Liaison Officers for the Luftwaffe who were equipped with Signal communications.

IV A. Progress of the Operation

16 December: At 0530 hours started the very strong artillery preparation on the whole front. Till 0600 hours the artillery fired on the enemy advance positions and continued harassing fire on enemy batteries, reconnoitered by the observation batteries.

The attack of the infantry that started at 0600 hours, was backed up by light and heavy batteries. As it was still too dark for the forward observation posts to see anything, the fire had to precede the infantry. Heavy batteries continued harassing fire on enemy batteries. The preliminary operation was carried out by special assault troops (infantry and engineers). The infantry advanced without difficulty at all points of the breakthrough. The enemy artillery started fire only after 0800 hours. From the sector of the 12 Volks Grenadier Division it was reported that an overpass was blown up near Losheimergraben, that could not be repaired by their forces. Engineers of the I SS Panzer Corps were sent out immediately, who repaired the bridge temporarily and built an emergency bridge for the tanks. At about 1300 hours, the infantry had made a general advance of 4 km into the enemy positions. Isolated assault troops reported retrograde movements of the American infantry corps. However the Army was of the opinion, that only the dug-in outpost positions were drawn back to the main resistance line, but not that the whole main resistance line was withdrawn. At road crossings and forest trails, where tanks were backing-up the American infantry, the resistance was tough and the attack made only slow progress. Tank emplacements had to be bypassed. The condition of the roads was bad, they were partly mined, and the terrain was very muddy, which made the commitment of the tanks off the road almost impossible. In order to exploit the initial success of artillery and infantry, the Army ordered the commitment of panzer divisions of the I SS Panzer Corps, with the instruction to commit first only armored infantry and engineers for the backing up of the infantry and to commit the tanks afterwards.

During the morning, the Army shifted their Command Post to Marmagen.

At about 1700 hours the situation was as follows: The LXVII Army Corps that had broken through approximately 2–3 km into the enemy positions, had great difficulties in overcoming the terrain. The Army had reckoned with these difficulties and ordered the Corps to continue the attack even during the night, and pointed out that enemy attacks from the area of Elsenborn southwest had to be smashed by all means. Two assault gun brigades were brought up to the Corps to assist.

The 12 Volks Grenadier Division, the attacking group of the I SS Panzer Corps, backed up by armored infantry of the 12 SS Panzer Division, had made good progress. The operations were not yet finished, the American resistance was particularly tough and the losses very high in the area of Losheimergraben. The attack group (3 Para Division) had met at the beginning stiff resistance, but a motorized group of the 1 SS Panzer Division was advancing on the road Honsfeld–Möderscheid. Details were still missing.

The I SS Panzer Corps received orders from the Army to continue the attack with the infantry during the night and to fall in the next morning as early as possible with the panzer divisions. In no case was the 12 SS Panzer Division to be engaged in fighting against the enemy, who eventually would attack from the north. An Army engineer battalion was made available for the repair of the bridge in the area Losheimergraben.

The II SS Panzer Corps was informed about the situation and instructed that, in case of a favorable progress of the attack of the 1 SS Panzer Division, a division of the II SS Panzer Corps would be committed behind the 1 SS Panzer Division.

During the night 16/17 December, the first part of the II SS Panzer Corps was advanced to the line Gemünd–Stadtkyll.

There were no attacks of the enemy air force on 16 December and the poor flying weather was favorable for the Army. The enemy artillery activity had been comparatively weak, although a stronger artillery group were reported in the area of Elsenborn.

Our artillery displaced to change their position; this was started already by mid-day.

17 December: A portion of the attacks had continued during the night. The LXVII Army Corps with 326 and 246 Volks Grenadier Divisions [sic] had opened the road Monschau–Mützenich, and a strong combat team was advancing past Höfen toward Kalterherberg.[5] Monschau was to be bypassed. On orders of Field Marshal Model, this German town was not to be fired on by artillery, in order to spare the lattice-work houses.

In the morning, the Army ordered the Corps to open the road Kalterherberg–Elsenborn and to attack the forces situated around Elsenborn (artillery and reserves). Till the late evening hours, this was impossible, the road being effectively blocked by abatis and mines.

The 277 Volks Grenadier Division was to continue their attack on both sides of Udenbreth past Krinkelt–Wirtzfeld for a later assault on Sourbrodt, south of Elsenborn. The division was reinforced by its assault gun company [six StuG III] that had not been ready for the commitment on 16 December (because the last parts of this detachment could only be extricated during the night 15/16 December). It was to be expected that the division with their attack in the direction of Elsenborn would gain terrain and contain the enemy forces that were situated in this area. The division had particular difficulties with the terrain.

In the morning, a message of the I SS Panzer Corps reported that the combat team of the 1 SS Panzer Division had broken through at 0400 hours but no more detailed information was available.

The 12 Volks Grenadier Division, that presently was attacking Hünningen, was ordered now to cooperate with the 12 SS Panzer Division and to open the road across Weismes in the direction of Malmédy, while the 3 Para Division was to take part in the attack, echeloned in depth and toward the left, pushing in the direction of Manderfeld.

At noon 17 December, the Army believed that the breakthrough of the 12 SS Panzer Division past Büllingen and the south border of Malmédy would be successful, and had given orders in the afternoon to the II SS Panzer Corps that the 9 SS Panzer Division be ready for the march, and that the road across Losheim be reconnoitered for this division. The 9 SS Panzer Division, if necessary, was to be committed on the left side of the 1 SS Panzer Division, under command of the I SS Panzer Corps, for an attack past Losheim, Amel (Ambleve) and Vielsalm. St. Vith was to be bypassed, because it was considered as the first objective of the enemy bombers. The intention of the Army was, regardless of actual attachments and plans, to win space to the west.

Since 0930 hours, the enemy artillery activity was stronger than on the preceding day, but our artillery could break up the infantry effectively from the new position. On 17 December, the enemy air activity was not appreciably stronger than on the day before. However, it was evident that the difficulties of the terrain for our advance were much more important than expected.

On a very muddy and hilly terrain near Büllingen the 12 Volks Grenadier Division met strong enemy forces with antitank guns and several tanks, and till the afternoon did not advance past the hills south of Büllingen. The I SS Panzer Corps reported that roads to bypass such resistance were reconnoitered. No further reports were received from the 1 SS Panzer Division, because the staff was on the march. In order to receive more rapidly messages from the I SS Panzer Corps, the Army had already sent out a liaison radio station, and sent another armed radio detachment immediately after the 1 SS Panzer Division.

Through an air force liaison officer radio communications existed with the parachute group von der Heydte, although other communications were not yet possible.[6] Several assault detachments of the 'Operation Greif' were operating in the enemy rear zone. The 2 Panzer Division (5 Panzer Army) in their attack north of Bastogne, and the LXVI Army Corps, bypassing the Schnee-Eifel with two foot divisions, made good progress.

On the whole, the enemy situation was as expected. The enemy had not reckoned with such a strong offensive which evidently had provoked a great confusion. Except some isolated combat teams (east of Elsenborn and Büllingen), the resistance was not very strong. Concentrated artillery fire under co-ordinated direction was not yet applied and there was only isolated commitment of enemy air force over the front. However the supply troops reported strong air activity in the rear zone that prevented the bringing up of the supply. On 17 December, however, these raids had no influence on the supply of the troops. The objectives, planned by the High Command, were not yet attained, but there were no reasons for worry. The Army had expected great difficulties for the first days, and believed that the Maas could not be attained before the evening of the 3rd day.

18 December: The LXVII Corps had advanced forward very slowly with the northern combat team. The roads were mined and obstructed with tree blocks and mines. Enemy resistance gradually became more fierce in the path of these divisions.[7] It was clear to the Army at this time, that the expected goal – breakthrough on both sides of Monschau and the cutting off of the road Monschau–Eupen – would not be reached. The Army found it impossible to reinforce this Combat team. Because of a series of train destructions, an expected heavy Panzerjäger battalion did not arrive.[8] The Volks Grenadier Divisions were too weak for this type of attack and were not sufficiently reorganized.

It contented the Army however, when these divisions blocked off the forest exits of the Hohes Venn on both sides of the road Eupen–Monschau, and closed in the Americans who stood in readiness for an attack in the direction of Urftalsperre–Euskirchen. A solid block in the sector of Monschau was important to the Army, as it was not possible to have a successful engagement step by step in the heavily impassable wooded country. The attempts, to win the roads from Monschau to Euskirchen to the camp at Elsenborn, and from there the roads from Büllingen to Weismes, were continued in cooperation with 277 Volks Grenadier Division, which continued the attacks near Udenbreth.

The 277 Volks Grenadier Division advanced well forward on 18 December, and took the heights north of Wirtzfeld. With this the Division was freed and together with the 12 Volks Grenadier Division could attack in the direction of Elsenborn. This was ordered for the 19 December. The attacks – Monschau and Elsenborn – had to be under the direction of LXVII Corps.

The 12 Volks Grenadier Division had together with the 12 SS Panzer Division taken Büllingen after a hard battle. Both divisions fought for the village Bütgenbach against a strongly defended enemy, who for the first time attacked with tanks. The 3 Para Division was over Herresbach–Heppenbach. The 1 SS Panzer Division had taken Trois-Ponts and was advancing. The weather cleared about noon. Employment of allied air forces began to develop. As was later seen the spearhead of the 1 SS Panzer Division was attacked.

It was important for the Army to support the 1 SS Panzer Division to win further terrain to the west before the enemy succeeded in bringing up stronger forces, and to prevent the building up of a solid defense front eastwards or westwards of the Maas. The enemy counteroffensive started about noon on the 18th. From intercepted radio broadcasts of the American MPs, it was to be seen that troops movements from the sector of Aachen in the direction of Verviers and eastwards of Lüttich were beginning. The movements of the troops showed obviously that besides an Armored Division only Engineer and antitank guns battalions were on the march, that the objective was to block off the heights and the wooded terrain east of the Maas, between Lüttich and Namur. At the same time, it was heard that inconsiderate orders had been given against the many civilian refugees which filled the roads.

The Army order for 19 December was: enlarge the breakthrough area on both sides of Monschau and attack with the 12 Volks Grenadier Division and the 277 Volks Grenadier Division, the enemy situated at Bütgenbach and throw him back to Elsenborn. Later, with the 277 Volks Grenadier Division on the left, to establish a solid defense front on the line Monschau–Hohes Venn south of Verviers. Enemy breakthroughs over Monschau to the west and the southwest were to be prevented.

I SS Panzer Corps was to extract the 12 SS Panzer Division and attack with the 12 SS Panzer Division through Malmédy. The attack of the 1 SS Panzer Division was to be supported by all means and the supplies secured. The 3 Para Division for the backing up of the advancing 12 SS Panzer Division is to be committed for an attack over the Möderscheid, Faymonville to Weismes. With this order the Army had the intention to prevent under all circumstances that part of the 1 SS Panzer Division or the 12 SS Panzer Division that were committed in northern direction of Verviers from being engaged on their northern flanks.

The II SS Panzer Corps held itself in further readiness to move off with the 9 SS Panzer Division south of the I SS Panzer Corps. The I SS Panzer Corps informed Army in the night that it was not possible for the 12 SS Panzer Division to start the attack south of Bütgenbach because the road Büllingen, Möderscheid, Schoppen was for the most part impassable because of the mire. The Division also could not pull out its vehicles from the sector of Losheim, and that from here the entire road network was impassable and it would take a day to bring them up. The Corps asked for permission to attack once more with the 12 SS Panzer Division and the 12 Volks Grenadier Division in order to gain the road across Bütgenbach. That was approved, simultaneously an order to the II SS Panzer Corps was given to attack with the 9 SS Panzer Division and to advance past Krewinkel, Wischeid, Andler, Medell, Recht, Halleux or Vielsalm. In case this thrust should succeed, it was the intention of the Army, with the 1 SS Panzer Division and the 9 SS Panzer Division to cross over the Maas under command of the II SS Panzer Corps. Later, after mopping up of Bütgenbach and Malmédy, to follow with the 2 SS and the 12 SS Panzer Divisions under command of the II SS Panzer Corps. The Commander in Chief of Army Group B was in accord with the view of the Army that the 2 SS Panzer Division could be brought up past Prüm, Pronsfeld, Habscheid, and St. Vith. It is also to be taken into consideration, that the 2 SS Panzer Division temporarily would be attached to the 5 Panzer Army. The Army was pleased at the possibility of this solution, and during the night ordered road reconnaissance. The breakthrough of the 2 SS Panzer Division depended upon the freedom of the roads, and on the bringing up of the gasoline supply, necessitated for the bypassing of 2 SS Panzer Division.

For the improvement of the road in the sector of Losheim and south of Bütgenbach a Pioneer Battalion was detailed and put under the command of the Chief Engineer of the Army.

Unfortunately, the road repair Construction Battalion from the TODT organization did not leave for this important work until after great delay.

The weather was foggy, the enemy air force only made isolated attacks, and no larger action developed. Unfortunately the ground began to thaw in the early morning hours and the roads and trails then became marshy. The night hours were not cold enough to cause a refreezing of this mud and mire.

19 December: On that day the enemy countermeasures were quite obvious. The enemy resistance against the LXVII Army Corps was growing. Counterattacks were made in the north. The terrain captured during the preceding days had to be given up. Kalterherberg, south of Monschau, was taken. The 277 Volks Grenadier Division reached the road Forsterei Wahlerscheid–Rocherath. On the whole, no perceptible progress was made. On 18 December, a Volksartillery Corps was attached to the LXVII Army Corps and was moving up to the new positions.

The 12 SS Panzer Divisions and 12 Volks Grenadier Division of the I SS Panzer Corps could not advance against the increasing enemy forces. The terrain being very muddy, the infantry advanced only slowly, and the tanks could not be committed off the road. Enemy antitank guns and tanks were well emplaced. Stronger artillery fire and the difficult terrain would probably prevent our breakthrough past Bütgenbach, because it was no more possible for the attacking forces to move into the assembly positions. Evidently the two divisions did not find the appropriate terrain for the attack, the battalions could not advance on the muddy ground and had to use the roads, where they were exposed to the enemy artillery. The heavy enemy artillery fire temporarily caused much disorganization within the two divisions. Tanks, that during the morning hours had found a bypassing road south of Bütgenbach, broke down in the mud at the west end of the village and only at night could be removed from there with great difficulties. A further advance was impossible with these ground conditions. Therefore, the Army gave order in the afternoon that the 12 SS Panzer Division cease the attack, be extracted rapidly and assembled in the area Baasem–Losheim–Manderfeld, and be sent either after the 1 SS Panzer Division or the 9 SS Panzer Division.

The 3 Para Division had well advanced (obviously they met upon weak enemy forces that fell back at their approach) and their advanced echelons had reached Schoppen. The Corps was given order to veer with the Division and to take Weismes. This operation would have relieved the divisions that attacked near Büllingen, and besides the relief of the 1 SS Panzer Division, the establishment of a key point for a defensive front toward north would have been possible.

The division either did not understand the importance of this order or the division was not brought up rapidly enough. The enemy occupation of Weismes (on 20 December) was strong, and the division was not strong enough to take it.[9] They did not advance farther than Faymonville. The 1 SS Panzer Division had pushed past La Gleize toward Stoumont and taken Cheneux. At noon the armored spearheads were attacked by enemy fighter bombers. With the advance of the 1 SS Panzer Division, the difficulties of the Hohes Venn, in spite of the bad road conditions, were overcome. This success had to be exploited rapidly. Therefore, the 1 SS Panzer Division was given order to continue their forward movement, fanning out on a wider front, and the I SS Panzer Corps was to secure the gasoline supply.

In the evening it was reported that the Kampfgruppe Peiper, advanced combat team of the 1 SS Panzer Division, had been attacked, and that also the parts that were following, were engaged against enemy forces, that had pushed past Spa toward La Gleize. It was possible now, that not only the Kampfgruppe would be cut off, but that the entire 1 SS Panzer Division would have to turn north against the approaching enemy forces.

The Corps gave an order to keep contact between the 3 Para Division and the Kampfgruppe and to commit a mobile security detachment in the line west of Faymonville, south of Malmédy, in order to protect the flank and to reconnoiter toward north. The reconnaissance detachment of the 12 SS Panzer Division [Kampfgruppe Bremer] and the supply troops were to be employed for this security mission.

The Army considered the possibility of committing the 3 Para Division for the flank protection on both sides of Malmédy, but then made a different decision because:

    a. The important road Weismes–St. Vith would thus be clear for the enemy.

    b. The parachute division had not arrived in time.

If possible, all the fighting parts of the division were to be relieved, far out on a wider front and to be committed for an attack on Stoumont. It was important to act rapidly and to overcome the difficulties of the roads.

Evidently, the command of the division did not keep the contact with Kampfgruppe Peiper, or their reconnaissance activity toward north was not sufficient, because they believed that the 12 SS Panzer Division was advancing on their right side.

As an exact copy of the orders for the 'Operation Greif' had been captured by the enemy, the bigger part of the reconnaissance detachments of this group could not be committed, and the planned surprise action against the enemy units could not be carried out. No contact could be established with the Parachute group von der Heydte.

At noon, the II SS Panzer Corps was given order to move up the 2 SS Panzer Division past Prüm, Habscheid, St. Vith (if 15 Army decided), otherwise past Habscheid, Burg Reuland, Bochholz. Army Group B had the intention to commit this division either with the 5 Panzer Army, or only to move them up to their sector and to attach them to the 6 Panzer Army. In the sector of the 5 Panzer Army the roads were better and would facilitate the commitment of the 2 SS Panzer Division at the side of the 9 SS or even beside the 1 SS Panzer Divisions. This movement, however, could not be accomplished in time, because the Führer Begleit-Brigade and the 116 Panzer Division blocked the roads south of St. Vith. The 2 SS Panzer Division could only be committed in the morning of 23 December.[10]

Enemy situation: Several days had passed before the enemy started to take countermeasures. From intercepted radio messages we know that:

    a. a defensive front was to be established west of the Maas;

    b. advanced obstacle construction units (engineers, antitank units and some tank detachments) were to be committed east of the Maas between Verviers and Dinant;

    c. units from the area of Aachen were moving up for commitment against the north flank of the Army.

As long as the weather prevented a stronger enemy air activity, it was still possible to break through the enemy defensive front, that was being established, and to destroy the enemy armor. The advantage of the Allies – better vehicles and a greater number of divisions – could be eliminated by rapid action and the greatest efforts.

20 December: The enemy resistance on both sides of Monschau was increasing. Assault detachments, that had crossed the Laufen-brook (north of Monschau) and the Schwalm (southwest of Monschau), had to be withdrawn. The LXVII Army Corps with the 277 and 12 Volks Grenadier and the 3 Para Divisions had taken to the defensive. This defensive front extended approximately in the line Simmerath – east of Monschau – Schwalm – Hill 475 (east of Kalterherberg) – Hill 550 northeast of Elsenborn – Wirtzfeld – south of Bütgenbach – Hill 557 (north of Ondenval) – Baugnez – Stavelot. It was important for the LXVII Army Corps to hold this line, because otherwise the supply of the 1 SS Panzer Division would become even more difficult. Manderfel and Möderscheid were already under intermittent artillery fire.

The 3 Panzer Grenadier Division was brought up to the Army in order to be committed near Elsenborn, if required by the command. The advanced parts of this division arrived on 21 December near Sistig. Without reinforcement, the 12 Volks Grenadier Division could not make a further attack near Bütgenbach.

The 12 SS Panzer Division was in the area assigned for the assembly. However, the bad roads delayed the assembly of the troops that was accomplished only on 23 December. A comparatively high number of tanks broke down during the operation. Orders for their repair were given immediately. The vehicles, many that had seen extensive use during the long war and often had unskilled drivers, were not always satisfactory.

The 1 SS Panzer Division, on 20 December, could not establish the contact with their advanced Kampfgruppe Peiper, that was being attacked by strong enemy forces and, during the night 20/21 December, had to withdraw to Cheneux. Nor was it possible to bring up the gasoline supply to this combat team by road. Therefore supply by air was requested. The I SS Panzer Corps had ordered the regrouping of the attack groups of the 1 SS Panzer Division and expected the success of the attack, that was to establish the contact with the Kampfgruppe the next day. Again it was quite obvious, that the terrain did not permit the commitment of tanks off the roads. Isolated antitank guns and tanks, dug-in at road crossings, often prevented any advance on both sides.

The II SS Panzer Corps was on the march. The 9 SS Panzer Division had a long delay at a blown up bridge near Andler. They advanced dismounted and mopped-up the north sector of the forest of Ommerscheid, where some enemy forces were still situated. The march on the muddy terrain and the carrying of the heavy infantry weapons and ammunition exhausted the troops completely.

The 5 Panzer Army, that had the possibility to advance with their right wing, took Born (north of St. Vith) with the Führer Begleit-Brigade. This success and the advance of the LXVI Army Corps cleared the enemy from St. Vith. Thus an important road junction in the left Army sector could be utilized. St. Vith was not to be occupied, because strong enemy air raids on this town were expected as soon as the weather changed. An engineer construction

battalion was brought to St. Vith, in order to secure the passage or the out-
flanking of this town.

The Army expected that the 1 SS Panzer Division would break through
again, and intended to attach the 9 SS Panzer Division to the I SS Panzer Corps.
It was also suggested that the Führer Begleit-Brigade should be attached to the
II SS Panzer Corps, and that this Corps (277 Volks Grenadier Division and
Führer Begleit) should attack south of the I SS Panzer Corps. Army Group B
approved of this suggestion, but did not yet pronounce a final decision. The
Army recognized that the continuation of the operation in the present direction
would meet upon great difficulties:

a. The forces that were to be committed for the isolation of Elsenborn
were too weak, even if the 3 Panzer Grenadier Division would also be committed. Thus the advance of our defensive flank to the line Monschau–Spa was
in question.

b. We had to reckon with the fact that two more days would pass, before
the 9 and 2 SS Panzer Divisions could be committed.

c. In spite of the greatest efforts and the commitment of all available
forces, it was impossible to repair the roads in the rear zone, in order to establish
an orderly method of re-supply.

Therefore on 20 December, the Army submitted the following suggestion to
the Commander in Chief of Army Group B: either to commit all available
panzer divisions in the direction of Huy–Dinant, or – and that seemed more
appropriate to the Commander in Chief of the Army – to advance north on the
good roads Houffalize– La Roche–Lüttich and to push into the enemy defensive
front, that was being built up, and in joint operation with 15 Army to attack
the rear of the enemy forces situated between Aachen and Lüttich, regardless of
the endangered flank at Elsenborn–Malmédy.

The Commander in Chief of the Army Group B did not approve of this
suggestion, but wanted to submit it to higher Headquarters. The Army never
received an approving answer. Maybe that the suggestion could no more be
carried out, because the mobile divisions [9th Panzer and 15th Panzergrenadier
Divisions] necessitated from the 15 Army for this attack had been extracted in
the meantime and committed in another sector.

21 December: The Army consolidated their defensive front and tried to
bring up the panzer divisions as rapidly as possible to the main resistance line.
All available forces, even the German civilian population, were committed, in
order to overcome the difficulties of the roads. The military police services
worked very hard and did an excellent job in those days. In spite of all the orders
that were issued on that subject, the troops – Panzer Divisions, artillery,
antiaircraft – never got rid of unnecessary vehicles, that were not capable of
cross-country driving, especially in the Eifel-mountains, and often delayed all
traffic for several hours.[11]

There was almost no enemy air activity over the sector of the fighting troops, because of the weather conditions, and enemy air activity was particularly strong over the rear zone. Trains, road junctions and supply traffic and dumps were bombed. Between 21 and 23 December, the Command Post of the LXVII Army Corps was bombed and had several casualties but could continue to work.[12] These air raids caused sensible delays in the bringing up of the supplies, that often had to be carried out during the night. Moreover, the supply dumps of the Army Group B had to be shifted often and gasoline supply columns, that were already in route, arrived late or not at all. One had to live from hand to mouth, and it happened very often that a tactical success could not be exploited, because the gasoline or ammunition did not arrive in time, or in too small quantities. The fuel consumption per 100 km was much higher than calculated before, because of the bad road conditions. If some of the supplies arrived at all in the main resistance line, it was due to the untiring activity of the truck drivers and the energy of the staff of the supply services.

The LXVII Army Corps was regrouped for the attack against Elsenborn. The troops were to attack Weywertz as follows: Parts of 246 Volks Grenadier Division past Kalterherberg, the 3 Panzer Grenadier Division and 277 Volks Grenadier Division across the road Foersterei Wahlerscheid, Rocherath, the 12 Volks Grenadier Division and parts of the 3 Para Division past Bütgenbach. Then in a joint operation, these forces were to push past Elsenborn toward the road Sourbrodt, Weismes. The attack was scheduled for the 23 December. On 22 December, parts of the 3 Panzer Grenadier Division were to be attached to the 12 Volks Grenadier Division.

The 1 SS Panzer Division had not succeeded in establishing the contact with Kampfgruppe Peiper, which was heavily attacked and encircled in a sector that was comparatively narrow. This made even a supply by air almost impossible.

The 12 SS Panzer Division was still assembling. The II SS Panzer Corps and the 9 SS Panzer Division were advancing past Recht toward the Salm-sector. The 2 SS Panzer Division that originally was to be attached to the 5 Panzer Army, was moving toward Bochholz. The march was delayed, because the division was stopped several times by march columns of the 116 Panzer Division and the Führer Begleit-Brigade.

The Parachute Group von der Heydte was instructed by an air force liaison officer, that the contact could not be established, and that the commander of this group was to fight his way through to Monschau (several messengers had re-joined friendly lines moving in the direction of Monschau), or to surrender after having fired the last round.

22 December: The LXVII Corps carried out further preparations for the planned attack on 23 December. Besides some local thrusts, enemy attacks did not materialize. Only the enemy artillery became heavier, its fire on the road

Honsfeld, Möderscheld made it untrafficable. The Army pushed on with the completion of the road Losheimergraben–Honsfeld, Amel.

With the I SS Panzer Corps the enemy pressure became greater, which weakened the attacks made for the relief of the Kampfgruppe Peiper. They did not succeed in establishing contact. The Army ordered the I SS Panzer Corps once again, to free the Kampfgruppe Peiper by all means and to prevent troops and valuable material from falling into the hands of the enemy. Supply by air was not sufficient, and it was attempted to supply badly needed motor fuels by means of armored vehicles.

These attempts also failed. Kampfgruppe Peiper suffered heavy casualties because of the fierceness of enemy artillery fire. As it was later reported, Obersturmbannführer Peiper arranged on 22 or 23 December a truce of several hours, in order to exchange the wounded.[13]

The II SS Panzer Corps with the 9 SS Panzer Division in their advance on Vielsalm had to march on foot because of the bad roads, while the first parts of the 2 SS Panzer Division had made contact with the enemy at Cierreux. Here, the Army had perhaps a possibility to 'kill two birds with one stone' namely:

   a. Tear open the enemy defense front on the line La Gleize–Bra–Erezee–Marche.

   b. Help the Group Peiper through a thrust over Manhay–Werbomont. (At the same time exploiting the good roads which lay in the northwest direction of the sector Maas–Lüttich–Huy.)

The Army ordered therefore, that the II SS Panzer Corps throw the enemy out by a quick thrust and win the sector Aisne [River] between Mormont and Erezee. It was intended, then with the 2 SS Panzer Division to win further terrain over this sector. The Army figured on the attachment of the 116 Panzer Grenadier Division or the Führer Begleit-Brigade.

The line of separation to the 5 Panzer Army was changed through a new order from the Army Group B, and now ran over Prüm–Bleialf–Samree – along the Ourthe–Andenne [River]. The Army proposed to the Army Group B that the LXVII Corps be placed under the 15 Army, because they were still tied in too far to the rear.

23 December: The attack as scheduled, of the LXVII Corps started in the morning hours. It had, except some local improvements of the front no success. The road Krinkelt–Foersterei–Wahlerscheid was opened and the important heights west of this road were taken in possession. Strong shock troops had also occupied the Hill 598, south of Kalterherberg. They had, however, to give it up again during the night of 23/24 December. The 3 Para Division announced next that Weismes and Oberweywertz were taken. However, this proved to be false. The Army expected no success in the course of the day, from a continuation of the attack on 24 December, because the 3 Panzer Grenadier Division had to be given up to the 5 Panzer Army. The Army proposed to the

Army Group B to carry on the attack on 27 December after renewed preparation. The Army had to be prepared for an attack, that would be launched across the line north of Monschau and Malmédy against their deep flank and the supply bases. Therefore, only part of the divisions appointed for the operation could attack, because otherwise the front would have been too much exposed. Only after a very careful improvement of the position could the fighting part of the divisions be extricated.

With the I SS Panzer Corps the situation had developed so that it no longer appeared possible to relieve the Kampfgruppe Peiper from the enemy pressure. The 1 SS Panzer Division was engaged with an essential part to secure the northern flank in the sector Weismes–Stavelot. The necessary motor fuels did not arrive. The Army ordered the Group Peiper to break through the encirclement to the east and to hold the sector directly eastwards of Trois-Ponts. The first part of the 12 SS Panzer Division were moving past Scheid toward St. Vith. Next, they had to be assembled in the sector of St. Vith behind the II SS Panzer Corps. Because of a lack of motor fuel, the march past Prüm behind the 2 SS Panzer Division as suggested by the Army, could not be carried out. The shortage of motor fuels caused especially great difficulties in the period 23/25 December.

The II SS Panzer Corps crossed over the Salm with the 9 SS Panzer Division at Salmchâteau and attacked with the 2 SS Panzer Division over Baraque de Fraiture in the direction of Grandmenil. At Les Tailles and Baraque de Fraiture they ran head-on into an American Armored Battalion.[14] From the mentioned shortage of motor fuels, the division was no longer able to thrust further to the west. In the afternoon, the LXVI Army Corps, that had advanced on both sides of the Schree-Eifel – commanded by General Lucht – with the 62 Volks Grenadier Division and the 18 Infantry Division were attached to the Army.

The Corps was on a march over St. Vith and Burg Reuland to the Salm sector. The Army gave the Corps the order to turn to the north and to clean up the country on both sides of the Salm from the enemy, with the intention to relieve 1 SS Panzer Division through the division on the right side and to extend the defense flank toward west with the division that advanced on the left side of the Salm. It remained to be seen whether the II SS Panzer Corps could advance further beyond Baraque de Fraiture.

24 December: The enemy air force immediately appeared with clear weather. The heavy bombardment of the rail and road junction center of St. Vith, Münstereifel, Prüm, and Stadtkyll was especially disagreeable, since it considerably slowed down the movement of the supply traffic.

In the sector of the LXVII Corps there were no other engagements. The combat team Peiper of the 1 SS Panzer Division of the I SS Panzer Corps fought its way back to Wanne. All ordnance material and non-expendable supplies – panzers, guns, etc. – were destroyed or they fell into enemy hands. Through this were the fighting possibilities of the 1 SS Panzer Division seriously impaired.

The proposed plans of the Army – the commitment of the 9 SS Panzer Division – were thereby revoked.

The II SS Panzer Corps reached Arbrefontaine with the 9 SS Panzer Division and the 2 SS Panzer Division took Manhay. Reconnaissance located enemy blocking positions in the woods north of Vaux Chavanne. LXVII Corps was advancing on both sides of Vielsalm and only met upon enemy resistance.

The enemy situation: The overall picture of the enemy was that he was gathering together his forces in preparation for an offensive, and was grouping together for countermeasures. The advance was not always carried on without incidents, despite the best of materials. The plans of the enemy seemed clear through his building up of blocked positions along the line Malmédy–Stoumont–Werbomont–Erezee–Marche. His front took advantage of the woods and the hilly terrain through which flowed rivers and streams, could be held with relatively weak infantry forces.

The enemy forces which were formerly gathered west of the Maas, now appeared gathered east of the Maas, either to strengthen the defense front or to be ready for an attack. Parts of mobile forces appeared in the region of La Glaize and north of La Roche. Their strengthening, especially near Malmédy, had to be taken into consideration. These could either thrust to the rear of the path of the army – II SS Panzer Corps – or could operate against the standing forces by thrusting in the deep flanks of the Army in the sector around Elsenborn by a push in the direction of the Moselle, in order to cut off Army Group B in a joint operation with the forces assembled in front of 7 Army. The gathering of enemy forces did not yet appear complete, and the Army had to figure on winning further space to the west by a further thrust, and to compel the enemy to use his troops.

The II SS Panzer Corps was therefore ordered not to halt, and to thrust forward in the general direction of the crossroads southwest of Durbuy. Simultaneously the Army Group B was asked that the 116 Panzer Division be placed under the Army. The subordination was not allowed, and in return the 3 Panzer Grenadier Division was taken from the Army. It was foreseen that another Panzer Division must be given to the 5 Panzer Army. In the evening hours, the Army shifted its command headquarters towards Meyerode – 8 km NE of St. Vith.

25 December: The day proceeded without any special engagements.

The 12 SS Panzer Division was placed under the 5 Panzer Army in order to clear up the situation at Bastogne. The 5 Panzer Army had taken Hotton with the 116 Panzer Division. The 2 SS Panzer Division had received the order to thrust out in the direction of Durbuy, early on the 26 December.

The Group Skorzeny was taken out and transported back to Grafenwöhr. Commitment with the 5 Panzer Army was contemplated but not carried out, because through the captured order, surprise no longer appeared possible.

26 December: The enemy air force activity was for the first time especially strong. They had the intention to halt our offensive.

The LXVII Corps was placed under command of the 15 Army. The contact between the two units was to the right of the 15 Army at Baugnez – 3 km SE of Malmédy. The LXVII Corps had thrown back a weak enemy force with its two divisions, and went into a defensive position on a direct line Baugnez–Stavelot–Trois-Ponts–Reharmont. I SS Panzer Corps gathered together with the 1 SS Panzer Division north of St. Vith. The 1 SS Panzer Division was put under the 5 Panzer Army on 26 December. With the 9 SS Panzer Division the II SS Panzer Corps had won the heights eastwards of Bra, and with the 2 SS Panzer Division, the heights eastwards of Erezee-Soy. Meanwhile the situation had improved at Bastogne; the army still contemplated further on assistance to the 5 Panzer Army.

27 December: The I SS Panzer Corps was given along with the 12 SS Panzer Division to the 5 Panzer Army for the commitment at Bastogne. The intent no longer remained with the Army, to carry through a thrust to the west, chiefly since they could not figure on another panzer division being placed under them. The II SS Panzer Corps tried once more to make a thrust on the enemy defense front, between Bra and Hotton. However, the enemy had already become so strong, that all of these local thrusts proved unsuccessful. Moreover, the enemy air force was out in full strength since the weather had cleared up considerably. Movements during the day were often not possible. As our air force did not succeed in coming through to our advanced parts, the troops – as happened already often in the West – remained without air defense. Our antiaircraft operated successfully but could not provide relief. In order to protect the supply routes, the AA regiment had divided itself into small groups on the roads, was well camouflaged and thus managed to keep low flying fighter bombers more discreet.

28 December: Since the Army took the defensive approximately on the following line: Baugnez–Trois-Ponts–south of Bra to Hotton with the LXVII Corps and the II SS Panzer Corps.

IV B. The Enemy Countermeasures

The Army was greatly weakened by the departure of the I SS Panzer Corps. We had to expect that the enemy would feel out the long flank and try to make a breakthrough at the weakest spots. Therefore, it was expected that the enemy would choose to attack with either the right wing Prüm or over Malmédy to St. Vith. Here was also the weakest spot of the Army, and especially on the boundary of the 3 Para Division at Baugnez. This point was looked upon with the greatest anxiety. In order to have at least a mobile reserve, the tanks (that were in repair) of the armored regiment of the 1 SS Panzer Division, and that after the breakthrough from La Gleize were being re-equipped with difficulty –

with two maintenance companies – were shifted into the wood northwest of Ober-Emmels.

A company of these Panzers were always held in readiness. However, this security measure was not necessary, because the enemy had not yet attacked at Malmédy as expected, but had chosen the 'smallest solution' (attack in the direction of La Roche–Houffalize).

The enemy attacks between 29 December and 4 January 1945 were seen by the army as reinforced reconnaissance. They were, except some local penetrations, resisted with our supporting artillery. The main attack was directed against: Stavelot and the line Grandmenil–Hotton. The enemy attacked more at front between Hotton–Marche. However, the front could, in general, be held. The Army took its HQ to Thommen – 10 km SW of St. Vith – on 3 January.

The beginning of larger attacks were expected to begin on 4 January. For support at Bastogne, the 9 SS Panzer Division had to be given up. By the night of 3/4 January the Army had only the 2 SS Panzer Division as mobile troops at its disposal and for defense only Volks Grenadier Divisions. It was a Panzer Army in name only.

On 3 January, the Army was reinforced with the 12 Volks Grenadier Division, which came from Bütgenbach to Rodt. To the West, the strongly projecting curved salient could be held until about 8 January. The strength of the Army was overburdened, the front so stretched that it was almost torn apart. Great anxiety was caused over the motor fuel situation. The available motor fuels went to the 5 Panzer Army, because in general the motor vehicles had only enough motor fuel at their disposal to go about 20 km. In case of a strong penetration, it was not known whether or not it would be possible to evacuate all guns, panzers and assault guns.

On the 3 January, the boundary of the 5 Panzer Army was fixed as follows: Marche–La Roche course over the Ourthe–Houffalize–Weiswampach–Prüm. At the same time the 116 Panzer Division was placed under the 6 Panzer Army.

Simultaneously the Army received the order that, with the beginning of the evening of 9 January, the projecting, curved front on the line Stavelot–Dochamps–Samree–Bastogne was to be drawn back in marches over the next four days. On 8 January the staff Group Felber of the Army – a few days later called XIII Corps – was subordinated and inserted to the right of the LXVII Corps. They were henceforth disposed as follows:

XIII Corps in the sector Baugnez–Mont le Fosse.

LXVII Corps in the sector Mont le Fosse–Erezee.

II SS Panzer Corps in the sector Erezee–Marche.

8 January–12 January: The withdrawal did not run according to plan at all points, the enemy pressure particularly from both sides of the Ourthe on La Roche was very strong and it had to be given up on 11 January. The enemy air force was very active during the attacks.

On 12 January, the Army held on a shorter front. The attacks in eastward direction had ceased. The Army calculated on an enemy regrouping and with attacks through Malmédy on St. Vith. This was not the case, however, and the enemy pressure from Stavelot and Bodeux was increasing. Local breakthroughs – especially on both sides of the Salm sector – could be resisted, but enemy pressure forced the Army until 16 January to withdraw to the general line – Ondenval–Halleux–Lieurneux–Wibrin–Nadrin. The available tanks of Kampfgruppe Peiper, 20 Panzer IVs and Vs, were placed under the XIII Corps.

Meanwhile, the release of the SS panzer divisions from Bastogne was ordered. Part of the 12 SS Panzer Division was in the sector Amel, the 2 SS Panzer Division on right wing of the LXVII Corps south of Salmchâteau, the 1 SS Panzer Division was gathered in the sector eastwards of St. Vith. Breakthroughs northwest of St. Vith were prevented. On 19 January, the Staffs of the I and II SS Panzer Corps, the 1, 2, 9 and 12 SS Panzer Divisions were gathered in the sector east of Prüm. The Command Post of the army was moved on the 18 January to Steffeln nearby.

On 20 January, the Army received the order to load on train transports, for commitment in Hungary. The first part of the movement to the loading stations commenced. The last committed parts – part of the 9 and the 2 SS Panzer Divisions – were extracted on 24 January.

The movements to the loading stations – Wiesbaden, Koblenz, Bonn–Köln – were delayed by enemy air attacks and snowdrifts on the Eifel roadnet. The III Flak Corps provided protection against enemy air attacks during the loading. However, the loading was mostly carried out at night and without incident.

V. Material Losses (Armored)

	Panzers	Armored vehicles	Guns
1 SS Panzer Division	40 [59]*	50 [9]*	12
2 SS Panzer Division	30 [19]	20 [9]	6
9 SS Panzer Division	30 [51]	20 [16]	4
12 SS Panzer Division	30 [51]	30 [36]	6
SS Panzer Battalion 501	20 [13]	– –	–
SS Panzer Battalion 502**	4 [–]	– –	–
TOTAL LOSSES	154	120	28

* Numbers in brackets were obtained by the editor by comparing the on hand strength reported by the German divisions on 17 December 1944 and 11 January 1945. Numbers for 'armored vehicles' are just for StuG and Jagdpanzer.

** There is no evidence that SS Pz Bn 502 participated in the Ardennes Offensive. Krämer is probably referring to SS Pz Bn 506, which operated with Sixth Panzer Army with only some half-dozen Tigers.

VI. Battle Experiences

1. The scope of the retraining of almost all of the combined units was not achieved.

2. The retraining could not be accomplished because of the following reasons:

   a. Hindrances due to enemy flyers,
   b. Insufficient training of officers and noncommissioned officers,
   c. Insufficient night training,
   d. Lack of motor fuels (because of this, there were no road practice exercises in close assembly).

3. The cooperation of all arms – especially important in Panzer units – was not practiced sufficiently.

4. The Signal Communications and the Troop Signal Communications Platoon – Radio Operators – could not hold sufficient practice because of the secrecy. Through this they failed to have the necessary speed in writing down and setting up the radio messages.

5. The training of the motor vehicle drivers was hindered because of a shortage of motor fuels. Basic training was especially important in the 'Eifel Country.'

6. Motor vehicles of all types were used together. The providing of spare parts caused the greatest difficulty. The motor vehicles were not sufficiently mobile for cross-country use.

7. The Panzers had proved very useful, except the Panzer VI – the Tiger. It was not mobile enough in the Eifel Country. The most successfully used Panzer in this terrain was the Panzer IV.

8. There was almost no terrain reconnaissance because of the ordered secrecy.

9. a. The Panzer units operated too far to the north. It would have been better if they had operated to the south of the Schnee-Eifel, where better initial results could have been had that would have improved the morale of the troops. A more advantageous 'middle-line' would have been: Bastogne–Marche–Namur.

   b. The terrain was inappropriate for the employment of Panzer units. A compact employment of all panzers of a division was not possible, therefore the shock power could not be exploited.

10. The air support of the troops was very slight or else there was none at all. Air cover support failed during the attack as well as for reconnaissance. Panzer Divisions without observation planes are blind.

11. Supplies were often lost because of the enemy air attacks on the interior. The supply routes were so long, so that motor fuels and ammunition had to be brought up from east of the Rhine. From 24 December, enemy air

attacks made the movements of supplies almost impossible. Because of this, often tactical successes could not be exploited.

12. The enemy countermeasures were more extensive than had been expected.

13. The enemy's cleverly organized strongpoints were defended longer than expected; especially when they were supported by tanks.

14. The change of position of the American artillery up to the time of opening fire lasted a long time. The coordination with their artillery observation was very fast.

15. The terrain was very cleverly exploited by the American infantry.

16. The enemy's building up of a defense front in the sector Lüttich–Huy–Durbuy–Aywaille in so short a time was a surprise.

17. The American counterattacks began either at 0900 or 1400. Night attacks were not common.

ENCLOSURE NO. 1

ORDER OF BATTLE OF THE 6 PANZER ARMY
15 Dec 44.

STAFF OF THE 6 PANZER ARMY
with Signal Regiment, Military Police Company, Security Company.

Commander-in-Chief:	General of the Waffen SS Sepp Dietrich
Chief of Staff:	Brigadier General of the Waffen SS Fritz Krämer
Artillery Commander:	Major General Kruse
	Major General of the Waffen SS Walter Staudinger
Deputy Chief of the General Staff:	SS Standartenführer Ewert

I SS Panzer Corps
with Signal Battalion, M.P. Company, Security Company.

SS Panzer Detachment No. 501 (Panzer VI)

Commanding General:	Major General of the Waffen SS Hermann Priess
Chief of Staff	SS Obersturmbannführer Rudolf Lehmann
Artillery Commander:	(Arko 501) Lt Col Knabe

Heavy SS Artillery Detachment No. 501, SS Observation Battalion No. 501, 2 Volksartillery Corps (Army), 2 Mortar Brigades (Army), 1 Heavy Artillery Detachment (Army) 210 mm howitzer.

1 SS Panzer Division   Commander: SS Oberführer Mohnke

12 SS Panzer Division (attached 506th Panzer Detachment (Army))
           Commander: SS Oberführer Kraas

3rd Parachute Division (Air force)   Commander: General Walter Wadehn

12 Volks Gren Division   Commander: Brigadier General Engel

277 Volks Gren Division   Commander: Colonel Wilhelm Viebig

II SS Panzer Corps

with Signal Detachment, Security Company, M. P. Company, 502nd SS Panzer Detachment (Panzer VI).

Commanding General:	General of the Waffen SS Bittrich
Chief of Staff:	SS Obersturmbannführer Keller
Artillery Commander:	SS Oberführer Bock
2 SS Panzer Division	
Commander:	Brigadier General of the Waffen SS Heinz Lammerding
9 SS Panzer Division	
Commander:	SS Oberführer Sylvester Stadler

LXVII Army Corps

Commanding General:	Major General Hitzfeld
Chief of Staff:	?
326 Volks Gren	
Division Commander:	Brigadier General Kaschner
246 Volks Gren	
Division Commander:	Colonel Peter Körte
	1 Volksartillery Corps
	1 Volks Werfer Brigade
	1 Heavy Artillery Battalion
	2 Assault Gun Battalions
	1 Heavy Antitank Battalion.

ENCLOSURE NO. 2

STATE OF REEQUIPMENT AND REORGANIZATION (ESTIMATE) 15 DEC 1944[15]

Division	Personnel	Material	Tanks & Assault Guns	Carriers	Antitank	Guns
1 SS Pz Div	90%	80%	35 Pz IV	120	24	36
attached			35 Pz V			
501st SS Pz Det			42 Pz VI			
2 SS Pz Div	80%	80%	45 Pz IV	120	36	42
			48 Pz V			
9 SS Pz Div	75%	75%	40 Pz IV	100	24	36
			48 Pz V			
12 SS Pz Div	90%	80%	40 Pz IV	120	36	36
attached			45 Pz V			
560th Pz Det (Army)						
501st SS Artl Det	90%	90%	–			12
502nd SS Artl Det	90%	90%	–			12
502nd SS Pz Det	50%	50%	12 Pz VI			
12 Volks Gren Div	80%	80%	12 Assault Guns		24	36

3d Para Div	75%	70%	—	12	36
277 Volks Gren Div	75%	75%	6 Assault Guns	24	36
326 Volks Gren Div	80%	80%	6 Assault Guns	24	36
246 Volks Gren Div	80%	80%	6 Assault Guns	24	36
1 Volks Artl Corps					60
1 Volkswerfer Brig					?

ENCLOSURE NO. 3

ORDER OF BATTLE OF THE 6 PANZER ARMY
8 Jan 1945
(STAFF OF THE 6 PANZER ARMY SAME AS
on 15 Dec 44)

XIII Army Corps

Commanding General: Infantry General Felber
62 VG Division   Part of the 1 SS Pz Division   18 VG Division
                  1 Volks Artillery Corps
                  1 Volks Werfer Brigade
                  326 VG Division (being brought up)

LXVII Army Corps

Commanding General: Infantry General Lucht
12 VG Division   9 SS Panzer Division
                  Parts of 560 VG Division
                  1 Volks Artillery Corps
                  1 Volks Werfer Brigade

II SS Panzer Corps

Commanding General: General of the Waffen SS Bittrich
2 SS Panzer Division   116 Panzer Division

Notes

1. 'An Interview with Fritz Krämer', ETHINT-21, 14–15, 1945; also ETHINT-22 and 23; all quotes from ETHINT-21. Coverage of Sixth Panzer Army artillery is given extensive treatment in 'An Interview with Generalleutnant Walter Staudinger', ETHINT-62, 11 August 1945; Walter Staudinger, 'The Artillery Command of the Sixth Panzer Army During the Ardennes Offensive, 1944–1945', B-347; Staudinger, 'Artillery Leadership and Artillery Assignment During the Course of the Ardennes Offensive', B-759; and F.W. Bock, 'Die Ardennenschlacht', P-109d. Bock was the artillery commander for Arko 102.
2. John Toland's interview with Jochen Peiper, interview notes on file at the Library of Congress in the John Toland Papers.
3. Hechler, 'The Enemy Side of the Hill', see note 7, Introduction, part one of this book.
4. Two regiments of the 3FJ Division, the 8th and 9th, were in line. The 5th FJ Regiment would not arrive until the following day.
5. Krämer is incorrect on this account. Although originally scheduled for the initial assault, the 246

VG Div was still in transport from 15th Army. The chief of staff probably means 272 VG Div, which, although fought-out, was fighting the US 78th Division just to the north of Kesternich.
6. Krämer is in error on this point. The radio carried by SS-Obstf. Harald Etterich from 12 SS Pz Div, who was to function as the artillery liaison, was broken in the jump and it would be 20 December before OB West had any idea of what had become of von der Heydte's battle group.
7. Actually resistance was fierce in this sector from the beginning. 326 VG Div estimated it took 20% casualties in the action at Höfen on the first day alone.
8. The missing unit comprised Jagdtigers of the schwere 653 Pzjäger Battalion, which had been blocked in rail transport by air attack.
9. Another reason resides with the poor morale of the 3 FJ Div, which was less than keen c these attacks.
10. Parts of the 2 SS Division had begun moving onto the battlefield on the 19th.
11. Krämer here refers to the curious situation during the advance, where many German formations took on captured US vehicles, which further clogged the roads.
12. This is not completely true since II SS Panzer Corps had to take over a number of functions of LXVII Corps for several days.
13. There is no evidence that a prisoner exchange like this took place.
14. It was, in fact, a hodge-podge of American units under the command of Maj. Arthur C. Parker III (11 tanks and a reconnaissance platoon from 3rd Armored Division, and several howitzers from 589 FA Battalion, half-tracks from 203 AAA Battalion and a few towed tank destroyers from 643 TD Battalion.
15. Krämer's original estimates are given in this table. More accurate numbers based on OB West situation maps are given in *Battle of the Bulge* by Danny Parker.

3

The Fifth Panzer Army During the Ardennes Offensive

BY General der Panzertruppen Hasso von Manteuffel

Introduction

General Hasso von Manteuffel was one of the most important of the German generals in the Ardennes, and he easily may have been the greatest battlefield commander of those participating. Heir to an old Prussian military family, von Manteuffel enjoyed an extremely distinguished career for a person of such diminutive stature (he was five foot two inches in height).[1] Von Manteuffel had entered officer candidate school at Berlin-Lichtefelde Academy at the age of 14, and was wounded when he was old enough to fight on the Western Front in 1916. After the war, the avid horseman became a major exponent of the panzer forces as espoused by Heinz Guderian. He worked for Guderian as the Inspectorate General of the Panzertruppen, beginning in 1934. When war broke out, von Manteuffel claimed a front-line command in Russia and fought with great distinction in a thrust that nearly reached Moscow in 1941. He later commanded a division in North Africa and then returned to lead the elite Grossdeutschland Panzer Division in Russia. His prowess there was so remarkable that Hitler personally promoted him directly from division commander to leadership of the Fifth Panzer Army. 'In every facet,' wrote his commander on the Eastern Front, 'an outstanding leadership personality'.

More than any of the other generals, von Manteuffel was able to influence Hitler's decisions regarding the Ardennes operation. He tried unsuccessfully to convince Hitler to settle for the 'Little Slam' – a description von Manteuffel borrowed from bridge parlance – as opposed to the 'Grand Slam' to Antwerp, for which he held out little hope of success. But that failing, the little panzer general (his friends called him 'Kleiner'), in a meeting on 2 December successfully convinced Hitler to alter several aspects of the plan. He was particularly worried about jeopardizing the surprise element with the artillery barrage that Hitler, with his Great War experience, had envisioned:

> I felt that such a [prolonged] barrage was a World War I concept and completely out of place in the Ardennes, in view of the thinly held lines. We had artillery observers with all the attack companies and we planned to lay down concentrated fire on known enemy strong points. I had a lengthy argument with Hitler concerning the artillery support, because he wanted to have a long barrage lasting until 1100, when the assault would jump off. I finally convinced him that such a plan would merely be an alarm clock for the American forces and would alert them that a daylight attack was about to follow. I told him that our

infantrymen were not the same calibre as those who had invaded France, and that they did not meet the required standards to achieve a breakthrough in daylight. I pointed out that it was well known that the American guards or sentries were usually asleep in the early morning hours and therefore, the time to attack was before dawn. Hitler agreed to this plan, and we formed assault companies in each division, picked from the best men available. These assault companies were given additional night assault training ... Dietrich, on the other hand, employed a heavy artillery concentration for approximately half an hour before his attack. Personally, I think this was a waste of ammunition.[2]

But if set against the offensive's far-reaching goal of Antwerp, von Manteuffel pursued the success of the operation with all the fervor which was typical of his personality:

> I never expected to reach the Meuse River in two or three days, but rather, I felt if all went well, we should be able to reach it in four to six days. Everything was right for the attack: the plans, ammunition, supplies etc. But the whole thing hinged on the inexperience of those who had conceived the attack and the lack of training of those who were to execute it ... Our initial attack was made on a wide front, with elements of all the panzer divisions in the assault wave. My theory was that if we knocked on ten doors, we would find several open.[3]

Von Manteuffel also requested the use of searchlights to create artificial moonlight on the night of the assault to help his assault companies feel their way forward. The idea, von Manteuffel explained to Hitler, was to bounce the searchlights off the low-hanging clouds to cast a low level of illumination. But listening intently, the German leader asked von Manteuffel how he knew there would be clouds. 'My Führer,' the diminutive panzer general reminded him, 'you have already assured us we will have cloudy weather.' Hitler could only agree.

Danny S. Parker

The Fifth Panzer Army

Assembly and Marching into position of the Units of the Fifth Panzer Army

It was important to bring up the combat troops into their initial positions shortly before the attack to prevent the enemy's knowledge of our intentions until the attack was well under way. For this reason the assembly of the panzer divisions took place far behind the front, namely, fifty to sixty km east. Only during the night of 14 Dec the panzer divisions moved up about fifteen km, the infantry divisions to about five to eight km behind the front, in order to proceed during the night of 15 Dec into their initial assault positions, which were to serve a few hours later as assembly points to launch the offensive. Difficulties that arose due to the fact that units of the 5 Pz Army were assembled in the 7 Army area, so that they first had to be diverted north, whereas units of the 7 Army were to proceed west, were in due time eliminated, according to arrangements between the Army staffs.

Careful planning was necessary with regard to the bringing up of the divisions and correct timing of the troop movements. The darkness and narrow roads – partly in bad condition with steep inclines and sharp turns – offered difficulties one had to tolerate to keep to 'correct timing', i.e. to be ready for combat action under all circumstances at the right time and in the right positions. Everything had to be arranged accordingly.

Traffic control east of the line Prüm, Pronsfeld, Waxweiler, Neuerburg was carried out by the Army. West of this line the Corps headquarters had to make the necessary arrangements. The individual lines of advance were in charge of traffic control commanders, having telephone connections with the army respectively. Therefore, any disruptions were quickly noticed by the superior command post, enabling them to take action if necessary. In this way it was also possible to get an immediate idea of the course of the march movements. The roads of advance to the front were used as 'one way roads' to avoid traffic from the opposite direction; similarly, other roads were restricted exclusively for the transport to the east. At difficult points (of which there were many in this area, containing few excellent roads but plenty of crossings) plans were made in advance to provide available prime movers, auxiliary headquarters and sand to take care of expected icy road conditions. At the same points, motor-vehicles repair units were also kept in readiness. The traffic control authorities were specially ordered to carefully camouflage all vehicles which were put out of action, so as to prevent the reconnaissance of the enemy from drawing conclusions. In spite of these efforts a great deal of road obstruction took place during the offensive. These difficulties were not only due to bad road conditions, the terrain, and the cold weather, but also to the training status of the troops which was not always satisfactory because only limited exercises were possible during the training period due to the lack of fuel.

In planning a time-schedule it had to be considered that all units of the attack-troops were to be brought up in such a manner as required by the order of succession and subsequent commitment to study after the breakthrough had been achieved. It was necessary, therefore, that the divisions combined their units into small battle groups previous to the time of moving into the assembly area. Formation of such battle groups also facilitated the concentration into few command posts as it was more practical to have only a few places from where orders could be given. Preparations of the divisions for combat action also was facilitated by the fact that the divisional artillery, the Volks Art Corps, mortar brigades and pioneer units were already moved up as 12 December to their positions or to their respective assembly areas. The emplacement of artillery and mortar detachments as well as the storage of ammunition into these areas went according to plan.

The general headquarters had to envisage the moving into position of the subordinated bridge columns.[4] There were available for the LXVI Corps two reserve columns; to the LVIII Pz Corps, one engineer and half a pontoon column; to the XLVII Pz Corps 1 engineer and 1 pontoon column; in addition, the 2 Panzer and Panzer Lehr Division included one motor vehicle column each [for load capacity of the bridge columns see p. 161 note 4]. Beyond that, plenty of lumber for the construction of bridges was made available to avoid the use of equipment of the bridge building columns at the Our and the Clerf. Equipment was to be saved up for possible construction of bridges over the Ourthe and over the Meuse. Transportation of lumber for emergency bridges caused difficulties because of lack of space. A solution was found by unloading bridge columns using their vehicles; in addition, loading parties were also made available so that the loading process of lumber provided for the emergency construction of bridges could be carried out as quickly as possible. By order of the Corps the Div bridge commanders were assigned to direct the crossing of the Our after completion of emergency bridges. Their task was to maintain a constant flow of troops across the bridges, to call upon troops ready for crossings at fixed points determined beforehand, and to prevent unwelcome concentrations of any kind at the bridges. Telephone lines were made available to them so that they could fulfill their task. In addition engineer units stood ready to enable the bridge commanders to repair any damage to bridges within their areas.

The 26 VGD occupied the most favorable position for moving into the assembly area, its outposts still standing west of the Our. It could therefore prepare its assault companies for crossing by building infantry foot bridges across the Our, at the same time giving an early start to the transportation across the Our over pneumatic pontoons of heavy weapons and horse-drawn infantry carts.

The LVIII Pz Corps and the XLVII Pz Corps, as well as the newly brought up divisions finally took over command in their sectors in the evening of 15 December, about 2200 hours. Therefore the sector of the LXVI Corps narrowed accordingly.

The fact that the 560 VGD brought up from Denmark had not yet arrived with all units, made the assembly for the LVIII Pz Corps to positions more difficult. An infantry regiment of grenadiers, the assault gun company and one engineer company had not yet arrived.[5] They reached their position so late and in such small formations that the Division was only complete by 22 December.

Prior to the beginning of the Offensive the 5 Pz Army of the LXVI Corps and the 18 and 26 VGD were assembled in a subsequent sector. Behind were assembled:

The 62 VGD in the vicinity of Schönecken

Führer Begl Brig in the vicinity of Daun

116 Pz Div in the vicinity of Mohn (15 km northeast of Gerolstein)

560 VGD north of Bitburg, on both sides of the Nimsbrook

2 Pz Div in the vicinity of Grosslittgen (8 km northwest of Wittlich)

Pz Lehr Div in the sector of Lutzerath-Mayen.

In addition every Corps area contained a Volks Art unit and a mortar brigade as well as the pioneer detachment.

Only during the night of 14 December the 62 VGD, 116 Pz Div, 560 VGD, and 2 Pz Div were moved closer to the main line of battle. At the start of the Offensive there were available:

To the right: The LXVI Corps with 18 VGD to the right and 62 VGD to the left.

In the center: The LVIII Pz Corps with 116 Pz Div to the right and 560 VGD to the left.

To the left: The XLVII Pz Corps with 2 Pz Division to the right and 26 VGD to the left.

At the start of the Offensive, on 16 December only the following were lined up for action: the Pz Lehr Div and the Führer-Begleit-Brigade. During the night of 15 December the Pz Lehr Div was moved closer to the front, namely into the area Kyllburg–Waxweiler.

It was the duty of the 26 VGD to secure the initial assembly, which forced the Inf Rgt 78 to remain in the attack sector of the 62 VGD, the 116 Pz Division, the 560 VGD and the 2 Pz Div until it was relieved during the night of 15 December by parts of the before-mentioned attack Divisions. Only on the evening of 16 December did the regiment join its division.

On 15 December at 1800 the staff of the high command of the 5 Pz Army took up its command post at Dackscheid northeast of Waxweiler. The night of 15 December was dark and frosty. Shelling by enemy artillery was just as heavy as on other evenings and nights. The enemy infantry kept quiet, so it could be presumed that the assembly and preparation for action had taken place unnoticed by the enemy. Apparently the surprise move had been successful. Reports of the Corps on the completion of the moving action into assembly points arrived in time at army headquarters. Final disclosure of the Offensive to the troops came during the evening hours of 15 December when the foremost outposts were informed of the impending attack.

The following orders were made:

To LXVI Corps:

The corps is to force the Our River crossing near Schönberg and Steinebrück then take St. Vith so as to advance deeply echeloned at and across the Meuse on both sides of Andenne. Rapid forcing of the Our Crossing is decisive, so as to take St. Vith by combined action of both subordinated divisions and to advance with increased speed across the Meuse.

To LVIII Pz Corps:

The Corps will cross the Our in the sector Burg Reuland–Kalborn and will gain, advancing by way of Houffalize, crossings over the Meuse in the sector Andenne–Namur with the upmost speed.

To XLVII Pz Corps:

The Corps will cross the Our in the sector Dasburg–Gemünd, passing by the Clerf sector, so as to advance echeloned in depth to and across the Meuse in the sector Namur–Dinant.

The breakthrough of the enemy positions and the cutting off of the Schnee-Eifel: a. LXVI Army Corps

16 December: At the right: the 18 VGD, reinforced by an assault gun brigade of 3 companies which according to my memory carried 30 assault guns on 16 Dec,[6] thereby reinforcing Division's strength to about 42 pieces, penetrates with a combat unit in the northern part of Schnee-Eifel between Ormont and Schneifelhaus, in order to advance over Roth–Auw–Schönberg to St. Vith; also to advance with a smaller combat unit from positions in the southern part of the assault line of the Division to disperse, at first by way of Brandscheid, enemy groups located in the Bleialf sector. This combat group will further penetrate enemy lines which had not been attacked in the direction of Schönberg, in the Schnee–Eifel sector, to cut them off. Assault guns will also be assigned to this combat group. The right combat group carries the main assault, employing about two-thirds of the Div strength, because the capture of Schönberg will greatly reduce the task of the left combat group thereby leading to the collapse of the Schnee–Eifel front. In addition the right combat group would soon be able, after penetration of the foremost enemy outposts, to gain a passable road. Both combat groups must be supported by artillery at close range. The main body of the advance guard is to be kept close by to advance rapidly to St. Vith over Schönberg. The left combat group is also assigned to the Division. At that point close liaison is of greatest importance for a coordinated effort by the Division.

To the left: The 62 VGD is charged as follows: The Division will break through the enemy lines, starting from the sector Habscheider Müehle–Losenzeifen, to force a crossing of the Our near Steinebrück over Gross Langenfeld–Heckhuscheid, later take St. Vith, joining the 18 VGD. The main assault follows the road Habscheid–Winterspelt–Steinebrück. The plan of the offensive, as ordered by the army, allowed troops to advance as of 0400 hours, so as to infiltrate the army strong points; the artillery was permitted to start firing at 0530 hours.

Moving into the assault positions during the night of 15 December took place without interference by the enemy. Its nightly harassing fire was typical of the preceding days, so we could rightfully assume that assembly and shifting of our forces had not been noticed by the enemy. The arrival and assembly of units of the 18 VGD was considerably delayed in spite of timely relief by the 62 VGD, as these forces were withdrawn from the left wing and forced to march long distances in complete darkness and on bad roads to reach the assembly area. However, these delays did not cause any disadvantages because of the very successful infiltration tactics of this Division during the early morning of 16 December.

Many strong points were by-passed. There was only a gradual resistance later on. Enemy shelling in this sector was insignificant, even after the attack was well under way. Until noon, the right combat group fought its way to the east of Auw, by-passing Roth and Kobscheid. The battle was mainly fought by infantry, assisted by a few assault guns and heavy infantry weapons the troops were able to carry with them. The crossing of the Westwall's 'dragon's teeth' was difficult at first in spite of careful preparation by the Division Headquarters and our forces. Due to enemy resistance the road over Roth was not available. The first reports of enemy counteraction against the advancing troops came from a northern direction east of Auw. In the center of the Schnee-Eifel, which was deliberately spared during the assault and which was screened by the Division training school, complete silence prevailed between Schlausenbach and the Halenfelder Forest. During the course of the day, withdrawals by the enemy were not observed.

In the sector of the left combat group the method of attack proved also successful and several strong points were taken. However, the resistance increased with the approach by the attacking troops to Bleialf. This resistance came from positions east and south of the village and exerted a flanking effect from the direction of enemy positions, not at first attacked. This was in the woods of the southern Schnee-Eifel, which had the characteristics of a primeval forest. Not until dusk did we succeed in taking Bleialf, whereas the right combat group forced Auw late afternoon. At Roth and Kobscheid enemy units were surrounded and mopped up during the night in order to clear the road for the bringing up of further combat units, especially heavy infantry weapons and artillery. The advance guard was brought up during the afternoon, so that it could be launched against Schönberg during darkness.

The 62 VGD had two regiments employed in the first line; of the 183 Rgt, one battalion was reformed into a 'mobile unit' and one battalion set up as

Division reserve. The replacement battalion was reorganized into a combat battalion to join the Division forces during the offensive.

The assault plan at the right sector also proved its worth. Our forces captured several strong points as well as the heights to the south of Eigelscheid, thereby penetrating the edge of the woods near that village. However, during the late morning resistance grew. Gross Langenfeld, into which 190 Regiment penetrated, was lost again, and the troops encountered very strong resistance from the woods along the road to Winterspelt and south of the road. A battalion of a regiment at the left flank advanced into the woods east of Heckuscheid. There heavy hand-to-hand fighting developed along the river. The battalion at the left of the regiment encountered already strong resistance east and south of Heckuscheid, which could not be overcome during the day. The mobile detachment was engaged early in the afternoon in the sector held by the right combat group. However, it was unable to overcome the enemy's resistance along the road to Winterspelt, not even with the aid of the 190 Regiment. In the evening, the following situation developed based upon reports by the Corps:

The 18 VGD succeeded in penetrating the enemy's front line and the isolation of the Schnee-Eifel sector could be expected if Bleialf was taken and this combat group continued to push forward to Schönberg, in order to form a pocket. The mopping up of the Schnee-Eifel was to be left to other forces, because everything depended on the reinforcement of the 18 VGD for its main task, to thrust towards Schönberg and St. Vith, i.e., to form a strong concentrated force before the enemy succeeded in bringing up reinforcements. When it became known that the left wing of the right neighboring army [Sixth Pz Army] had gained only little ground, anxiety increased. Reconnaissance patrols still reported the wooded area and the heights to the southwest of Manderfeld as well as Wischeid still occupied by the enemy. Flanking fire endangered our advance from Auw to Schönberg and furthermore the important road of advance of the Division over Roth and Auw. It was also necessary for the corps to strength the attack of the 62 VGD by combining all available forces and ammunition along the road to Winterspelt, in order to capture a bridge near Steinbrück in an undamaged condition.

The Army was unable to reinforce the corps: I considered the existing forces and equipment as sufficient as long as we were able to successfully concentrate and employ all units.

The number of prisoners was small; the enemy losses of dead and wounded according to troop reports was considerable. Our own losses at the 62 VGD were higher than expected. The day's achievements at this corps did not come up to expectations. Our time schedule fell behind but I hoped to make it up by continuing our attacks through the night.

17 December: In the morning of 17 December, due to the energy of the commander of the 18 VGD, we succeeded in taking Schönberg. The bridge

across the Our was undamaged. During the afternoon, Heuem, Atzerath and Setz were taken and our foremost units advanced as far as the Walleroder Mill along the road to St. Vith. In the early morning the left combat group succeeded in launching a successful attack against Bleialf. At first the latter group continued to advance in the direction of Schönberg. But the offensive was held up by many attempts of enemy units to penetrate to the West across the road of advance which were threatened with encirclement in the Schnee-Eifel sector. The deep woods, filled with crevices, rendered reconnaissance and infantry combat quite difficult, so that a union with the main body of the Division near Schönberg did not occur until darkness.

For 17 December the Division commander of the 62 VGD planned only to hold enemy forces near Gross Langenfeld and Heckuscheid so as to employ the main body of the forces and equipment to push on by way of Winterspelt, Wallmerath toward Berg. The brave Regiment 190 took the heights north of Winterspelt. North East of Ihren, the mobile battalion invaded Wallmerath beating the enemy back to the western part of Winterspelt. The forces of this battalion attacking to the south of the road of advance, succeeded in repulsing the enemy from the wooded sector at Heckhalenfeld. However, this village which the Regiment 183 had for the second time taken, was lost again to the enemy. Once more, the losses of the Division were heavier than expected owing to the heavy fighting in the woods. The enemy put up a fierce resistance and profited by the terrain which was very favorable for a defence. His artillery fire also indicated plentiful ammunition.

The engagements of the first two days resulted in the breakthrough by the corps of the front enemy defense lines; encirclement of the enemy positions in the Schnee-Eifel made itself felt. These enemy troops could only force their way through the terrain away from the roads, which were in German hands. Also, during this and the following day, enemy units of various strengths were attempting to infiltrate through Regiment 293 from the east to the west under cover of darkness. However, the forceful defense against the attacking units of our two divisions indicated that only small forces of the 106 Division were being encircled.

Although the success of the corps in the early morning led to the assumption that the delay in the time schedule could still be made up, the course of events during the day proved otherwise. In spite of exemplary tactics from the troops and their leaders, we were unable to carry the attack with the necessary vigor by capturing St. Vith, which would also have decisive influence on the engagements of the left wing of the 6 Pz Army. For the 6 Pz Army breaking the resistance in the St. Vith sector was of great importance because these units of the Army had advanced little beyond the initial front lines.[7]

For the following day the task of the corps remained as in the original assault plan. I myself considered the commitment of the Führer Escort Brigade to reinforce the Corps.

The Breakthrough of the Enemy Positions and the Cutting Off of the Schnee-Eifel: b. LVIII Pz Corps

LOCATION OF THE ENEMY

During the last 14 days before the start of the offensive the sector of the LVIII Pz Corps located in the hinterland had been only under occasional harassing bombardments by the enemy. The section could be regarded as 'quiet'. It was opposed by units of the 28th American Division. The following crossings over the Our were contemplated within the Corps center: Burg Reuland, Oberhausen, Ouren and Kalborn. With the exception of Kalborn, the front extended so far to the east of the Our that the Corps command post counted on the fact that the bridges of Burg, Reuland, Oberhausen and probably the two crossings near Ouren were undamaged because they were needed by the enemy for the transportation of their own supplies.[8] According to reports by reconnaissance patrols the Kalborn bridge was destroyed. Therefore, the Corps massed its forces in the northern sector. An attempt was to be made to take these bridges in an undamaged condition. The engineer and half bridge columns as well as the emergency bridge equipment were therefore lined up behind the northern sector. Because the enemy had not included the Our in his defense sector, but set up defense lines east of the river, the Corps had to figure on strong enemy forces particularly in the northern sector. Therefore, it was absolutely essential to take the crossings by a surprise attack before the enemy garrison recovered to take up the defence. Any softening by artillery fire of the enemy positions was therefore abandoned, instead 'infiltration' tactics were to avoid a premature alarm of the enemy and take advantage of surprise.

PLANS AND HISTORY OF THE BREAKTHROUGH

Mission of the Corps: 'The 116 Pz Div will break through the enemy positions in the sector Heckuscheid–Lutzkampen, taking immediate possession of the Our crossings in the sector Burg Reuland–Oberhausen (with the main body at Oberhausen). After that the Division will advance further northwest crossing the Meuse in the sector Namur– Dinant. The panzer reconnaissance unit of the Division will be at the disposal of the corps in the northern part of the Hof forest.'

The Division was instructed to find its route of advance to the north of the Ourthe. Local resistance, expected at Houffalize and La Roche, was to be bypassed. It was also pointed out that an advance to the south of the Ourthe was a strong possibility, if an advance north was too difficult, whereas it probably had a better chance of success to the south of the river.

Plan of the Division: The division intended to employ on the right Panzer Gren Rgt 60, which was to pierce the enemy positions between Heckuscheid in order to take possession of the crossing near Burg Reuland. The Pz Gren Regt 156 with a subordinated antitank gun battalion on the left sector, was charged with the breakthrough of enemy positions on both sides of Leidenborn and to be first to win the crossings near Stupbach and Oberhausen. The regiment employed an assault company which was to be followed by the main body of the regiments one hour after assembly of such assault companies at 0530 hours. At any breakthrough, the panzer regiment reinforced by a panzer engineer company was moved forward into the Hofswald, to be used subject to developments at the sectors of either one of the two Pz Grenadier regiments.

Developments During 16 December: The assault company of the Pz Gren Regt 60 encountered tenacious resistance in the wooded area to the northwest of Berg. The assault company of the Pz Gren Regt 156 succeeded, by bypassing Lutzkampen, in gaining ground in the direction of Oberhausen. Lutzkampen was captured by a following regiment. Northwest of Lutzkampen the enemy resistance made itself felt again. The danger increased that the attack would be stopped. The tank regiment, brought up behind the regiment, was delayed by the 'dragon's teeth' Westwall fortification to the west of Leidenborn and entangled itself in unfavorable terrain. Intended support by tanks was therefore impossible. West of Lutzkampen we observed a second line of defense running as far as Sevenig, which due to flanking fire, gave us plenty of trouble.

At about 0930 hours, the right attack group of the 560 VGD captured the southern crossing of the Our near Ouren, having bypassed the strongly defended Sevenig. At that point, the Corps turned all units of the 116 Pz Div towards Ouren during the afternoon and gave orders to stop the attacks against Burg Reuland and Oberhausen. However, due to a counterattack by the enemy in the afternoon the 560 VGD lost the Our crossing gained earlier. In the meantime, the attack of the 116 Pz Div became effective and joining forces with the Pz Gren Regt 156 to the right and the Pz Gren Regt 60 to the left, reached the Our in the evening on both sides of Ouren at several places.

The tank regiment, which had forced its way through the 'dragon's teeth' west of Leidenborn, penetrated the American positions at Lutzkampen and could effectively support the Division's attack at Ouren. Units of the Pz Gren Regt 60 covered the right flank of the Division to the north.

The enemy covered the rear zone of the Division with sporadic artillery fire which increased during the afternoon concentrating on Lutzkampen.

THE 560 VGD

Tactics Planned by the Corps: 'The 560 VGD will break through the enemy positions in the sector Lutzkampen–Kalborn, taking possession of the Our crossing near Ouren. The Our is to be crossed with a smaller combat group near the bridge site of Kalborn.' The Corps reserved for itself the decision to route the further advance of the Division on the western bank of the Our, depending on developments.

Plans of the Division: The Division, which started the battle with only two thirds of its effective strength, formed two combat groups. The right and stronger group, the Regiment 1129, was committed to force the Our crossing of Ouren. The weaker regiment group, Regiment 1128, was to take the Our crossing to the southeast of Kalborn. Due to the very rough and uneven terrain and bad roads, the success of the attack was not at first expected. The combat group Kalborn was assembled to give the attack of the Division the necessary width and depth to relieve the main thrust of the Division in the direction of Ouren.

Events of 16 December: At 0930 the right combat group of the Division aided by its assault company succeeded in capturing the southern one of the two crossings of Ouren, bypassing Sevenig. The report, resulting in changed operations by the 116 Panzer Division, arrived at noon. During the afternoon counterattacks by the enemy threw the company back to the eastern bank of the river and further to its original assault position. However, the thrust of the 116 Pz Div made behind the combat group once more regained the eastern bank of the Our on both sides of the Ouren. The left combat group of the Division had an unexpected success. It succeeded in forcing the crossing to the south of Kalborn close to the destroyed Our bridge. By exploiting this success and penetrating in the afternoon as far as Kalborn on the heights of the western bank of the river, the crossing was secured after a hard battle. Thus, a bridgehead was formed that could be of special importance for the continuation of the attack.

Final Situation on 16 December: About 2200 the Corps Headquarters was faced with the following situation: The attacks launched with its main body to the right in the direction of Burg Reuland did not lead to any success. The attacks launched after the shifting of the center of gravity in the direction of Ouren were met with stiff resistance by the enemy and had resulted in counterattacks so that here too our attempted crossings of the river were frustrated. The attack carried as far as the river. However, on the following day continuation of the offensive with the use of our own massed artillery promised success.

The 560 VGD had succeeded in crossing the Our southeast of Kalborn and in capturing the village Kalborn, a success which had not been included in the objectives of this first stage. Due to the destruction of the Kalborn bridge, the very steep highway of approach with its sharp curves and the mining of the roads, it could hardly be expected that construction of a bridge at this spot could be completed before the night of 17 December or early on 18 December. Therefore, the corps headquarters decided to stand by its decision made on 16 December at noon to cross the Our with center of gravity at Ouren.

The left neighboring corps captured the Our crossing near Dasburg and constructed an emergency bridge on this spot. Details on the load capacity of the bridges at Ouren and approach roads leading to these crossings were unknown; therefore, we contemplated the bringing up of the 116 Pz Div on the following day in case the Corps found it impossible to cross either at Ouren or at Kalborn within a short time. On the evening of 16 December the commanding general requested the commander in chief for freedom of action with regard to this question. Decisions should be made based upon further development of the attack of the 116 Pz Div against the crossings of Ouren and their condition as well as the assault roads condition. The commanding general reported that on the following morning he would make a personal investigation on the spot.

The reconnaissance battalion of the 116 Pz Div made available for the corps in the southern part of the Hofswald, received orders early in the evening of 16 December to cross the Our to the western bank over Irrhausen and Dasburg, in order to force a crossing of the Our for its Division, and further to dispatch well equipped reconnaissance units in the direction of Burg Reuland as well as Ouren.

The Breakthrough of the Enemy Positions and the Cutting off of the Schnee-Eifel: c. XLVII Pz Corps

LOCATION OF ENEMY

The 28 American Division was opposite the Corps front line. During the last weeks the Division had tried to establish contact only in single raids against the German positions. Artillery of the enemy was frequently employed, using a large quantity of ammunition for sudden shelling raids against German positions, strongpoints, and our communication lines. We observed frequent changes of positions of the batteries.

German combat outputs were located in the attack sectors of the 2 Pz Div on the eastern bank of the Our, whereas the 26 VGD had their outposts on the Western banks in the sector. Reconnaissance indicated that the enemy had only small outposts at the eastern bank of the Our; it was presumed that in case of a German attack the enemy would only offer stiff resistance along the highway Fischbach–Marnach. On the other hand, we figured on the existence of stronger and massed American outposts at the front line of the 26 VGD, as here the enemy did not have the protection of the Our between his lines and the German positions.

These differences in the enemy's front line resulted in various methods of attack in the corps sector. The 2 Pz Div was to infiltrate into the thinly held enemy positions attacking with many spearheads and to push the enemy outposts beyond the Our.

In the sector of the 26 VGD the Our did not offer any protection to the front lines of the enemy. At this point his outposts were more numerous and equipped with heavy weapons. Therefore, we reckoned with immediate and effective defensive action. The attack of this division was therefore to be launched from 0530 to 0550 hours, preceded by a short artillery bombardment.

PLANNING AND DEVELOPMENT OF THE BREAKTHROUGH OF 2 PANZER DIVISION

Mission of the Corps: 'The 2 Pz Div, in its sector along a broad front, will cross the Our by means of a bridge to be built near Dasburg. After establishment of a bridgehead across the Clerf at Clerf, the Division will advance without stopping northwest by way of Noville toward the Meuse in the sector Namur– Dinant.

'The Panzer Lehr Division, which is to follow close behind the assault of the 26 VGD, will take up positions to the left of the 2 Pz Division aiding their advance beyond the Meuse, after having crossed the Clerf over Bastogne, which is to be bypassed in case of strong enemy resistance.'

The Aim of the 2 Pz Division: The Division with the Pz Gren Regt 2 to the right, the Pz Gren Regt 304 to the left, and crossing the Our on a broad front, intended to use the road along the heights Fischbach–Marnach and after the capture of Urspelt and Reuler to take Clerf using both regiments. Forming a bridgehead near Clerf a further advance northwest of Noville was to be made immediately with all available forces.

Events on 16 December: At the beginning of the attack, the Division was able to break through the American outposts and to gain ground quickly. The Our was crossed without great difficulties. At first heavy infantry weapons, later on also motorcycles and single Volkswagens were ferried over to the western bank. However, numerous obstacles and obstructions delayed a quick supply of these supporting weapons. Due to the very strong currents of the river, the building of a bridge proved to be difficult. However, the artillery fire of the enemy was weak. Our own armored infantrymen attacked without waiting for the arrival of their heavy weapons. This caused considerable losses when enemy counterattacks were launched. Our own tanks, assault guns and anti-tank guns had not yet been ferried across and the situation became serious. At 1500 the bridge at Dasburg was completed. This bridge was made by the Pz Engineer Battalion 600, which used the bridge building equipment allotted for this purpose. The first tanks were rolling across the bridge in order to reinforce the attack of the armored infantry riflemen. The advance was very slow, however. The road Dasburg–Clerf was blocked in great depth by obstacles which were built in Autumn 44 by ourselves during the retreat. This fact caused considerable congestion on the bridge and at the approach roads leading to it, handicapped our attempts to gain ground.

Early in the afternoon the armored infantrymen reached the road Fischbach–

Marnach against the startled enemy. Here the resistance grew stronger and more effective. Marnach was only captured during the late afternoon after a renewed attack by the armored infantry supported by our own tanks, which had arrived by that time. In the east of Urspelt–Reuler attacks of the Division after nightfall were pinned down due to resistance of the enemy.

26 VGD

The Mission of the Corps: 'The 26 VGD was to cross the Our in its sector on a broad front. A bridge was to be built near Gemünd. The Division was to move quickly to take the crossings over the Clerf, especially at Drauffelt, so as to advance to the north without stop.'

The XLVII Pz Corps employed the Pz Lehr Div, following close behind the 26 VGD, to launch a thrust to the west as soon as possible over Drauffelt, to Bastogne. In case of stronger resistance near Bastogne the capture of this place was assigned to the 26 VGD, so as to free the Pz Lehr Division to reach the Meuse quickly.

The Plan of the Division: Even before the start of the offensive the Division intended to force its way to the front enemy lines then whenever possible to infiltrate these positions. From 0530–0550 hours the enemy infantry positions were to be heavily bombarded; these twenty minutes were to be used to move sufficiently close to the enemy lines for the onslaught. After another short bombardment to be directed against points of penetration by means of radio of the advanced observers, our own infantry had to break through on a broad front. The orders of the Division follow:

The Gren Regt 77, bypassing Hosingen in the north was to advance to the north of the road Hosingen, Bockholz toward Drauffelt, to establish a bridgehead.

Füsilier Regt 39 was to advance from the wooded terrain by way of the Hosingen road to the north of the Wahlhausen road pressing forward to the north of the road Holzthum–Consthum toward Lellingen and Wilwerwiltz. The regiment was to avoid extended engagements with the enemy at Wahlhausen, Holzthum and Consthum.

The right wing division of the 7 Army joining at the left, the 5 Parachute Division, had orders to hold the same level of advance as the 26 VGD.

The sector of the 26 VGD, the center of gravity, was held by the 77 Gren Regt. The Division wanted to commit the reinforced Reconnaissance Battalion 26 after the completion of the bridge Gemünd over Hosingen to seize the road for the Pz Lehr Div, which was assembled near Neuerburg. The commitment of the 78 Gren Regt, all portions of which had to be withdrawn from a former position, at nightfall on 16 Dec depended on the development of the situation.

Developments on 16 December: At first the 77 Gren Regt gained ground. Hosingen, which was held under our own fire, was bypassed to the north. The

Regiment continued its attack against Bockholz and the woods south of it. Gradually the American resistance grew stronger. East of Bockholz and to the south of the woods the attack stopped entirely.

Füs Regt 39 had also succeeded in breaking into the American positions. It forced its way with the right (I) battalion into the wooded area north of Wahlhausen and continued assaulting the nearby village. The I Battalion, trying to eliminate the resistance in the wooded area to the north, by sweeping southward and by a pincer's movement, diverted with strong portions to the south, therefore, both battalions were now attacking the village Wahlhausener. The village was captured and the attack continued to the southwest. In the afternoon the regiment's advance was slowed by the enemy, who was being constantly reinforced, located 1 km to the southwest. A withdrawal of portions of the I Battalion, to divert them again to their original western direction, was impossible during the day due to the close contact with the enemy. Besides, the Americans started to counterattack from the Weiler–Merscheid area, as well as from the south of Hochscheiderdickt.

By 1600 hours the Gemünd bridge was completed by the engineer battalion of the Pz Lehr Div using the B-bridge equipment. The foremost battalion of the Inf Regt 78, which was brought up in the late afternoon, received orders to move forward into the northern part of the woods, two km to the west of Eisenbach. The division planned to employ this battalion between regiment 77 and 39 for the attack against Pintsche, Wilwerwiltz, while the battalion following it was to capture Hosingen, still held by the Americans.

In spite of the completion of the Gemünd bridge, the contemplated use of the road from Eisenbach to Drauffelt was at first impossible because on the western bank of the Our, a deep abatis and two huge mine craters to the north and south of Eisenbach made any traffic impossible. This fact and the situation in the sector of Füs Regt 39 caused the XLVII Pz Corps to commit the reconnaissance of the Pz Lehr Div, joined by the Füs Regt 39 in the afternoon of 16 Dec in the left sector of the 26 VGD over Wahlhausen, Holzthum, Consthum in order to form a bridgehead near Kautenbach. According to a report (not being confirmed afterwards) portions of the 5 Fallsch Jg Div were already fighting their way to the crossing. The Füs Regt 39, by regrouping of its forces, had already prepared to carry out this plan. After nightfall it disengaged from the enemy, leaving behind outposts to the southwest of Wahlhausener Strasse, then taking positions in the woods north which were cleared by the enemy to continue the attack in the originally western direction. Late afternoon, portions of the regiments established contact with portions of the 5 Fallsch Jg Div in the vicinity east of Weiler.

For this purpose the reconnaissance battalion of the Pz Lehr Div was subordinated to the Regiment 39, and the new formation was called 'Combat group Kaufmann.' The combat group was to start the attack during the night.

The moving up of the battalion of the Pz Lehr Div proved difficult due to heavy traffic on roads soon turning muddy.

PZ LEHR DIVISION

The Mission of the Corps: 'The Pz Lehr Div holds itself ready to advance by order of the Corps, following behind the 26 VGD by way of Gemïnd to Drauffelt, toward Bastogne and the Meuse into the sector Namur–Dinant. It is essential for the Division to take up positions as soon as possible to the left of the 2 Pz Div, advancing over Noville. In the case of strong resistance, Bastogne is to be outflanked, its capture is then up to the 26 VGD.

'Consideration is given to possible support of the engagements of the 26 VGD between the Our and the Clerf with portions of the Pz Lehr Div. The reconnaissance detachment of the Division is to stand ready for disposal of the Corps near Neuerburg.'

Only portions of the reconnaissance battalion of the Pz Lehr Div crossed the Our. They were subordinated to 39 Füs Regt to advance over Holzthum to Kautenbach. On 16 Dec due to the heavy congestion of the roads leading to the Our the Division had not yet been assembled.

FINAL SITUATION ON 16 DECEMBER

At 2200 the XLVII Pz Corps reported the following: 2 Pz Div fighting to the east of Urspelt–Reuler; 26 VGD fighting to the right of Bockholz; in the center with Gren 78 (minus one battalion) was advancing from the forest two km to the west of Eisenbach in the direction of Pintsche.

To the left with combat group 'Kaufmann' (Füs Regt 39, portions of the AA of the Pz Lehr Div) were advancing from Wahlhausener Strasse toward Holzthum. Portions of the artillery of the 2 Pz Div and the 26 VGD were changing positions on the western shore of the Our. 5 Fallsch Jg Div to the left fought for Weiler and Merscheid. All possible means were employed to eliminate obstacles west of Dasburg.

The Clerf was not reached at any point. The enemy was unquestionably surprised by the attack; he offered, however, in many places tenacious and brave resistance in delaying and skillfully fought combat tactics. His counterattacks, which started at once, partly supported by small armored groups, resulted at many points in critical situations. Hosingen held out, making the support of the 77 Regt extremely difficult.

The tenacious resistance of the enemy together with the road blocks placed by the enemy, difficult terrain, poor roads which were in places almost unpassable by mud, were the most essential reasons for the slowing of the attack. The congestion on the roads leading to the Our was also one of the reasons why the Pz Lehr Div, with the exception of portions of the AA, had not yet crossed the Our by 16 December.

The Battle for St. Vith (LXVI Army Corps)

The Night of 17 Dec and 18 Dec: The suggestion by Field Marshal Model, to employ the Führer-Begleit Brigade held back as Army reserve for the attack against St. Vith corresponded with my plans regarding the use of this brigade. Originally it was not the intention of the Army command to employ this brigade in the corps sector, but in the center of gravity of the Army, namely, in the sector of either one of the two armored corps after the breakthrough to exploit this penetration. The commitment of this brigade in the sector of the LXVI Army Corps meant, therefore, nothing less than giving up of the idea to use this armored mobile unit which eventually could have a very unfavourable effect on the quick development of the main attack. On the other hand, the capture and therefore the elimination of St. Vith was of the greatest importance both for our own Army and especially for the 6 Pz Army. For this reason Field Marshal Model heartily welcomed the employment of the brigade at this place because he anticipated favorable reactions on the further conduct of battle at the left wing of the right neighboring Army.

We planned, in case of rapid capture of St. Vith, to employ portions of the 6 Pz Army or the Führer-Begleit Brigade itself from the St. Vith area to the north in order to outflank the enemy who was stubbornly defending himself. In addition the capture of the town made it also increasingly difficult for the enemy to reorganize his forces. I agreed to the employment of the brigade at the LXVI Corps, in the hope that this well trained and equipped force could bring a quick decision in the St. Vith sector. In a few days they would have been ready for further action by the Army.

The Brigade which my chief of staff finally assembled early on the morning of 17 Dec were now set in motion in anticipation of further action. During the night of 17 Dec orders were given to advance by way of Prüm–Bleialf to Schönberg for operations with the LXVI Army Corps. The weather was sufficiently light to permit the bringing up of the Brigade which was expected to arrive at noon on 28 Dec. The Brigade was ordered to use this advance route on account of its light traffic, offering by far less difficulties as the routes Roth–Auw and Auw–Andler, which were holding up supplies due to traffic tie-ups, steep grades, and mud holes. Due to these circumstances neither on the night of 17 or 18 Dec was the 18 VGD able to bring up essential portions of its artillery or heavy weapons so that it made only very slow progress towards St. Vith. At noon, 18 Dec, while visiting their staff at Schönberg, they were still more or less jammed on the road; on the road leading over Andler–Schönberg up to three columns were standing side by side, because portions of the 6 Pz Army had moved here without being authorized to do so.[9]

I met the division staff at Walleroder Mühle and the combat group at Schönberg, where the left combat group of the division, had joined her in the afternoon after fighting to clear the roads from Bleialf to Schönberg. The enemy portions in the Schnee-Eifel surrendered one after another; small detachments were still advancing under darkness to the west. About 1600 hours the Division commander of the 18 VGD reported that there was a stiffening of resistance to the east of St. Vith near Prümerberg. Here the enemy appeared with tanks which evidently tried to force the line of defense of the town to the east. I also witnessed a small thrust supported by tanks along the road which was, however, stopped by our assault guns.

There were reports from the 62 VGD that early in the morning the enemy resistance at Gross Langenfeld had slackened but that the enemy still defended himself during the forenoon at Heckuscheid and at Winterspelt. The brave Regiment 190 took Ihren in the course of the morning, also the dominating height to the east. Regiment 164 mopped up Winterspelt in the course of the morning and pushed ahead as far as to the Our crossing near Steinebrück, which was undamaged. The left flank of the Division advanced in the river valley to the west of Heckuscheid as far as Heckhalenfeld. Reconnaissance employed by the Division reached the area Auel–Steffeshausen, where the enemy was reported near Bracht and Burg Reuland. Local counterthrusts coming from Elcherath and the Our valley meant that the crossing point near Steinebrück was once more lost during the afternoon. The bridge was later destroyed by the enemy.

At the command post of the 18 VGD I discussed with the Commanding General the conduct of battle for the attack on St. Vith. Based upon the reports of the troops and of the Corps, I expected the start of the battle on 19 Dec. I had the impression, and developments during 18 Dec confirmed my observation, that even the foremost portions of the Division were only fighting along the road Muehle–Prümersberg. I therefore ordered the immediate employment of reconnaissance on a broad front toward St. Vith, committing the arriving elements of the Führer-Begleit Brigade over Wallerode and Meyerode toward the road Büllingen–St. Vith, and by the 18 VGD from Wallerode as far as Vollmersberg, by activating portions of all regiments of the Division possessing the necessary fighting strength. For this purpose, the regiment of the division, fighting on the left, was to be brought up quickly at Schönberg where it assembled. This regiment, after clearing the road Bleialf, lost too much time with the reorganization of the units. Furthermore, all combat units of the Division, especially the entire artillery, were to be brought up with great speed from Auw–Andler, or to bring the Führer-Begleit Brigade forward unimpeded and quickly through Schönberg and Heuem, into the area Medell–Wallerode to prepare it for action for the attack by way of Emmels toward Sart-les-St. Vith. The 18 VGD was to start the attack depending upon the result of the reconnaissance and preparatory bombardment by all gun barrels, with a well supplied artillery, leaving behind a strong security until along the route of advance with two combat groups of equal strength toward the northern and southern part of St. Vith, which had to include Vollmersberg and Mailust. The attack was to be supported by the 62 VGD in such a way as to enable the latter to carry the attack by way of Lommersweiler–Neidingen–Gahlhausen against Neundorf.

My return trip to the army headquarters by way of Schönberg–Auw convinced me of the serious traffic situation so that in the evening I agreed to postpone the attack until 19 Dec, pointing out the necessity of continued strong reconnaissance in the indicated attack sector. The Führer-Begleit Brigade, whose spearhead had already arrived twelve hours late at Schönberg, reported further delays.

19 December: The 19 Dec was reserved for the preparation of the attack against St. Vith in the right corps sector. There was no progress made against the enemy. The expected results of reconnaissance proved disappointing as the infantry positions lacked any support by our own heavy weapons as well as by the artillery and assault guns. Due to heavy tank and artillery fire the road over Prümerberg was continuously barred by the enemy. While driving by way of Heuem and the road fork short to the east of Wallerode–Mühle I ascertained in the late morning that only small portions of the Führer-Begleit Brigade had reached the assembly area for the attack in the forest south of Medell and therefore ordered postponement of the attack until 20 Dec.

On the other hand the 62 VGD was successful on this day. The enemy had evacuated Gross Langenfeld during the night. Regiment 190 reached Dreihütten. The left regiment captured Elcherath as well as Hemmeres and crossed the Our near Steinebrück; it then pushed forward as far as Lommersweiler. According to reports from the Division, at the Bruessel Berg American tanks appeared for the first time for the defense of Steinebrück and artillery and mortar fire of the enemy were also stronger than on the previous days. These weapons seemed to be located near Grüfflingern and to the south of Neidingen. Contact with the 18 VGD was established at Setz. The division intended to construct in addition to the bridge over the Our (now destroyed) an emergency bridge near Halt Steinebrück, which was actually completed by 20 Dec.

In order to secure the support of the left neighboring corps (LVIII Pz Corps), the 62 VGD received orders to attack on 20 Dec over Grüfflingen toward Maldingen to block the road St. Vith–Beho–Gouvy. I believed the letting up of the attack against St. Vith, which was due to the fact that this Division did not attack in the direction of Neundorf as previously ordered, would justify this risk in view of reports and my own impressions on the enemy that the combat efficiency of the Führer-Begleit Brigade would be fully adequate for the support of the attack by the 18 VGD. Besides the attack of the 62 VGD against Maldingen created favorable conditions for the continuance of the attack after capture of St. Vith in the direction of the crossing of the Salm river.

With the exception of the 62 VGD, the result of 19 Dec in this corps sector was as a whole disappointing. I indicated that the enemy had made use of the time to reinforce his position near St. Vith. In my opinion the lack of success was not so much due to the enemy's strength in numbers and material, but rather in the fact that neither on 18 nor 19 Dec did we succeed in assembling sufficient forces for the attack and in securing combined use of all forces in this sector. The conduct of the panzer forces was excellent.

20 December: Recognizing the true situation, the Commander of the Führer-Begleit Brigade quickly gathered the portions of his brigade which had arrived by midnight (one infantry battalion and two assault gun companies) and still under darkness, ordered an attack from the area of Wallerode along the road to St. Vith. The attack was repulsed however, the attacking forces withdrew unimpeded by the enemy into the forests east of Emmels to reform their lines and take up the offensive after arrival of the main body of our own armor. Due to the unfavorable conditions of the roads, the arrival of the armored elements of the brigade was once more delayed so that the brigade commander decided to carry out the attack against Emmels in the early morning with freshly arrived infantry. This attack was successful; Nieder- and Ober-Emmels were captured and the road St. Vith–Ligneuville was successfully barred. Thanks to the initiative and bravery of his troops a favorable condition for further attack of the town was created. However, on the entire front line, from Wallerode as far as south of Prümerberg, the 18 VGD did not succeed in making any headway.

On the other hand, the 62 VGD also created favorable conditions for continuation of the battle for the town. The right combat group of the Division, which on 19 Dec had faced even more enemy tanks than during the previous days, succeeded in forcing the enemy back from Dreihütten in the direction of Gahlhausener Kreuz and to conquer the heights to the south of Breitfeld and close to the east of Neidingen Mühle. The attack of the combat group in the center of the division slowed up due to strong enemy forces who defended themselves tenaciously and skillfully on the slopes to the west of Neidingen, whereas the left flank of the Division captured Maspelt, its spearheads reaching the multiple road junction in the Grüfflingern forest to the east of Gross Hart. At this point these forces were also slowed up facing a tenaciously fighting enemy. Repeatedly the Division Commander reported flanking fire from the south approximately from the direction of Burg Reuland, Bracht, and Alster. The outposts near Amel and at Steffeshausen had no contact with the enemy.

The progress made at the flanks of the corps led us to believe that by 21 Dec the attack against the town would be successful.

21 December: The expected success did not materialize. So far neither the Führer-Begleit Brigade nor the 18 VGD had reached the front with all portions. The 18 VGD especially lacked artillery which had not yet arrived.

Nevertheless the Führer-Begleit Brigade attacked with all available forces in the direction of the objective. A battalion succeeded, skillfully taking advantage of the woods west of Ober-Emmels, in temporarily barring the road St. Vith–Vielsalm to the west of Sart-lez-St. Vith. Here prisoners belonging to the 7 American Armored Division were taken. Exploiting this success, the brave battalion penetrated to the direction of Commanster. However, conditions of the roads leading through a wood in the Wallerode–Nieder-Emmels area close to Sart-lez-St. Vith and south of it were exceedingly difficult for the bringing up, commitment, and use of the armored elements of the Brigade, so that no support by armor could be given to the battalion. The battalion was halted and used to block the road by occupying Sart-lez-St. Vith. On the retrograde march the battalion encountered enemy artillery near Hinderhausen whose close range fire compelled the small forces to withdraw. The battalion was incorporated into the brigade in the forests north of the village. The final blocking of the busy road was unsuccessful. Most of the prisoners escaped in the confusion and the captured motor vehicles were lost again.

Once more the 18 VGD could not make any progress against the enemy in spite of the fact that it had reorganized and moved its center of gravity into the area of Wallerode.

The 62 VGD, now attacking for the sixth day, was ordered to support the attack against St. Vith–Vollmersberg on 21 Dec. Its portions held fast in the center and to the left of the Division, facing a stronger enemy, employing not only artillery but also tanks and large calibre automatic weapons (antiaircraft guns used for ground purposes!) opposite Gahlenhausen in the dense woods of Grueefflinger Hart and Gross Hart. Furthermore, the enemy was still observed to the south of Maspelt. In the afternoon Regiment 183 took Breitfeld, but was repulsed near Vollmersberg. To the west of the road the spearheads moved hard to the south, the road of Gahlhauser-Kreuz, Gahlhausen but could not cross while attacking to the north. Regiment 190 was repulsed at the Bevonknapp and was also beaten back while turning to the south. At first the left regiment gained ground in the direction of Kleine Hart; however, owing to local enemy attacks to the north from the direction of Maspelt and Alster, the employment of the replacement battalion, reorganized into a combat battalion, was necessary in order to remedy the situation. During that action Maspelt changed hands several times. At dusk a crisis arose caused by enemy thrusts which threatened the left flank of the Division.

Under the ever increasing pressure against St. Vith from a northern, eastern, and southern direction, the enemy evacuated the town during darkness, after the 18 VGD before dark had finally succeeded in gaining ground by attacking from the Wallerode section the northern part of the town. During the night the Division penetrated the town from the east and occupied it.

The Army Corps received orders from the Army to block the road Trois-Ponts–Houffalize in the area Salmchâteau and near Bovigny to force the river near Salmchâteau and to keep it open for the further operations of the Army; the Corps was charged to secure its northern flank and besides, after having reached the Salm, to prepare itself for the withdrawal of the Führer-Begleit Brigade as a reserve.

22 December: During the night heavy snowfall set in. Early in the morning of 22 Dec, after the reorganization of its troops and the bringing up of three armored companies (about 25 tanks) the Führer-Begl Brigade repeated the attack against Sart-lez-St. Vith. One battalion attacked the village from Ober-Emmels, the other battalion, taking advantage of the forests of Buchenberg and the village in order to permanently block the route from St. Vith to the west, from the area west of Ober-Emmels. The battalion, launching its onslaught from Ober-Emmels, was repelled by heavy and well placed artillery fire and was forced to withdraw into the wooded parts northeast of the village. The battalion attacking the west of it took the place firmly in its hands.

Exploiting the snowfall, the 62 VGD during the darkness broke through the enemy lines of security at several points, its right flank reaching St. Vith and the area Mailust by 0700 hours on 22 Dec, with the center part of Neundorf as well as the heights 'Auf dem Gericht' and the village Thommen. Pursuing the enemy, withdrawing at the frontline, this division succeeded until nightfall, despite its nightly engagements and marches, in advancing with the infantry and the engineers, as far as Commanster, Beho and Braunlauf supported by antitank units of the Division. Reconnaissance felt its way forward as far as Bovigny which achievement deserved highest recognition. Due to the bad road conditions and the exhaustion of the horses, the artillery of the Division could not follow these movements. At the time the artillery lagged far behind and was finally brought up over St. Vith. During the night, the construction of an emergency bridge near Beho had begun.

The 18 VGD reorganized its forces in St. Vith, but its main body did not advance further than Sart-lez-St. Vith. During the day the Fhr-Begl Brigade did not gain any ground either, in the direction of its assigned task (Salm sector).

23 December: On 23 December the Brigade attacked the Salm sector, advancing by way of Hinderhausen, Commanster, Rogery, Cierrieux, but encountered strong armored forces of the enemy hard south of Salm château, which repulsed all attempts at crossing of the river.

The VGD succeeded in crossing the Salm near Honvelez and by joining all other forces in taking Provedroux by assault. Thereby the road across the river was opened to the Fhr-Begl Brigade by use of the incompletely destroyed 70 ton bridge south of Salmchâteau. In the afternoon the Division was holding the line Provedroux–Honvelez–Bovigny.

The 18 VGD reached Poteau to protect its deep right flank and stopping, together with portions of the 6 Pz Army, American fire from the north against St. Vith. The activity of the enemy air force, which started on 22 December, hindered somewhat the movements and engagements of the Corps at a few places but not decisively. On 23 December in the afternoon I met Field Marshal Model near the command post of the VGD 62. He discussed with me the situation and advised with regard to the attack of the 6 Pz Army. The 5 Pz Army, after reorganizing her forces, was to shift its center of gravity in the attack to the left, in order to exploit the success achieved by the 5 Pz Army on the Salm for continued advance as the continuation of the attack was explicitly demanded by the Führer. Consequently the LXVI Army Corps was immediately transferred to the 6 Pz Army, which appeared to be most practical because it gave me a chance to devote my whole energy to the attack in the center of gravity of my army and to the approaching Battle for Bastogne.

Since 15 Dec about 8000 officers and men were taken prisoners by the LXVI Army Corps; furthermore, the stocks of light infantry weapons, ammunition, food supply, and motor vehicles of the encircled portions of the 106 Div were also taken.

RETROSPECT OF THE BATTLE OF ST. VITH

The moving up of the divisions into the assembly areas, as well as especially the relief of the 18 VGD from its former sector with its subsequent reorganization for the attack, proved to us that in the Schnee-Eifel it would take twice as long for the attack as was estimated. Consequently, I reckoned that the battle for St. Vith get under way by the night of 17 Dec. Events have proved that I was right, inasmuch as the spearheads of the 18 VGD reached Wallerode Mühle on 17 Dec in the afternoon. However, the coordination with the left combat group was not realized. Before the beginning of the attack it was planned to move forward weak portions of the right combat group of the 18 VGD with the support of some assault guns from Schönberg along the road to Bleialf in order to facilitate the advance of the left combat group. This plan was not executed, as we did not succeed in routing the 18 VGD over Roth, Auw, and Schönberg with all its combat units. On 17 Dec this far-reaching attack would have caused complete collapse of the Schnee-Eifel front and by 18 December would also have made it possible to assemble sufficient forces for fighting the still rather small groups of the enemy. There was too little reconnaissance and commitment of the VGD on 18 and 19 Dec and more only sufficient forces were brought up because of the traffic congestion which up to this time had not yet been completely eliminated. This was also the cause of repeated postponements of the attack against the town.

The lack of marching experience of the Fhr-Begl Brigade made it impossible for the latter to overcome the difficulties of the roads which were caused by weather influences prevailing in that season in the necessary time. Its full fighting power could therefore not be committed. For example, no more than about twenty-five tanks or assault guns out of the eighty armored vehicles of the unit were ever in contact with the enemy. In general, the achievement of the troops and their leaders were excellent. The enemy had taken full advantage of the time element and by his successful battles for St. Vith turned the issue in his own favor.

The enemy had tied down more forces than anticipated. The Army had even to employ an additional group, which was needed at another place. By delaying actions in the area of St. Vith the enemy gained time for bringing up forces for the defense of the Salm sector and to stop the penetration at the northern flank.

The 62 VGD had to be employed finally for the direct support of the battle for St. Vith more to the north which was less favorable. Therefore, the LVIII Pz Corps fought with a completely unprotected northern flank.

The operations of the 6 SS [sic] Pz Army were unfavorably influenced. There was no doubt that an attack properly carried out by the Fhr-Begl Brigade on 18 and 19 Dec would have decided the issue of battle at the left flank of the 6 SS Pz Army.

This brigade could have been assembled by 19 Dec in St. Vith. The delay in time, which proved decisive, occurred after its departure from the road Schönberg–St. Vith to a highly unfavorable area for mobile troops to the north of the road (Wallerode–Meyerode–Born–Emmels).

The Advance of the LVIII and XLVII Panzer Corps to and Across the Ourthe

A. LVIII PZ CORPS

17 December: The reconnaissance detachment of the 116 Pz Div was able to capture Heinerscheid on 17 Dec and was supported by the Regiment 1128 of the 560 Div which had crossed the Our near Kalborn. In the morning the 116 Pz Div succeeded in crossing the Our near Ouren. The enemy offered tenacious resistance. The terrain was difficult to survey and favorable for the defense. The bridge was in a bad condition and its load capacity small. The road Lutzkampen–Ouren was completely covered with mud. Only tracked vehicles moved forward and they, too, only with great difficulties. At this spot the construction of a bridge and the necessary improvement of the roads would have caused considerable loss of time. The bridgehead won was not deep enough for bridge construction, therefore the corps was rerouted to the crossing Dasburg over Irrhausen and Daleiden, after repeated requests for information with the Army. The disengagement from the enemy and the required reorganization of the forces was only completed on the night of 17 Dec because the bringing up of the forces on the bottomless roads required plenty of time. Fortunately, however, the bad weather made the enemy air activity impossible.

The 560 VGD whose regiment 1128 had already reached the western bank of the Our, received orders to mop up the terrain to the eastern shore of the Our with all forces still available on the eastern bank of the Our. This resulted in very costly battles for the Division, especially during the capture of Sevenig which was fiercely defended by the enemy, resulting in heavy casualties to the 560 VGD due to its inexperience.

Engineering detachments were dispatched to rebuild and reinforce the approach routes.

Final situation on 17 December: According to reports received prior to 1200, the reconnaissance detachment of the 116 Pz Div had reached Asselborn. Enemy resistance and counterattacks supported by tanks were quickly repelled by the reconnaissance battalion. The scouting troops were employed against Houffalize. We felt that the front of the enemy was pierced and the situation was ripe for the advance to the west.

The mass of the 116 Pz Div was advancing over Dasburg towards the western bank of the Our.

The 560 VGD was still mopping up the enemy in the area Ouren–Sevenig whereas the Regimental Group 1128 of the Division had captured Heinerscheid. Small security detachments supported the right flank of the Division near Berg. The neighboring LXVI Corps at the right flank was still fighting in the Heckuscheid sector. The neighboring XLVII Pz Corps to the left had established bridgeheads across the Clerf near Clerf and Drauffelt. On 18 Dec the LVIII Pz Corps intended to bring up all available forces behind the 116 Pz Div for a further advance to the west.

18 December: While the main body of the 116 Pz Div was assembled in the sector Heinerscheid until the nightfall of 18 Dec its reconnaissance detachment advanced fighting continuously over Hachiville, Tavigny and was close to Houffalize with an enemy engaged in delaying battle tactics. Until nightfall the Regiment 1128 of the 560 VGD reached the sector Asselborn and Sassel following close behind the reconnaissance detachment of 116 Pz Div. The eager desire to advance shown by soldiers of the Division, the majority of whom were very young and were fighting for the first time, was excellent in spite of bad weather and road conditions. The Regiment 1129 was still fighting in the Ouren–Sevenig sector with the enemy, who was still holding out. At Kalborn the construction of a bridge was started. On the night of 18 Dec the remaining portions of the 560 VGD east of the Our arrived, to join the division.

19 December: On 19 Dec the 116 Pz Div had received orders to advance as far as possible to the west by way of Houffalize, La Roche. Strong enemy resistance expected at Houffalize was supposed to be bypassed. At Houffalize in the morning of 19 December the reconnaissance battalion of the Division met enemy resistance. The detachment observed movements of strong forces on the road leading from Houffalize to the north. It received orders from the Division to withdraw to the south by way of Bertogne. Houffalize was to be captured by rear portions of the Division. During the day the Regiment 1128 of the 560 VGD had overcome the last enemy resistance in the sector Ouren–Sevenig, taking up positions for an attack at Weiswampach over Ouren. At night after stiff resistance, Weiswampach was captured. The main body of the Division followed the 116 Pz Div by way of Binsfeld, Ulfingen, Asselborn, Troine and its spearheads reached Buret after a forced march at nightfall. To continue the advance the Corps planned to employ the Division to the north of the Ourthe river. It was known that the right neighbor was still fighting at the Our. The left neighbor faced an enemy who was defending himself fiercely to the east of the line Noville–Bizory-Neffe. At Wicourt the 116 Pz Div made contact with portions of the 2 Pz Div and was able to assist the fighting of the latter.

20 December: During the night of 19 Dec the corps was informed by the 116 Pz Div that the Ourthe bridge located five kilometers to the northwest of Bertogne had been destroyed. Its reconstruction by engineers attached to the Division (engineer detachments of the Corps were not available) could not be completed until nightfall of 20 December. Therefore, the Corps had to decide to eventually activate the Division by way of the crossroad northwest of Flamierge against Champlon. It was known that Bastogne was held tenaciously by the enemy. Extensive enemy movements were reported along the road of Bastogne–Champlon. The demolition of the bridge near Ourtheville had to be expected if the Division were employed along this road. Traffic congestion had also to be taken into account if the 116 Pz Div advanced and either met or was drawn into the movements of the 2 Pz Div in the sector of the XLVII Pz Corps. In the meantime Houffalize was captured by portions in the rear of the 116 Pz Div. In this sector the enemy was withdrawing to the west. It was decided to take advantage of the 'soft spot' in order to quickly gain further ground to the west. Upon request by the Army, the Div was ordered to hold the line, going into action on the night of 19/20 Dec, attacking towards Samree over Houffalize.

The Regiment 1128 of the 560 VGD advanced on 20 Dec, fighting continuously from Weiswampach by way of Wilwerdingen, Hautbellin as far as the sector in the vicinity of Gouvy. The main body of the Division was started off by the Corps by way of Tavigny, Cetturu in the direction of Mont-Samree in order to avoid bottlenecks.

116 Pz Div which had taken up new direction during the night of 19 Dec, attacked vigorously. They were able to overcome the strong resistance of the enemy near Samree and to capture Dochamps in the evening of 20 Dec.

At night on 20 Dec the LVIII Pz Corps considered the enemy fighting in that sector as overrun and in the course of retreat. New enemy forces had not yet appeared. The Corps had to gain ground quickly, crossing the Ourthe in the sector Han–Hotton to the northwest, before the enemy was able to reestablish a new defense line in this sector.

It was known that the right neighboring army, in spite of heavy fighting near Vielsalm, was only making slow progress and the bringing up of the 2 SS Pz Div behind the LVIII Pz Corps was contemplated.

On 21 Dec the Corps therefore ordered the 116 Pz Div to attack Hotton over the Soy road and to gain the northwestern bank of the Ourthe to advance further toward the Meuse. The 560 VGD received orders to attack along the road Dochamps, Amonines and furthermore in the direction Petit Han. On 20 Dec the left neighbor, the 2 Pz Div, was still fighting near Champlon. Therefore both flanks of the far advanced corps were unprotected. Relying on the arrival of the XLVII Pz Corps, the Army clung to its decision to advance farther to the west.

21 December: The 560 VGD was attacked at its flanks while advancing by way of Samree–Dochamps in the direction of Amonines and along the road Vielsalm–Samree. Our own patrols on the forest northwest of the road Samree–Amonines contacted the enemy. A combat group of the Division employed by way of Cherain against Les Tailles encountered the enemy at the large crossroad two km north-northwest of Les Tailles, who evidently tried to keep these crossroads open for his retreating forces.

Enemy resistance stiffened also in front of the sector of the 116 Pz Div. In the afternoon the Division succeeded in crossing the road Soy–Hotton; however, attacks against Hotton failed. The portions of the Division located close to the north of the road Soy–Hotton were at first unable to gain ground to the northwest. These troops were soon pinned by the strong artillery fire of the enemy, especially from the dominating heights north of Soy. On 21 and 22 Dec the enemy succeeded once more in advancing his line to the south by way of the road and in establishing himself in the wooded area south of Melines and west of Wy. The course of the front line held by the 116 Pz Div, on 22 Dec, was not quite clear. Near Marcourt, four km to the northwest of La Roche, a group of about thirty tanks or armored scouting vehicles were observed, which had been cut off and had formed a circle to defend itself.

On the night of 21 Dec it was announced that the first portions of the 2 SS Pz Div had arrived. They reported to the Div command post of the 560 VGD at Nadrin. The Division was to attack, joining the II SS Pz Corps, over Grandmenil toward Barvaux, therefore in a northwestern direction. Furthermore it became known that the 2 Pz Div was attacking Marche from Champlon. Our patrols reported that La Roche was evacuated by the enemy.

In the evening hours the belief of the corps strengthened that the 116 Pz Div was unable to throw the enemy facing it and to gain ground to the northwest. The corps presumed that the enemy had brought up fresh troops. A confirmation by captured prisoners was not available. Due to the fact that the corps had to keep the advance moving under any circumstances and as the attack of the 2 Pz Div gave rise to hope that this could be achieved to the west of Ourthe

– possibly in conjunction and supported by the push of the 2 Pz Div – the 116 Pz Div received orders to detach itself from the enemy in the course of 22 Dec and, moving ahead over La Roche, to push forward northwest on the south-western bank of the Ourthe. On 22 Dec the 560 VGD received orders to continue its attacks over Amonines in the direction of Grand Han.

During the night of 21 Dec the 2 SS Pz Div was subordinated to the Corps. It was ordered by the Corps to march under protection of its open right flank, to advance along the big road Houffalize–Grandmenil toward Barvaux.

For the first time the sky started to clear up so that we had to expect immediate enemy air attacks.

22 December: In connection with the diverting of the 116 Pz Div by way of La Roche to the western bank of the Ourthe, the arrival of the 2 SS Pz Div created a new task of the 560 VGD. On 23 Dec the Div had to take over the sector of the 116 Pz Div during the withdrawal of some of its units, meanwhile on 22 Dec advancing its main front line to the road Soy–Hotton. At night on 22 Dec, the Division succeeded in reaching, with a combat group, the forest exit to the east of Amonines whereas another combat group followed up an advance to the northwest of the 2 SS Pz Div as far as to the sector northwest of the large crossroad two km northwest of Les Tailles. The execution of the originally planned attacks at the direction of Grand Han would make it evident that due to heavy losses during the last days the combat power of the Division had sunk considerably. It was no longer strong enough to attack Grand Han over Amonines.

2 SS Pz Div gained ground astride the road of the large crossroad 2 km to the northwest of Les Tailles toward Grandmenil. On this occasion bitter fighting developed with an armored group of the enemy located on the crossroads 2 km to the northwest of Les Tailles. Overcoming this resistance the Division met further opposition during its drive on Odeigne. The villages Freyneux and Lamormenil lying further to the west were also occupied by the enemy. From this point the enemy contacted the flank and rear of the group of the 560 VGD, fighting in the Amonines sector, thereby forcing this Division to push forward to defend the woods east of Amonines to prevent any enemy penetration of the flank and the rear of the forces drawn up at Amonines.

In the earliest hours of the morning of 22 Dec the 116 Pz Div tried once again to capture Hotton. Thanks to the skillfully directed defense by the enemy this attempt also failed. Over exertion may also have affected our troops. Since 16 Dec they had been on the march or fighting steadily for over a week and any relaxation was very limited. Already at noon on 22 Dec the reconnaissance battalion of the Div was started off on a march by way of La Roche with the task to guard there the Ourthe crossing for the Division and to gain the dominating heights to the south of Menil–Verdenne. Information gained from the reconnaissance battalion arriving at night indicated that the enemy occupied a running front line to the south of the line Hampteau–Menil–Verdenne which, however, seemed only thinly occupied.

On 22 Dec the weather was clear; the activity of the enemy air forces was increasing.[10] In the course of 22 Dec the Corps expected to advance to the northwest with the support of the 116 Pz Div between Hotton and Marche.

On 19 Dec when the Army decided to leave the 26 VGD at Bastogne in order to use it in the drive to the west with the armored forces of the XLVII Pz Corps – although realizing the importance of Bastogne's possession by the enemy – serious doubts arose for the first time as to whether the objective could be reached. In the evening of 22 Dec, it was quite certain that our plans could not be realized. It is true forces of the XLVII Pz Corps had reached approximately the line Buissonville–Rochefort. The question arose whether we would succeed in advancing this pointed spearhead and widen it sufficiently to achieve strategic results as the attack of the 6 SS Pz Army already bogged down. The left wing of the LXVI Corps was still fighting at Vielsalm. In the sector of the LVIII Pz Corps we did not manage to cross the road Erezee–Soy–Hotton to the northwest; the attack against Hotton had failed. The pressure exerted against the northern flank of the LVIII Pz Corps, running along Erezee–Malempre and beyond it, was increasing. Finally we had to avoid the resistance of the enemy in the sector of the XLVII Pz Corps at Marche in order to keep up the drive forward to the west. The question whether or not the Seventh Army would succeed in withstanding continued pressure of the enemy from the south remained the source of constant anxiety. We were therefore anxious to know whether the 116 Pz Div would succeed in gaining ground to the northeast past Marche in the direction of Baillonville. The success or failure of this thrust would probably decide the question as to whether the Meuse could be reached (considering a 'small solution') to facilitate a turn to the northwest of the river by the two Pz Corps and thereby achieve a strategic success by relieving the LXVI Corps and the 6 SS Pz Army.

23 December: During the day the 2 SS Pz Div fought its way forward without being able to break through. The combat group of the 560 VGD chosen to seize Amonines could not overcome the strong enemy resistance. On the other hand, another combat group of the Division succeeded in advancing once more to the main front line of battle as far as just south of Melines. During the day portions of the 116 Pz Div were withdrawn, last were those fighting near Werpin.

By nightfall the 116 Pz Div, whose reconnaissance battalion had already moved to the southwestern bank of the Ourthe, reached with the Pz Gren Regt 156 and the main body of the artillery the sector of Grimbiemont by the evening. The remaining portions were brought up during the night to the new operational area. The bridge at La Roche, which was only slightly damaged, was repaired. The reconnaissance battalion reported that the enemy was digging in;

this battalion also observed that it was faced by the newly arrived 84 American Division. In order to dominate the road Hotton–Marche, the 156 Pz Gren Regt was employed on the same day to attack in the direction of Verdenne. The Regiment reached the woods to the northwest of Verdenne.

On the following day, 24 Dec, the Division was given orders to pierce the enemy positions and to push through by way of Baillonville toward Ciney, in order to establish contact with the 2 Pz Div and to protect its right flank.

24 December: On 24 December the enemy launched counterattacks against the sectors of the 2 SS Pz Div and the 560 VGD. Both Divisions were unable to advance. The 560 Division succeeded, during the attack against Freyneux and Lamormenil launched to relieve its flank, in capturing Lamormenil. However, it was lost again in the evening.

The attack made by the 116 Pz Div failed; the breakthrough was not achieved. The Pz Gren Regt 156, which succeeded in making a local penetration in the area to the northwest of Verdenne, was able to dominate the road Hotton–Marche with its artillery. Another combat group of the Division was able to capture Verdenne and to gain the ground to the north and northeast of the village. Therefore the enemy succeeded in the entire sector of the LVIII Pz Corps to hold his lines intact and not only to establish a strong defense, but to undertake counterthrusts of his own. Nevertheless, the attacks of the 116 Pz Div had to be continued because it became necessary to relieve the 2 Pz Div which had advanced far to the west. The casualties of the Division on 24 Dec were considerable. The Corps asked the Army to bring up the Führer-Begleit Brigade to take position on the southern bank of the Ourthe in order to capture Hotton which had been contested for a long time and thereby to support the advance of the 116 Pz Division. On 24 Dec there was lively fighter bomber activity by the enemy.

25 December: The 560 VGD, which had orders to change over to the defense, was fighting off enemy attacks against the line Soy–Hampteau. The Division held the line it had reached. The SS Pz Div was commanded to secure the right flank of the Corps along the line of the crossroad, two km northwest of Les Tailles–Odeigne–Oster. Oster was to be attacked and captured. The attack failed.

The attacking columns of the 116 Pz Div met a heavy enemy counterattack which the Div could hold off only by employing its available resources. The Division suffered heavy casualties. A combat group of the Div, which on the previous day advanced as far as to the north of Verdenne, was surrounded. Verdenne was lost.

On the following day the Corps was promised that the Führer-Begleit Brigade would be subordinated to its command. It was a clear, cold wintry day on 25 Dec during which the enemy battled our own units continuously, making extensive use of its air forces.

26 December: Attacks of the enemy against the 2 SS Pz Div and the 560 VGD continued. The 560 VGD was driven back as far as the line north of Magoster to the north of Beffe.

The Führer-Begl Brigade, arriving early in the morning, received orders to attack Hotton as its first objective. The road Hotton–Marche was to be blocked supporting the attack of the 116 Pz Division. The Brigade, advancing along the Ourthe, succeeded in the late morning to capture Hampteau, but in view of the situation at Bastogne had to be called off and the brigade was diverted with all possible speed toward Bastogne. For this reason the Army was forced to give up a successful operation. A further thrust of the 116 Pz Div was not out of the question. The Div succeeded in establishing contact with the combat group which had been cut off north of Verdenne by bringing up a small armored group. However, it failed to restore continuous liaison.

Therefore, on the following day the LVIII Pz Corps gave orders that the Div should make every effort to free the encircled group. On 26 Dec the front line of the Corps ran from the crossroads to the north of Les Tailles–Odeigne–Freyneux–the forest to the north of Dochamps–Amonines–north of Magoster–north of Beffe–Hampteau–wooded outskirts south of the village Menil–Verdenne and finally the northwestern edge of the forest to the southeast of Marche. The enemy air force was very active.

27 December: on 27 Dec the 2 SS Pz Div was again put under the control of the II SS Pz Corps. The enemy attack launched against the 560 VGD and the 116 Pz Div increased in strength. The 560 VGD lost Magoster and was driven back as far as the northern outskirts of Beffe. The frontline of the 116 Pz Div had to be withdrawn. The Div had contact with portions of the 9 Pz Div, which since 20 Dec had been operating with the XLVII Pz Corps. The weather was clear and enemy air forces were attacking our own ground forces the whole day.

B. XLVII PZ CORPS

17 December: On 17 Dec the 2 Pz Div did not succeed at first in breaking the resistance of the enemy at Urspelt and at Reuler. Not until late afternoon did a battalion of the 2 Gren Regt to the right flank (Battalion Monschau) succeed – starting from the north – to advance to the south on the Clerf and to cross the river on the railroad station of Clerf. At that point, the resistance in the before mentioned village ceased. On the whole, it was probably a question of a general withdrawal behind the Clerf, which was, due to the general situation, ordered by the American command because at the front line of the 26 VGD the enemy resistance slackened approximately at the same time.

The Battalion Monschau penetrated into the village Clerf from the north and at 1700 was able to capture the southern bridge of the village, which was undamaged.

The Division established a bridgehead at Clerf and after mopping up the area behind it, reformed its ranks. At that locality pockets of resistance of the enemy were still holding out, defending themselves fiercely, so that on 17 Dec the village could only be crossed by armored cars.

The 26 VGD at 0500 hours had sufficiently eliminated the road blocks and demolitions to make limited traffic possible on the road leading from Eisenach to Hosingen. Portions of the artillery of the Panzer-Jäger battalion and the heavy flak detachments were drawn up to support the envisaged attack of the II/78 against Hosingen. Before dawn the Gren Regt 77 had captured Bockholz. The Regiment continued progressively attacking American resistance northwest of Bockholz and south of Munshausen.

The 1/78 pushed its way through against strong enemy resistance to the southeast of Bockholz in the direction towards Pintsche.

Combat group Kaufmann (Füs Regt 39 and portions of the Reconnaissance battalion of the Pz Lehr Div) captured Holzthum and fought for the possession of Consthum.

On this day, too, wet and cold weather prevented the enemy from employing his air force.

At 1100 hours Hosingen fell: twenty officers and three hundred men of the American garrison were taken prisoners. In the afternoon the enemy resistance slackened also at the sector of the 26 VGD. Late at night the 77 Gren Regt captured Drauffelt; the 78 Gren Regt also took Pintsche. Consthum (combat group Kaufmann) fell also. The combat group continued to attack Alscheid, however reaching the Clerf in the afternoon which was crossed only after midnight by the combat group without meeting resistance and subsequently penetrated into Alscheid encountering no resistance.

According to a report made by the liaison officer of the 5 Fallsch Jg Div portions of the Div were attacking the Our crossing at Kautenbach.

By order of the XLVII Pz Corps the Pz Lehr Div had to exchange the reconnaissance battalion, subordinated to Combat Group 'Kaufmann', for the Pz Gren Regt 901. The order issued in the afternoon, was only executed during the night of 17 December. The corps wanted to have the reconnaissance battalion at its disposal to commit it as originally planned by way of Eschweiler and Derenbach against Bastogne. The main body of the Pz Lehr Div was to follow the 2 Pz Div with the Pz Gren Regt 902, one armored and one artillery battalion across the bridge Dasburg–Marnach; the Pz Gren Regt 901, one armored and one artillery battalion across the bridge Gemünd–Hosingen was to follow the 26 VGD.

The exchange of the reconnaissance battalion for the Pz Gren Regt 901 and the fighting of the Combat Group 'Kaufmann' for the possession of the crossing of the Clerf to the east of Alscheid, terminating only at midnight on 17 Dec, proved that the Pz Gren Regt 901 would only be available to the Pz Lehr Div at a later time and that it must follow behind.

However, the heavy congestion of the roads in addition to the bad state of the roads was also the reason why the available portions of the Pz Lehr Div including the Pz Gren Regt 902, which had been brought on by way of Dasburg, and the reconnaissance battalion did not yet cross the Clerf on 17 December.

Both Divisions, the 2 Pz and 26 VGD, established bridgeheads at the crossing points planned across the Clerf. On orders, they were to advance to the west with as strong a force as possible. Both Divisions encountered considerable road congestion which increased by advancing portions of the Pz Lehr Division. To a large extent the congestions continued to the west of the Clerf, especially in the area Knaphoscheid–Drauffelt. They were partly responsible for the late arrival of the Pz Lehr Div at Bastogne. Speed was urgently needed, the more so, as according to an intercepted radio message on 17 Dec the American 101 Parachute Div was alerted and ordered to attack Bastogne. On midnight 17 Dec the situation of the XLVII Pz Corps was as follows:

The resistance of the enemy had slackened. On the entire front line of the Corps the enemy withdrew behind the Clerf area. We succeeded in establishing bridgeheads at Clerf and Drauffelt. The breakthrough seemed about to be realized. The question was 'to keep the enemy on edge' and to follow through without delay to prevent him from taking up new defense positions. Sending in the Panzer units, in particular the Pz Lehr Div, was therefore of the highest importance, especially in view of the approaching engagement with the American 101 Parachute Division.

The LVIII Pz Corps together with the 560 VGD had captured Kalborn. The left neighbor (5 FJ Div) was successfully attacking the Clerf crossing at Kautenbach.

From the point of view of the Army it appeared that despite the success achieved on 17 Dec the aim of the Army to get to and across the Meuse with the advance guards during the night of the third day of the attack was already imperiled. As far as time was concerned the objective could be achieved only under the most favorable conditions, provided the American resistance west of the Clerf could be easily overcome by our own advance guards.

18 December: During 18 December the weather again prevented the use of the enemy air forces. This was fortunate since road congestion started to cause the greatest difficulties. The 2 Pz Div reached Hamiville at about 2000 hours with its most advanced portions, meeting weak resistance. Late in the afternoon, in the area to the north of Brachtenbach it encountered a combat command of the 9 American Armored Division which was thrown back.

The Gren Regt 77 was ordered by the 26 VGD to attack Oberwampach; the Gren Regt 78 (including the main body of the Division artillery, the engineer battalion, portions of the antitank company and signal battalions was to attack Niederwampach and the Füs Regt 39 Derenbach.

Because on 18 Dec the Clerf crossing point at Kautenbach had not yet been captured by the 5 FJ Div, and during the day the enemy started to bring up groups equipped with tanks from the Wiltz valley in a northern direction, the division used the Füs Regt 39 to safeguard its southern flank. Conforming to its projected plan of attack, it was to build up a defense flank along the line Alscheid–Erpeldange–Wiltz–Noertrange with the front to the south. Here the regiment also remained on 18 December. The Div reached its objectives only on the night of 18 Dec; however the forces were not yet reorganized and for the most part were without combat vehicles. The whole day harassing fire including surprise shelling was concentrated on Eschweiler, Derenbach, and Niederwampach and on the roads connecting these villages.

On 18 Dec at 0900 the Pz Lehr Div, with its advanced guards (the reconnaissance battalion), followed by the Pz Gren Regt 902, crossed the Clerf near Drauffelt and advanced west under occasional harassing fire. The line of march extended from Eschweiler, Derenbach, starting far back to the south as far as Erpelange. At 1800 the Division (minus Pz Gren Regt 901) reached the sector Niederwampach. At 2100 continuing its advance it took the road Benonchamps, Magaret (the Corps had recommended the use of the road over Bras which was in a better condition). We did not start from Magaret toward Bastogne before 19 Dec, having previously mopped up Magaret by dawn. At daybreak the Division commander observed personally preparations of American forces organized for the defense of the heights southwest of Magaret. According to reports by the natives a strong group of American tanks (about forty), including artillery, had passed through Magaret in the direction of Longvilly on 18 December at about 1900. Therefore, the XLVII Pz Corps had only advanced between 8–13 km to the west, reaching Hamiville with the 2 Pz Div and with the Pz Lehr Div at Niederwampach. This was the area in which the 26 VGD joined the Pz Lehr Div on the night of 18 Dec. They were met by portions of the Ninth American Armored Div north of Brachtenbach and it was confirmed that on the night of 18 Dec portions of the American 10th Armored Div were advancing westward on the road to Magaret. The situation of the Pz Lehr Div turned out to be very unfavorable. The speed of the advance of the Div was held up due to bad road conditions.[11] All difficulties previously enumerated in these reports are undoubtedly true. However, the question remained whether an immediate attack by portions of the Division in a southern direction would not have led to success; in other words, it would have flung open the way from the south to Bastogne. The fact that the Pz Lehr Div did not immediately turn south, which in all probability would have led to success, indicates a breach in the leadership of the Panzer Div. Independent maneuvering was an essential part of the speed and mobility of this arm.

19 December: At night the 2 Pz Div resumed their attack against Noville according to their original order. Bourcy, occupied by the enemy, was captured at 0530; the edges of the woods, one km to the east of Noville, were reached by an attack at 0830 hours. Noville, which was occupied by stronger forces, could not be captured. The division did not yet have all its portions available, the rest of which, due to road congestion, only arrived in the course of the day. The XLVII Pz Corps had the following orders:

– The 26 VGD, after having reached the road Noville, Bastogne, was to attack on both sides of Arloncourt to penetrate into Bastogne from the north.

– The Pz Lehr Div, attacking by way of Magaret–Wardin was to penetrate into Bastogne from the east and advance beyond to the west.

The attack was delayed because fierce fighting developed at noon with a combat command of the American 10th Armored Div. It had advanced during the previous evening in a westerly direction; our patrols observed this force to be resting on 19 Dec in the sector of Longvilly. This combat command, which in the course of the morning had also attacked the southern flank of the 2 Pz Div, was presumably charged with supporting a defensive front to the east of Bastogne.

The result of the battle was the complete destruction of the combat command, fifty armored vehicles and tanks were reported destroyed, twenty-three tanks, fourteen armored cars, fifteen guns on self-propelled mounts, twenty-five trucks and thirty jeeps fell into our hands. Portions of the Pz Lehr Div and the 2 Pz Div took part in the fighting, a major part of which was carried by Regt 77 of the 26 VGD.

Due to this engagement with the combat command involving heavy losses to the enemy, the attack of the 26 VGD and the Pz Lehr Div, as ordered by the XLVII Pz Corps, could not get under way before noon. The enemy had gained valuable time to establish a defense line to the east and to the southeast of Bastogne facing the east. According to our reconnaissance the enemy's intention was not of establishing small security outposts, but of the organization of a strong defense line supported by artillery.

The 26 VGD started to attack as late as 1300 with a combat group from the area east of Niederwampach. In the afternoon, the attack bypassing north of Magaret bogged down in front of Bizory, which was defended by strong forces. Reconnaissance patrols who temporarily penetrated into the village were driven out again. Another combat group of the Division (Regt 77) advanced by way of Arloncourt, which was captured (here we found remnants of the combat command) – to wooded area south of Foy. At night this attack, too, bogged down with the result that the Div was facing east of the road Foy, the village of Bizory who was offering fierce resistance.

At 1700 hours Pz Lehr Div had captured Neffe and advanced further to Mont which, however, could not be captured. The combat group belonging to the reconnaissance battalion of the Div[12] and ordered to attack Wardin, could not take this village before nightfall. Marvie, according to reports by reconnaissance patrols, was also occupied by strong enemy forces.

On the night of 19 Dec the XLVII Pz Corps along the line to the east of Noville – east of Bizory – west of Neffe faced an enemy who put up tenacious resistance. Our problem was whether we should gather all forces to capture Bastogne on 20 Dec or go back to the original plan for the 26 VGD to capture this place while employing the Panzer Divisions for a further advance west, bypassing Bastogne. The Corps, therefore, consulted the Army regarding this question. The importance of Bastogne, if held by the enemy would hinder all movements to the west and cripple our entire supply. This fact was emphasized to all at the conference prior to the attack. If it could not be overrun or captured by a surprise raid it would tie down our forces. Our own forces were considered insufficient in numbers and combat strength for both tasks to advance to the Meuse and protect the long southern flank, including Bastogne. Besides, Bastogne offered the enemy a threat to bring up forces to start an assault from this area which could seriously endanger the German attack. All incentive for capture of Bastogne existed even more so now that the Seventh Army did not contain the strength originally envisaged. However, on the other hand, the XLVII Pz Corps would have to give up temporarily its advance to the west in order to capture Bastogne.

Therefore the Army gave orders for the 2 Pz Div to take Noville and to advance without delay further to the west. The Corps received orders to employ the Pz Lehr Div once more for the attack against Bastogne from the east. Even so, the Division was to have forces available to advance to the west by way of Sibret. The task of the 26 VGD was to continue the attack from the positions reached and after reaching the road Noville–Bastogne to capture the latter from the north.

The LVIII Pz Corps and the 116 Pz Div had already reached Houffalize early on 19 Dec and reconnaissance by noon had advanced to Bertogne 7 km west of Noville. This fact played its part in bringing about this decision by the Army. In addition to all previous considerations, it became necessary to exploit the success of the 116 Pz Div to secure joint operations of the two Pz Corps for the thrust to the Meuse. Also, during the day the 5 Fallsch Jg Div had captured Wiltz giving us hope that Füs Regt 39 might soon be available for the attack on Bastogne.

20 December: At 1400 the 2 Pz Div succeeded in capturing Noville by an enveloping action from the north after taking Rachamps. At midnight the advance detachment of the Div reached Ortheuville along the Bastogne–Marche road. There the Ourthe bridge fell undamaged into our hands. The Div advanced from Noville by way of Foy, which was held by the enemy. It was taken and its garrison fell to the south. Advancing from Foy after leaving security detachments, the Div turned to the west.

The attack to be made by the 26 VGD was delayed because of the dense fog which, while it prevented any action by the enemy air force, also did not permit observation and commitment by our artillery. The Füs Regt 39 was approaching and was made available to the Div south of Arloncourt.

Between 0900 and 1000, by orders of the XLVII Pz Corps, the Regts 77 and 78 were temporarily subordinated to the Pz Lehr Div. It was the new task of the 26 VGD to penetrate Bastogne from the southwest with all available forces by way of Wardin (which had been captured in the meantime by the Pz Lehr Div) and then proceed over Remoifosse. The Pz Lehr Div was to attack the town from the southeast with its center of gravity on its left wing near Marvie. At the same time, the Corps sent word to the Div that portions of the 5 Fallschirm Jäger Div were advancing by way of Lutremange and Harlange toward the highway from Bastogne to Martelange.

For the execution of the ordered attacks, 26 VGD had Füs Regt 39 available, supported by portions of the Div artillery and the Pz Jg Company. The reconnaissance battalion, which was still attached to the Pz Lehr Div was again subordinated to the Div. Finally, the engineer battalion, the replacement training battalion and the combat school were to be brought up to the Div. The Div intended to commit the reinforced Regt 39 over Lutrebois, Remoifosse and to attack to the north from the Assenois sector so as to penetrate Bastogne from the south. The reconnaissance battalion[13] was to attack Bastogne from the area Senonchamps to Mande St. Etienne from the west. However, we could not expect the arrival of the reconnaissance battalion in the Senonchamps area before evening.

Therefore the Pz Lehr Div was in the lead at the eastern front of Bastogne. It was now attacking, using the Regts 77 and 78 which had started the attack at 1100 east of the road Foy–Bizory and attacking with its own forces from Neffe toward Mont from Bras over Wardin to Marvie.

The advance of the portions of the 26 VGD surrounding Bastogne from the south was delayed by road blocks in the wooded area to the south of the road Bras to Marvie. All vehicles of this combat group had to be rerouted over Doncols and Lutremange while the fighting forces advanced by foot. On the road Doncols–Lutremange, which was in a very bad condition, road congestion disrupted traffic. Portions of the Pz Lehr Div and of the 5 Fallsch Jg Div became entangled and were pressed together so that it was difficult to reorganize them.

Until midnight the situation of the XLVII Pz Corps was as follows:

The 2 Pz Div was well ahead. Ourtheville had been captured by the reconnaissance battalion. However, fuel began to get scarce. The Pz Lehr Div captured Bizory (Regt 77). Regiments 77 and 78 were now close to each other along the road Foy–Bizory, but owing to strong enemy resistance made little progress. The attack from Neffe to Mont did not gain any ground. Wardin was captured. Marvie, notwithstanding our own attacks, was still tenaciously held by the enemy. Since late afternoon the combat group of the 26 VGD was engaged in battle to the west of the road Bastogne–Martelange. Salvacourt and the heights to the west of it were captured. The attack against Assenois gained ground slowly. The resistance to the south of Bastogne was not as strong as on the eastern front of Bastogne. The right neighboring corps moved the 116 Pz Div to the northern bank of the Ourthe and had advanced from Houffalize which was now completely in our own hands by way of Samree and as far as Dochamps. The right flank of the Seventh Army had to close in on the highway Bastogne–Martelange in its drive to the west.

For 21 Dec the Army had given orders that the 2 Pz Div and Pz Lehr Div were to advance further to the west with all available forces. They had to leave behind:

2 Pz Div   – security detachments in the western and northwestern sector of Bastogne;

Pz Lehr Div – the forces stationed between the roads Bastogne–Bras and Bastogne–Remoifosse (Pz Gren Regt 901).

These forces were subordinated to the 26 VGD; also the regiments 77 and 78 were again under the command of the Division. It was the task of the 26 VGD to continue the attack at Bastogne with the center of gravity in the south and southwestern sector.

21 December: On 21 Dec the weather cleared up so that during the afternoon a restricted number of fighter bombers appeared over the battle area for the first time.[14]

The 2 Pz Div made only little progress, due to fuel shortages, and had to be content to widen its bridgehead across the Ourthe to Tenneville which was established by the reconnaissance battalion. The reconnaissance battalion had to repulse attacks from a southeastern direction against the bridgehead in the sector Flamierge and east of Amberloup.

In the sector of the Pz Lehr Div the relief of its elements for the advance to the west was complete. By nightfall, the Div gained ground as far as Morhet. The reconnaissance battalion together with the engineer battalion advanced as far as Amberloup–Tillet– Gerimont (here American supply column in strength of sixty trucks and 22 jeeps were captured). Our reconnaissance reported that the roads leading from the east and the northeast to St. Hubert were blocked.

Early in the morning the 26 VGD succeeded in capturing Sibret after a heavy battle. The Div fought its way forward against fierce resistance by the enemy. By night they had reached the line from the Bois de Hazy – the southern part of Assenois – close to the south of Villeroux – eastern edge of Bois de Fragotte – northern edge of Bois de Valets. We failed to capture Senonchamps and to gain the large road to the north of it. However, the road was covered by our fire. In the southeast and north of Bastogne the portions of the 2 Pz Div and Pz Lehr Div were relieved according to orders. Neither to the east nor in the north did our attack gain much ground. The right wing of the Div was now approximately one km to the northwest of Recogne joined up to Champs by security detachments of the 2 Pz Div. The ring encircling Bastogne was only open between Champs and Senonchamps.

According to a report from the Seventh Army, the 5 Fallsch Jg Div had established a defense line of its flank at Hollange–Remichampagne. An advance guard was said to have crossed the road Bastogne–Neufchâteau near Vaux les Rosieres to the west without meeting the enemy.

In the course of the day a negotiator of the Pz Lehr Div was sent to Bastogne to demand its surrender. The demand was rejected. On the night of 21 Dec the XLVII Pz Corps gave orders charging the 26 VGD with the entire front encircling Bastogne. Pz Gren Regt 901 of the Pz Lehr Div and two artillery battalions of a Volks Artillery Corps (the latter being brought up) were subordinated. The remaining security detachments of the 2 Pz Div between Champs and Senonchamps were to be relieved by the Division. The encircling ring between Champs and Senonchamps was to be closed, the attacks against Bastogne with center of gravity from a southwestern direction were to be continued. In order to continue this attack the encircling ring in the eastern, northern and northwestern sectors had to be held by weak forces. The attack was to be made with the Füs Regt 39 and the Reconnaissance Battalion 26. The support of all available artillery was to be employed (with the division artillery of the eastern sector used for the forming of an artillery group in the sector Salvacourt–Sibret). Two artillery battalions of a Volks Artillery Corps were to be brought up, to replace the guns withdrawn from the eastern sector.

According to the picture given by the reconnaissance on 21 Dec at night, no forces of the enemy had been up from the west to face the 2 Pz Div. In the afternoon, the LVIII Pz Corps, with the 116 Pz Div, had crossed the road Soy–Hotton.

22 December: Before dawn, the first portions of the Pz Gren Regts arrived in the bridgehead of the 2 Pz Div. However the tanks of the Division were still pinned down due to lack of fuel.

The enemy had set up demolitions on the road Bastogne–Marche west of Champlon. Only after a bitter contest did the demolished place fall into our hands.

On 22 Dec the activity of the American air force was steadily increasing. The main body of the 2 Pz Div advanced along the highway towards Marche. One combat group of the division proceeded over Nassogne towards Hargimont. The forces of the division proved insufficient for a successful attack against Marche, which was being occupied by strong enemy forces. Therefore, the Div left behind a Pz Gren battalion reinforced by antiaircraft artillery to seal off Marche and advanced with all major forces south by way of Hargimont. It was feasible to capture Hargimont by attacking from the east and south. From Hargimont the Division advanced further to the west and at night was able to take Buissonville and Jamodenne. There was heavy fighting going on for Aye, which changed hands several times. The Pz Gren battalion had the further task to seal off the sector Aye in order to keep open the road Hargimont, Harsin, for the advance to the west, as ordered by the division. On its march to Rochefort, the Pz Lehr Div encountered strong resistance by the enemy at St. Hubert. Only at 0100 hours could the place be taken.

Between 0700 and 0800 the Füs Regt 39 and the Reconnaissance Battalion 26 launched an attack in the sector of the 26 VGD. It made only slow progress against fierce enemy resistance. In the course of the day, heavy fighting took place which put portions of the division in a critical position. The enemy temporarily succeeded in counterattacking, using armor to break through the Bois Bechu and the Bois de Hazy to the east of Assenois, and to gain ground as far as to our own artillery positions north of Clochimont. At dusk, the Div was facing the enemy along the line south of the Bois de Hazy and Boiz Bechu on the northern outskirts of Assenois (which was lost temporarily), then turning to the north Benonchamps (which was captured by the reconnaissance battalion), northern edges of the Bois de Fragotte and Bois des Valets. However, the breakthrough as far as the road Bastogne–Marche, which was still being used by single American vehicles, was not successful. At this time the Regt 77 encircled Bastogne in the north from Recogne to Champs. The Regt 78 adjoining on the eastern front as far as Mont did the same. The southeast of Bastogne was still held by the Pz Gren Regt 901.

In the course of the afternoon single vehicles were set on fire by tank or flak fire on the route Remichampagne, Morhet, while crossing the road Bastogne, Vaux-les-Rosieres from the south. It determined that a small group of enemy tanks, which had broken through from the south, kept under fire the named crossroad at the section about half a km to the north of Petit-Rosieres. Tanks of the Pz Lehr Div sent against them forced the enemy to retreat. During the day the 5 Fallschirm Jg Div had been attacked several times by American reconnaissance forces from the south. According to information received by the command post of the Div, there was no cause for anxiety. The Div further stated that its line of security was further advanced over Chaumont, Remoiville further to the south. The location of its advance detachment was Libramont.

The XLVII Pz Corps hoped to reach the Meuse with advance detachments of the 2 Pz Div on 21 Dec. On 22 Dec the neighboring 116 Pz Div on the right flank disengaged from the enemy and marched over La Roche toward Grimbiemont, seven km southeast of Marche. The XLVII Pz Corps intended to close the gap in the sector of the 26 VGD, especially in the western sector of Bastogne between Senonchamps and Champs by an attack of the Reconnaissance Battalion 26 and the Gren Regt 77 from the north and the south and during the darkness of 23 Dec to continue the attack to the southeastern outskirts of

Bastogne. At this place they were under the impression that the enemy had withdrawn his forces to carry out his attacks in the southwestern sector.

However, the over-all picture indicated that the encircling front of Bastogne would be forced to change over to defensive operations. During these days all attacks by the enemy were repulsed by the use of all available reserves. The losses on the 26 VGD during the fighting of the last few days were considerable and had decreased the fighting power of the Div to a great extent.

The question was undecided whether the surrounded enemy was attempting only to break through the encircling ring. It was possible that the enemy envisaged with these attacks, to join the forces pressing from the south in order to break the encircling ring of Bastogne.

Bastogne was supplied from the air on 21 and 22 December.[15] On both days supply flights were at first for parachute operations: some of the cargo-carrying gliders were shot down by antiaircraft artillery.

The Advance Against the Meuse

On 22 Dec when the 2 Pz Div had broken through the enemy's defense line between Marche and Rochefort near Hargimont. On capturing Buissonville and Jamodenne on the night of the same day, a favorable situation for a successful advance of the 2 Pz Div against the Meuse crossing point near Dinant seemed feasible. It was clear that this thrust was not without danger as it was launched from a pointed wedge driven westward by the 116 Pz Div and the 2 Panzer Div. The 6 Pz Army and the right wing of the 5 Pz Army (560 VGD) bogged down. There was no contact whatsoever with the LXVI Army Corps so that the Pz Corps was worried about adequate protection of its own deep right flank. In the sector facing the 116 Pz Div the enemy resistance grew stronger. The pressure against the 7 Army, entrusted with the shielding of the southern flank, was also increasing. On 23 Dec a critical situation developed for the 5 Fallsch Jg Div by a strong assault by reconnaissance forces of the enemy, directed from the south toward Bastogne, which was also felt in the sector of the 26 VGD. Finally Bastogne, which continued to be fiercely and successfully defended by the enemy, became not only a stumbling block to the rear positions, but a direct threat enabling the enemy to advance from the south and possibly establish contact with the forces employed at Bastogne. That town could then be used as a base for further operations to drive into the deep flank of our own forces.

23 December: The 2 Pz Div planned to employ all available forces against Dinant, sending the reconnaissance battalion ahead by way of Jamodenne, Hogne, Sinsin, Leignon, Conneux.

The XLVII Pz Corps was promised the 9 Pz Div which was being brought up. The time of the arrival was not yet certain. The Corps intended to use the 9 Pz Div for the relief of portions of the 2 Pz Div, still occupying Marche and Hargimont, and to let the Div follow close behind the 2 Pz Div. The 9 Pz Div was charged to protect the right flank of the 2 Pz Div against enemy attacks from the north and northeast to safeguard the right flank.

On the night of 22 Dec the reconnaissance battalion of the 2 Pz Div assembled at the appointed road. It was followed by 304 Pz Gren Regt, portions of an armored battalion, two artillery battalions, and one engineer company. A further heavy artillery battalion attached to a Volks Artillery Corps, first activated at Marche, was brought up.

During their advance these forces continuously encountered enemy forces attacking from the north so that portions had to stay behind to safeguard the flanks: this occurred at Hogne, Sinsin, Pessoux and Haversin (four km to the south of Pessoux).

On 23 Dec in the forenoon the situation became more serious when the enemy launched heavy attacks based at Marche supported by tanks. The enemy succeeded temporarily in gaining control of the road Bande–Hargimont. A battalion brought up during the course of the day proved insufficient to restore the situation by assault tactics. It had to be employed to strengthen the front line. The course of the front line was thereby improved and enemy attacks in southern and southeastern directions were beaten off.

Early in the morning the reconnaissance battalion reached Foy–Notre Dame which made it possible to break the resistance of the enemy by surprise; numerous vehicles and material of the enemy were taken.

At first, the forces of the Div following behind also made good headway, but soon had to repulse increasing pressure by the enemy from the north and northeast. This brought the advance to a standstill. The forces of the Division split into two groups, fighting against strong enemy attacks from all sides. One group west of Conneux, the other one south of the village. In the afternoon, the connection with the rear was also lost. In villages and other places security detachments and train elements established primarily of defense put up desperate defensive battles against superior enemy forces. These small split-up groups were the first to be destroyed. The two portions of the Div fighting near Conneux were able to establish contact and to unite. However, the lack of fuel and ammunition soon made itself felt and weakened their combat strength.

In the sector of the reconnaissance battalion, which at first was quite successful in overcoming the enemy's resistance, the situation became strained as well. Its advance had been countered by new and stronger enemy forces and was halted. It found itself in a critical situation, following behind and putting up a stubborn fight to its rear. Facing it was the American 2d Armored Division.

In order to describe the situation along the left flank of the 2d Panzer Division, it is necessary to turn back again briefly to the events of 22 December. The Panzer Lehr Div had taken St. Hubert on 22 December at 0100 hours. Near Bure and Tellin small engagements with enemy reconnaissance forces had taken place; it had been possible, however, to drive the latter back across the

Lesse. On the bridges across the Lesse near Han-sur-Lesse, Belvaux, and Resteigne small forces from the Division had been posted, and armored reconnaissance had pushed forward to the southwest by way of Wellin. Except for reconnaissance troops, no enemy forces had been sighted.

On the afternoon of 23 December the Division had advanced on Rochefort from St. Hubert in two Kampfgruppen, one coming from the right way of Masbourg and Forrieres, the other from the left via Grupont and Wavreille. At 1800 hours friendly reconnaissance reported that Rochefort was clear of the enemy; this report later proved incorrect. As the right Kampfgruppe of the Division approached the town, it unexpectedly encountered resistance. Not until midnight was it possible to penetrate into the town, where the enemy fought determinedly, particularly in the central sector, and inflicted heavy losses on our forces.

On 23 December the Division sent out reconnaissance in the direction of Libramont. These troops advanced by way of Bras-Haut and Serpont (over the back road through Seviscourt) and ascertained that Libramont was strongly occupied by the enemy. Enemy movements northward could not be detected, however.

For the Army advance, it was of vital importance that the Pz Lehr Div succeed on 24 December in gaining ground in the direction of the Meuse in order to relieve the pressure on the 2d Pz Division. Even at that late hour we might have been able to achieve a successful conclusion of the offensive which could be broadened extensively by rapid concentrated use of all available portions of the Army and the Heeresgruppe. We could hardly expect a favorable result of an attack by the 116 Pz Div in view of the strong enemy forces which faced this Div. I presumed, however, that it was in a position to hold the line, so that it could become the pivoting point of the continued offensive to the north. We awaited the arrival of the 9 Pz Div with greatest impatience because it was urgently required for the relief and the extension of the wedge forming the attack of the 2 Pz Div. The pressure against the 7 Army was steadily increasing. In the sector of the 5 Fallsch Jg Div, heavy engagements developed in the area Vaux-les-Rosieres. Portions of the Div, which formed a defensive flank facing the south along the line Remichampagne–Chaumont, were driven back in a northern direction and later incorporated by the 26 VGD near Chaumont. A further increase of this pressure by the enemy against the right wing of the 7 Army could endanger the forces of the Army facing the front to the north and stationed near Bastogne. This was another reason to push ahead the attack of the Pz Lehr Div and the early entry into action of the 9 Pz Division.

24 December: During 24 Dec the resistance of the enemy at Rochefort was overcome (by Pz Lehr Div). This opened the road for the Pz Lehr Div to the west. In the afternoon a spearhead of an advance detachment belonging to the

Div reached Ciergnon. The Division intended that all available portions of the Div follow this combat group.

The very active enemy air force made it increasingly difficult to bring up new supplies, fuel and ammunition and at the same time continuously attacked our ground forces. This made the situation of the 2 Pz Div especially difficult. The pressure of the enemy from the north in the direction of the road Dinant–Rochefort was increasing constantly. In the afternoon the enemy succeeded first in capturing Humain and, after dark, in penetrating Buissonville. The Division planned to pierce through to the reconnaissance battalion of the 2 Pz Div fighting at Foy–Notre Dame. However, the XLVII Pz Corps decided to exploit the Pz Lehr Div in order to free again the road Hargimont–Buissonville. The road was needed because single groups of the 2 Pz Div were bogged down due to lack of fuel. At 1800 orders were issued that the Pz Lehr Div was not to continue by way of Ciergnon.

Due to extreme shortage of fuel the arrival of the 9 Pz Div was so delayed that it could not be counted upon to relieve the 2 Pz Div. Late at night the commander of the 9 Pz Div reported at the Corps command post and held out the prospect of the arrival of the spearhead of his Div at Bande at 1000 on 25 December.

25 December: The day, a clear winter day, began with the heaviest air activity of the enemy. The 2 Pz Div continued in a very precarious position. In the course of the day Chauvanne was lost. Enemy tanks penetrated temporarily Harsin. To reach Hargimont it was necessary to use the road by way of Grune. The 3rd Battalion of the armored artillery regiment of the 2 Pz Div was taken by surprise while motoring north of Buissonville and for the most part annihilated.

The Pz Lehr Div succeeded in capturing Humain and Havrenne, which was retaken, however, by the 2 American Armored Div. The attack of the Div against Buissonville failed. At 1500 the foremost position of the 9 Pz Div reached the line Roy–Charneux– Hedree and attacked Marloie. The withdrawal of the 2 Pz Div, which had become necessary, was not approved. Therefore, the Div received orders to maintain with all possible means the connection with the reconnaissance battalion by advancing over Rochefort, Ciergnon, and Custinne. The 9 Pz Div was to advance with the arriving portions by way of Humain to Buissonville.

26 December: During the night of 25 December the 2 Pz Div had regrouped its forces still assembled at Marche leaving behind to safeguard this village only the battalion which was brought up to the Division on the previous day and an antiaircraft combat element of the Luftwaffe. The forces released from the front, a weak Panzer Grenadier Battalion, portions of an artillery battalion and a flak battalion, as well as portions of the Division engineer battalions, were withdrawn. At dawn this group assembled and marched by way of Ciergnon as far as to the southwest of Custinne. By the afternoon this group succeeded in fighting its way as close as 800 meters to the Conneux pocket in spite of strong activity by the enemy artillery and enemy attacks launched with the support of tanks. A breakthrough as far as the pocket failed due to tank-supported enemy attacks (according to the reports available here there were about eighty tanks). The group no longer had any antitank weapons available. A support of the combat by the encircled group failed on account of lack of ammunition and the immobility of the tanks pinned down without fuel. The reconnaissance battalion of the 2 Pz Div reported that it was attacked by forty-five tanks at Grand Trisogne. Other portions of the Div reached the V-turn of the road one km northwest of Sinsin.

Contact of the Conneux group with portions of the reconnaissance battalion had only been disrupted during the night of 23 December. The combat group of the Div which assembled in the early morning hours on 26 December and which also included the Div commander collected stragglers who confirmed that the battalion had succumbed to the superiority of the enemy. Other stragglers got into the Conneux pocket.

At 1500 the Army received the approval for the withdrawal of the 2 Pz Div. Thereupon the XLVII Pz Corps received orders to withdraw the 2 Pz Div to the bridgehead of Rochefort.

The Div commander remained another two hours in the area south of Conneux with the combat group of the Div brought up from Marche which had failed to reach the Conneux pocket by assault. Thereafter he had to withdraw in order not to be cut off with his combat group. The portions held in the Conneux pocket received orders to destroy all material and to fight their way out in the direction of Rochefort. The enemy followed only with great hesitation and did not attack the route of retreat. On 26 Dec, at midnight, the last portions of the fighting troops of the 2 Pz Div had crossed the Rochefort bridge in a southern direction. The strong artillery fire of the enemy near Rochefort caused additional losses at the time of the crossing of the bridge. During the night and on 27 Dec about 600 men returned from the pocket near Conneux. On the same night the withdrawn elements of the 2 Pz Div were sent into action at the bridgehead Rochefort and southwest of the city. On the night of 26 Dec the portions of the Pz Lehr Div, located to the northwest of the town Rochefort were also withdrawn to the bridgehead there. Thereby the XLVII Pz Corps also changed over to the defense.

The Battle for Bastogne

23 December: At Bastogne the troops belonging to the encircling front were forced to go over to the defense as early as 22 December. The 26 VGD was facing the enemy along the line southern third of the Bois de Hazy and Bois Bechu–northern outskirts of Assenois–Senonchamps–northern edge of the

Bois des Valets. Regiment 77 encircled Bastogne from the north and northwest of Recogne as far as Champs. On the eastern front the Regiment 78 adjoined as far as Mont. In the southeast of Bastogne the Pz Gren Regt 901 of the Pz Lehr Div still held the same line. The gap in the eastern sector of Bastogne between Senonchamps and Champs was to be closed up by an attack from the north by the Regiment 77 and from the south by the Reconnaissance Battalion 26. On the night of 23 Dec the southeastern outskirts of the town were to be attacked by Pz Gren Regt 901. In the course of 22 Dec the 5 Fallsch Jg Div had been attacked several times from the south by American reconnaissance forces. Therefore, the Div wanted to advance its security farther by way of Chaumont–Remoiville.

Thanks to the attacks by the Regt 78 and by Reconnaissance Battalion 26 we succeeded during the day in closing the encircling ring around Bastogne in the west. Mande–St. Etienne was captured and contact between Regt 77 and the Reconnaissance Battalion 26 was restored in the vicinity of Flamizoulle. The attack by the Regiment 77 was supported by an armored combat group of the 2 Pz Div, which after the successful attack of its Div was once more available. The Füs Regt 39 was pressed heavily by the enemy and incurred losses due to strong enemy artillery fire. During the day a crisis developed caused by a strong thrust of the American reconnaissance coming from the south against the front of the 5 Fallsch Jg Div (along the line Chaumont–Remoiville to the north of Cobreville). Portions of the young troops of this Div had given up their positions and were once more incorporated by the command post of the 26 VGD at Hompre. A combat group assembled by the 26 VGD – supported by four tanks and batteries located near Hompre – drove the enemy back. A number of enemy tanks were put out of action; the combat group pursued closely and blocked the roads and crossings near Chaumont and Remichampagne. Contact was established with portions of the 5 Fallsch Jg Div southeast of Chaumont.

The combat of the enemy was continuously supported by their tactical air force. At noon, Bastogne was again supplied from the air, on which occasion some airplanes were shot down.

The Pz Gren Regt 901 assembled about 1800 in order to launch the ordered attack. The Regiment penetrated into Marvie, another combat group of the Regt gained ground to the north along the road of Remoifosse. At about 2200 the attack ceased as its continuation did not hold much hope for success. The enemy had heavy losses in dead and wounded and lost a great deal in prisoners.

23/24 December: The development of the situation at the southern front indicated that the enemy was ready to risk everything to break through the encirclement of Bastogne from the south. The Army had no more forces to reinforce the southern flank of the curved front line projecting to the west. Furthermore, there was not sufficient fuel to bring up the artillery left behind at the line of departure. Even now the flank protection of the 7 Army proved to be too weak. The 5 Fallsch Jg Div was only able to send out security detachments possessing very little essential defensive power. The 26 VGD and the sub-ordinated Pz Gren Regt 901 were also weakened after 8 days of continued combat action.

At the same time armed forces asserted that a decision was necessary whether the attack to the west was to be continued with the aim to turn to the north after having reached the elevated terrain in the vicinity of Marche or whether Bastogne was to be captured first. In their estimate, they pointed out that the continuation of the attack along the southern routes of attack of the LVIII Pz Corps (116 Pz Div) was possible only after the assignment of new forces in adequate strength. However this attack was also greatly handicapped by the strong enemy resistance east of the Ourthe (south of the road Hotton–Grandmenil) and by the situation in front of the right wing of the XLVII Pz Corps (2 Pz Div). The small width of the attack together with the danger of enemy activity against the flanks did not permit a tactical extension. In their opinion the attack depended to a great deal on the increasing enemy activities from the south especially against Bastogne and against the only feebly secured flank between this town and Rochefort. The army arrived at the conclusion that reserves ready to be employed at once should be brought up by the supreme command in order to assist in the attack of the LVIII Pz Corps (116 Pz Div). In addition adequate forces and ammunition should be used to reinforce the defense south of Bastogne.

24 December: On 24 Dec at noon the Chief of Staff transmitted the demands of the Army by telephone to General Jodl. They were once more submitted on the night of 24 Dec by two further phone calls to the aide-de-camp of the Wehrmacht and Führer, who stayed during the night at the command post of the Commander in Chief of the Army, and again reported to the Armed Forces Operations Staff. They emphasized the unfavorable devel-opment of the situation in the areas of the former spearheads of the two Panzer Corps.

On the evening of 24 Dec the 2 Pz Div had to withdraw to the narrow bridgehead of Rochefort after the smashing of its brave combat group near Conneux. The 116 Pz Div succeeded in capturing Verdenne and the area to the north and northwest of the village and in dominating by artillery the road Hotton–Marche. The breakthrough of the American lines between Ourthe and Marche to the northwest failed. The enemy succeeded in re-organizing himself and changed over to counterattacks with increasing frequency.

At the front of Bastogne, the 24 Dec was devoted to preparations for the attack to be launched on 25 December. The 26 VGD, to which the 15 Pz Gren Div was subordinated, intended to use this Div as the center of gravity launching the decisive thrust in the western sector from the area Champs–

Mande–St Etienne. The attack was to be supported by containing attacks against the town from the east and southeast. The Reconnaissance Battalion 26 with added tank destroyers had the task to join in the attack in the center of gravity. The main body of the artillery forces of the 26 VGD and of the 15 Pz Gren Div and the additional reserve artillery which was being drawn up, were put under the unified command of the higher artillery authority of the army to assist in the attack of the 15 Pz Gren Division.

On the night of 24 Dec the Pz Gren Div was brought up to its assembly area. Its strength did not meet expectations. The following units were expected to join in the attacks:

– One and a half rifle battalions with small companies.

– One reconnaissance battalion consisting of 25–30 armored personnel carriers, 20 tanks or assault guns, one engineer company and two artillery battalions (motorized).

Starting on 26 Dec the arrival of a further 10–15 tanks, several rifle companies and batteries could be expected. The Army was promised support by the Luftwaffe. It consisted of the dropping of bombs on Bastogne on the night of 24 Dec by some airplanes.

25 December: On 25 Dec in the course of the early hours of the morning the Army was informed that Hitler had decided to continue the attack on the heights of Marche with all available forces. In addition to the 9 Pz Div and the 15 Pz Gren Div, the following forces were made available: the 3 Pz Gren Div and the 167 VGD. For the time being no decision concerning Bastogne had been made.

There, the attack planned for 25 Dec began at 0530. The 15 Pz Gren Div succeeded in breaking through to the east of Fond de Laval and between 0800 and 0900 in splitting up the enemy front. At this time the gap gained by the armored group of the Div was used as a springboard for the thrust against Bastogne. The Regt 77 to the left of the 15 Pz Gren Div had penetrated Champs with small elements, fighting their way forward between Champs and Longchamps. The reconnaissance battalion employed on the right of the 15 Pz Gren Div pushed forward astride the large road Mande–St. Etienne, and Füs Regt 39 attacked on both sides of the railroad and the road Neufchâteau–Bastogne, the Pz Gren Regt 901 advanced with strong assault detachments from the southeast toward the road Bastogne–Bras gaining ground. Champs changed hands several times. The Regiment 77 penetrated temporarily south of the village into wooded sections to the west of Rolle.

The attack of the Panzer combat group of the 15 Pz Gren Div gained ground against fierce resistance and reached the road Champs–Hemroulle. The sector of the forest to the south of the village and of Hemroulle were in the hands of the enemy. Our own losses were high. The reconnaissance battalion had to repulse enemy counterattacks gaining ground slowly. The Füs Regt 39 attacked against the enemy offering fierce resistance in the direction of Isle-le-Pre; the losses of the battalion were heavy. The assault detachments of the Pz Gren Regt 901 approached, advancing to the west of Marvie, the Marvie–Bastogne. At this place our losses were also heavy. Assault detachments of the Gren Regt 78 advanced on both sides of the railroad Bastogne–Bourcy approaching the exit of the woods west–northwest of Bourcy.

At 0900 numerous fighter bombers of the enemy took part in the ground battles. The consumption of ammunition of the artillery on both sides was considerable. The increasing losses forced us to employ our last reserves. At noon it was reported that portions of the armored combat group of the 15 Pz Gren Div were engaged in heavy costly battles at Hemroulle and on the road Hemroulle–Champs. At this time the advanced Pz combat group intended to push through to the south of Hemroulle toward Bastogne. At the same time, the armored infantry had to defend itself against heavy attacks in the wooded sections one km to the southwest of Hemroulle. Regt 77 had to give up Champs again. It intended to renew its attack to the south of the village.

A short time afterwards, it was reported that the armored combat group of the 15 Pz Gren Div had hardly any tanks left which were fit for commitment; they had been annihilated in the area close to Hemroulle. The whereabouts of the commander of the combat group was unknown. This sealed the fate of the attack and it was called off in the afternoon. The ground gained at various places was given up again if it proved unsuitable for defense.

The losses of the 15 Pz Gren Div and of the 26 VGD were severe. No doubt those of the enemy were also considerable. The failure of the attack proved to be the more painful as after 25 Dec the attacking divisions were no longer in a position to launch large scale attacks because of the losses suffered.

During the whole day of 25 Dec the 5 Fallsch Jg Div was engaged in defensive actions against enemy attacks launched from the southwest between the roads leading from Martelange and Neufchâteau toward Bastogne. The Div could maintain its positions along the line: road fork two km north of Bives–Remoiville–Hollange. By nightfall Chaumont was lost. The enemy pressure from the south continued in undiminished strength. Even after nightfall the artillery fire of the enemy in the area of Bastogne remained lively. Heavy surprise shelling caused great losses to our troops. A surprise attack at nightfall, attempted once more against Hemroulle with the support of ten tank destroyers, failed utterly.

The Army gave orders that the 26 VGD and the 15 Pz Gren Div were to change over to defense. On the night of 25 Dec, Field Marshal Model decided, after having received a request by the Army on 24 Dec, that Bastogne was to be captured first, but that the Führer-Begleit Brigade was to launch an attack hard to the west of the Ourthe so as to capture the elevated terrain to the east of the Marche from the north in conjunction with the 116 Pz Div. When it was pointed out that the forces available at the moment, including ammunition and fuel, were by no means adequate to repeat the attack against Bastogne, we were advised that reinforcements would be made available.

26 December: During the night of 25 Dec the block of minefields between Remoifosse and Sibret as well as in the area of Clochimont were reinforced. The 5 Fallsch Jg Div defended the sector from Sainlez by way of Grandrue–Remichampagne in the direction of Morhet facing the south. At dawn, the artillery fire in the Bastogne area started again. Germans and Americans were fighting against their respective positions, both expecting an offensive by the enemy.

At 0900 American fighter bombers – as usually the case during these days – appeared in great numbers and their activity was first of all directed against villages behind the front and artillery positions. During the morning, reports were increasing that the 5 Fallsch Jg Div had to repel strong enemy attacks from the south. At noon it became known that engagements with advancing enemy armor were taking place in the vicinity of Remichampagne. Portions of the Füs Regt 39 of the 26 VGD in Sibret and Assenois became exposed to artillery from a southern direction.

At about 1500, security detachments of the Füs Regt 39 which had advanced to the south reported that portions of the 5 Fallsch Jg Div had been forced by the enemy to withdraw to Sibret and Hompre, and that Clochimont stood under attack by tanks. Shortly afterwards the enemy smashed small elements of the 5 Fallsch Jg Div at Clochimont and started to advance on both sides of the road Clochimont–Assenois. Assenois fell at about 1700 hours. Ten to twelve tanks succeeded in breaking through by way of Assenois toward Bastogne. Sibret was also attacked. The gap behind the enemy tanks which had broken through was only closed by a weak defense screen of the 26 VGD. This was due to heavy losses the preceding day weakening the forces of the Div to such an extent that reinforcements from areas of the Bastogne front, which at that time were not under attack, was out of the question. The Pz Gren Regt 901 had established a defense line between the Bois Bechu and the Forest l'Ardosiere fronting the southwest. The remnants of the 5th Fallsch Jg Div had escaped to the east and continued their resistance on the edges of the woods east of the villages Salvacourt and Clochimont.

At dusk, our reconnaissance reported that all forces of the 5 Fallsch Jg Div had withdrawn from the sector between Salvacourt and Sibret. Late afternoon the Army had already decided to subordinate the Führ-Begl Brigade to the XLVII Pz Corps which had been attacking since the early morning hours from the southern bank of the Ourthe by way of Hampteau (the town already had been captured) against Hotton. The LVIII Pz Corps had received orders to cease the attack instantly and, in view of the imperiled situation south of Bastogne, to get the Brigade as quickly as possible to Bastogne. It was planned to have the

Brigade attack south of Bastogne from Sibret to Hompre in order to close the gap at the front.

The decision meant that the LVIII Pz Corps had to give up its plans to explore by attacking and to find out whether, and to what extent, it still would be possible to create the necessary conditions for the continuation of the general offensive by taking possession of the elevated terrain east of Marche. On the other hand, the order of Model represented only half a solution. He commanded the continuation of the attack in a western direction because Hitler ordered it; however, first he wanted personally to eliminate the greater danger: namely, Bastogne.

Now I made every attempt to take up a defensive position which was favorable as far as terrain and the effect of our weapons was concerned, even by giving up part of the terrain just gained in order first to clarify the tactical situation of Bastogne. Field Marshal Model agreed to all related requests of the Army, but as for himself did not get any liberty of action which could allow him to give up even one meter of the conquered area on his own initiative.

I prepared in advance to have my plans carried out and a request was made to place the west front under a single command; consequently, the Bastogne sector and the area to the west of it, which by this time had become the Army's center of gravity, was put under the command of the energetic General Freiherr v. Lüttwitz (XLVII Pz Corps).

Days before the supreme command had announced the arrival of a further corps headquarters whose task was to direct the battle for Bastogne. The two attacking corps (XLVII and LVIII Pz Corps) were not to be diverted from their main task, that is, the attack at and across the Meuse. The XXXIX Pz Corps under the command of the experienced, prudent and determined General of the armored forces, Karl Decker, arrived. It was subordinated by me to the General of the armored forces, Frhr v. Lüttwitz, who criticized this measure in his report. The practice to employ a further corps headquarters in a sector representing the center of gravity was nothing extraordinary and had been put into effect frequently. Considering our situation it was done for the following reasons:

(1) General headquarters was not in a position from a communication point of view to command as many divisions as were now assembled in the combat area of Bastogne; moreover, reinforcements were expected.

(2) The personal influence of the commanding general decreases naturally in proportion to the high number of divisions and the long distances from his command post to the heart of the battle. Therefore, a further command post was introduced.

(3) On the other hand v. Lüttwitz knew the area from the preceding days of combat and

(4) I, personally, was not in a position to stay frequently and for an

extended period in this combat sector as required by the present battle situation and the orientation of the new staff.

Furthermore, my operations staff was over-burdened to be able to effect coordination of all forces within the array; also the following problems had to be considered: regulation of arriving new elements; bringing up of the artillery and their regrouping; organization of supplies, which necessitated the search, transport and distribution of every cubic meter of fuel.

27 December: Changing to defensive tactics, the LVIII Pz Corps, together with the 560 VGD in the evening of 27 Dec, took up defensive positions south of Magoster, northern outskirts of Beffe, center of the woods between Beffe and Werpin. The 116 Pz Div held the sector Rendeux–Cheoux–Grimbiemont. The 2 SS Pz Div, hitherto subordinated to the Corps, was again put under the command of the II SS Pz Corps.

To the left of the 116 Pz Div, the XLVII Pz Corps with the 9 Pz Div adjoined at Charneux. The Corps planned to relieve the Pz Lehr Div by the 9 Pz Div located in the bridgehead of Rochefort and to commit the Pz Lehr Div between Han-sur-Lesse and Remagne. These steps were to relieve the increasing enemy pressure from the south. Small elements of the Pz Lehr Div were already assembled, forming strong points near Tellin, Mirwart, Smuid, Hatrival, Vesqueville, Moircy, and Remagne. At Tellin on 27 Dec, British forces made their appearance for the first time.

On the night of 26 Dec, Sibret was given up. At dawn the Führer-Begleit Brigade brought up by the LVIII Pz Corps took up positions in the Bois de Herbaimont. Expecting action by the American air force, the Brigade was to remain there during the day. Early on 28 Dec it received orders to advance Chenogne and to capture Sibret first; then by an attack at Hompre to close the gap on the southern front of the Bastogne encirclement and finally to unite at Hompre with the 1 SS Pz Div which had arrived there.

28 December: On 28 Dec the 560 VGD also was subordinated to the II SS Pz Corps, which at that time had extended its left wing as far as the Ourthe River. In its place, the LVIII Pz Corps took over the command of the 9 Pz Div. The front of the LVIII Pz Corps was now running from the northern edges of the woods to the west of Marcourt, south of Cheoux–Roy–Hargimont as far as Rochefort where on 28 Dec the 9 Pz Div held its bridgehead against all attacks of the enemy. Adjoining to the 9 Pz Div, the remnants of the 2 Pz Div which on 29 Dec were also subordinated to the LVIII Pz Corps protected the left corps flank from Han-sur-Lesse as far as Tellin. On 28 and 29 Dec the main pressure of the enemy was directed against the 116 Pz Div, which, with few exceptions, held its positions. However, the sector St. Hubert (Pz Lehr Div) was also under continuous attack, although the enemy was repulsed. All attempts failed to break through the wooded sections on both sides of Hatrival and to the west of Vesqueville toward St. Hubert by major attacks. At the left wing of the Pz Lehr

Div the advanced strongpoints Freux and Rondu were lost. The enemy infiltrated the wooded area northwest of Moircy and attacked Remagne for the first time.

The attack launched in the morning by the Führer-Begleit Brigade against Sibret failed. The 3 Pz Gren Div, having arrived in the meantime, attacked and reached the line Chenogne, southern outskirts of the Bois le Fragotte.

29/31 December: LVIII Pz Corps: during the night of 28 Dec Rochefort which had been under increasing enemy pressure and strong artillery fire was evacuated by the 9 Pz Div. On 30 Dec the front was running on the heights south of Rochefort. The enemy attacks from Rochefort and from Tellin caused a withdrawal at the front along the line Jemelle–Wavreille to the west of Bure. The 2 Pz Div had to take over some portions of the sector of the Pz Lehr Div.

XLVII Pz Corps: On 30 Dec the Pz Lehr Div lost Remagne; on 31 Dec, Moircy, too. However, until 31 Dec the Div succeeded to prevent the enemy from crossing the road St. Hubert–Morhet. Attacks against the line Bois de Fragotte–Chenogne were repulsed.

The Army's estimate of the situation was that the enemy intended to collapse our front, projecting in an arc to the west by attacking from the south and breaking through in the direction of Houffalize. This was indicated by the relaxing enemy pressure in the Marcourt–Wavreille sector and the attacks from the south, which were increasing in strength, particularly in the sector St. Hubert–Tillet. For this reason a withdrawal of forces from the front of the LVIII Pz Corps which appeared necessary was not possible, as the forces of the Corps were already used to the utmost. It was only possible to assign the 2 Pz Div to the sector Mirwart–Smuid which was the most we could do considering the weak forces of the Division. During the day, at the request of Heeresgruppe B, all available forces were put at the disposal of the army for the capture of Bastogne. Consequently the staff of 1 SS Pz Corps (Major Gen of Waffen SS Priess) and the 167 VGD, which since 24 Dec we held in reserve, were put under the command of the Army. Until 24 Dec this Div had been assembled in the area of Gerolstein and had also added a reinforced rifle company to the 26 VGD using motor vehicles. At first, marching by night, it reached the area in the vicinity of Ulflingen.

We further expected the 340 VGD which came from Roer. During the last days of Dec it arrived with two weak battalions and about two artillery battalions. Finally the 12 SS Pz Div was also subordinated, which was badly decimated and came from the 6 SS Pz Army. On or about 2 Jan 45 it arrived with its first portions at Bourcy, east of Noville. Its strength was negligible.[16]

A unified attack against Bastogne, which perhaps would have had a chance of success if we had succeeded in assembling our reinforcements for combat within 48 hours, did not take place because the promised support arrived with considerable delay and in much smaller strength than was anticipated. This limitation applied first of all to units of the Waffen SS which arrived only with weak fighting strength.

The original plan of the Army could not be carried out: namely, the attack from the west with the 3 and 15 Pz Gren Divs and portions of the 26 VGD at and south of the road Mande–St. Etienne–Bastogne. The 12 SS Pz Div was to attack on both sides of the road Noville–Bastogne and with the 1 SS Pz Div, 167 and 340 VGD by way of Lutrebois against Assenois by covering the eastern flank by attack launched by the Führ-Begl Brigade against Sibret. However, the supreme command stood by its original decision and, in spite of the altered situation, forced piecemeal attacks on our own front, none of which were successful, as the timing of the attacks was not coordinated although at some places local successes had been gained.

Only after the failure of the 1 SS Pz Div during the attack against Lutrebois which was to block the southern road leading to Bastogne did the supreme command agree with the opinion of the Army that even in this sector any assault tactics were doomed to failure because our troops, although giving their last, did not possess the required strength, equipment, and supply of ammunition to match the opposing enemy. Furthermore, the severe weather tried the troops exceedingly hard, who began to be affected by the difficulties in supplies.

The Army was not only forced to defend the sector at Bastogne but was afraid that the enemy would start a breakthrough from the area of Bastogne to Houffalize in order to unite with the forces assembled to the north of the Ourthe.

The Army tried, therefore, having ceased all attacks, to attain an immediate withdrawal of the salient far projecting to the west. It justified this with this fact: according to its estimate of the situation on 29 Dec 1944 so many enemy forces were assembled facing the northern and southern flanks of the salient that no adequate forces and means (fuel and ammunition) were available to prevent a breakthrough threatening to envelop Houffalize from both sides. Furthermore, the clear cold winter weather favoring ultimate air supremacy of the enemy air force forced us to operate only at dusk and to postpone marches, disposition of troops, transfer, and the transport of supplies under complete darkness. However, although the situations on both sides of the Ourthe and on the right wing of the Seventh Army towards the Wiltz became worse all the time a withdrawal was only reluctantly approved by the Supreme Command after the beginning of the enemy attacks on 3 Jan 45.

The fact that the fronts were held and that the enemy, in spite of tremendous superiority, did not succeed to penetrate anywhere was due to the valor of our troops and their commanders in all ranks. By counterattacking our division commanders again and again closed gaps opened by preceding battles and by offering strong resistance blocked the road to the armored reconnaissance units of the enemy.

An enemy counterattack made on 3 Jan 45 – and recognized as such – changed events and the conduct of battles at the army front lines completely. I informed the troops of my decision to fall back by fighting delaying actions, stressing the fact that by their mutual cooperation (neighborly understanding and help) liaison within the army was to be maintained to prevent a break-through by the enemy within the zone of our army.

Troops and leaders succeeded in achieving this in an exemplary way. Due to heavy snowfalls combat action could take place on both sides more or less only on or along the roads, and it became evident that motorized portions, reinforced by antitank weapons of all kinds (tanks, assault guns, antiaircraft, combat elements) and engineer units, during the darkness had to take over the pro-tection of movements and of prepared positions (Auffanglinie) where the troops during daylight were assembled and reorganized.

Lack of fuel and the huge lack of recovery and repair services of all kinds forced us to destroy or leave behind considerably more armor than was put out of action by the enemy during the entire attack. In this way artillery too fell into the hands of the enemy without firing.

Neither Field Marshal Model, nor I, or any other military leader doubted that our forces could no longer resist the enemy pressure. The plan and the suggestion of OB West, Heeresgruppe B and the Army had therefore the aim, after a short reorganization of the troops at the starting line of the attack on 26 Dec, to retreat to the Rhine in widespread withdrawal movements. This had been expressively requested several times by Field Marshal Model. Hitler refused to have any discussions whatsoever on this subject. The march batta-lions (reserves) which had been quickly and hastily assembled in the homeland were not uniformly organized, their uniforms, equipment, and arms were inadequate and when these new troops were sent to reinforce the forces on the retreat these troops could not even assimilate them. Other reinforcements were assembled in the communications zone of our army and then transferred to incomplete defense lines to cover the troops withdrawing from the west. These units had no heavy weapons, artillery, antitank weapons and engineers; therefore, they could not fulfill the tasks assigned to them.

The former attack troops, after continuous combat action for fourteen days under heavy fighting and unfavorable weather conditions, were at the limit of their efficiency when the Anglo-American counterattack began. The losses in men and material could not be replaced. Besides, the collapse of the offensive, which was begun with the greatest hope, affected the morale and paralyzed the will of resistance considerably. A great burden was added to the Army when, during the first days of January, orders were given to withdraw the units of the 6 Pz Army from the fighting front. The troops and their commanders did not comprehend this action: I protested against it in the sharpest manner. The explanation that these units were wanted for new tasks at the eastern front could not deceive the troops any longer to believe that during these decisive days once more the Heer had to bear the main brunt of the fighting, whereas the units of the Waffen SS first enjoyed what the frontline soldier usually called a 'rest'. The Supreme Command had once again forgotten to take into account the psychological effects on the troops.

The course of events on the front can be described as follows: At the end of Dec the attacks of the 9 and 12 SS Pz Div in the sector of Longchamps–Noville–Bourcy failed just as well as the attacks by the 340 VGD with portions of the 12 SS Pz Div between the railroad Bourcy–Bastogne and the road of Longvilly at the town in spite of initial local successes.

In the first days of January the attacks of the 1 SS Pz Div over Lutrebois and the southern road approach toward Bastogne were repeated; all of them failed. On the other hand, the 167 VGD, starting off north of it, was able to reach with its spearhead the wooded point to the south of Remoifosse. During the next weeks this Div was therefore the backbone in this sector because the 1 SS Pz Div, in spite of strong forces, was unable to commit its full fighting strength against the enemy.

At the end of Jan the enemy succeeded in reaching the road Nothum–Bastogne situated in the sector of the 7 Army, fighting his way thereafter by advancing from the south toward the crossroads east–northeast of Doncols, which action forced a withdrawal of portions of the Army located southeast of Bastogne.

On 5 or 6 Jan 45 XXXIX Pz Corps had to be transferred and the I SS Pz Corps shortly afterwards, therefore, on 13 Jan the LVIII Pz Corps took over command in the sector Neffe–Wardin–Bras–Doncols to the west of Nothum.

In the center part of the Army front the successes of the enemy forced a withdrawal of our lines along the highway Bastogne–Noville otherwise these portions would have been cut off. The success of the attack started on 3 Jan near Odeigne (lost on 5 Jan) and Samree led us to fear that the enemy would push through along the highway Les Tailles–Houffalize in order to unite with the portions attacking out of the area Bastogne and to the west of it. Houffalize was lost on 16 Jan; on the previous day St. Vith had again fallen into the hands of the enemy.

The successes at St. Vith and the advances of the enemy upon the adjacent army wing at the left flank compelled the withdrawal of the Army, as our frontline in the center was endangered by a pincer movement.

At first while preparing the retreat, the Supreme Command ordered the line Salm sector–Ulflingen–Clerf river to be the covering line. However, neither the latter nor the Our sector became useful as the area on both sides of the Clerf and the Our was heavily wooded and the reconnaissance, protection, and defense of such sectors required a great number of men; those were lacking. Therefore, the Army ordered to hold the assembly line which was used for the

(Previous) SS Oberstgruppenführer Josef
Dietrich, commander of the Sixth Panzer
Army in the Ardennes, photographed at
Berchtesgaden by Eva Braun while
Dietrich was commander of the 1st SS
Panzer Division.
(U.S. National Archives)

(Left) Awaiting judgement. No. 33,
General Fritz Krämer, the chief of staff of
the Sixth Panzer Army, sits during the
closing statements at the 'Malmedy' trial in

Dachau in 1946. Krämer would be
sentenced to life imprisonment, although
paroled by 1956. No.11, sitting next to
Krämer, is his commander in the
Ardennes, Josef Dietrich.
(U.S. National Archives)

(Above) Typical war-time pose finds Adolf
Hitler poring over a map. Peering over his
shoulder are Hermann Göring, Alfred Jodl
and (far right) Wilhelm Keitel.
(U.S. National Archives)

(Above) General der Panzertruppen
Erich Brandenberger speaks with a
young officer during the campaign in
Russia. Brandenberger would command
the Seventh Army during the Ardennes
campaign.
(Wenger collection)

(Left) Generalfeldmarschall Gerd von
Rundstedt (left) in charge of OB West in
mid-1944. He is accompanied by his
chief of staff, Generalleutnant Günther
Blumentritt.
(Wenger collection)

(Above) General der Panzertruppen Hasso von Manteuffel, the commander of the Fifth Panzer Army, confers with General Fritz Bayerlein over a map. Bayerlein would command the Panzer Lehr Division in the Ardennes. *(Wenger collection)*

(Left) Two SS grenadiers with the 1st SS Panzer Division pause to enjoy captured American cigarettes after routing the 14th Cavalry Group near Poteau, Belgium on December 18, 1944. One of the destroyed American armored vehicles can be seen in the background. *(National Archives)*

(Top) An armored SS reconnaissance
detachment advances past the
Kaiserbaracke crossroads between
St. Vith and Malmedy on December, 18, 1944.
(U.S. National Archives)

(Above) SS panzer grenadiers advance
across the Poteau crossroads,
18 December, 1944.
(U.S. National Archives)

attack on 16 Dec in readiness to serve as a covering line. Although desirable it was not possible to retreat to it in a few days as neither was there a chance to wheel back the infantry, nor was there enough fuel to transfer back the mobile, motorized elements. The danger arose, too, that the combat frontal lines could not be maintained much longer if the enemy would follow through quickly with strong forces.

During the following weeks there was only one thing to do, that is, to continue our withdrawal movements which had since then been carried out. The result was that the enemy, in spite of his superiority in numbers and his high maneuverability, did not succeed anywhere in piercing the front of the Army. Contrary to all requests of the OB West in the line of departure we found nothing that would have served to strengthen the defense of the Army, neither adequate ammunition nor material for the building of road blocks, mines, artillery or antitank weapons. The units inserted into their positions were alarm or combat units.

Therefore our forces had to carry the whole burden of continuous attacks and defensive actions for over five weeks. They did their utmost and held out. They were brave, dependable, obedient, conscious of their responsibility and loyal to the Fatherland in the hope and belief that by their conduct and their almost super-human efforts the political leadership of the Reich would be given the time to end the war.

On Looking Back

On the occasion of the breakthrough the following became apparent: The strategic and tactical surprise had been successful; the choice of the concentration area and that of the front sector to be attacked had been a correct one. The date and time of the attack as well as the plan of attack corresponded to the given circumstances and were suitably fixed. The enemy line of security had been pierced at many places, several undamaged bridges fell into our own hands. The enemy air force had not recognized our assembly for battle; it had thus missed the unique possibility of making use of its unlimited air supremacy to deal an annihilating blow to the German forces assembled and concentrated in a small area – the last German reserves. Our estimate of the enemy in the area of operations of the 5 Panzer Army proved right. Nevertheless, the Offensive failed. The reasons for this failure were in my opinion the following:

a. The number of forces launching the attack on 15 December was not in proportion to the objective [Antwerp] which had been placed too far ahead. The operation lacked the necessary personnel and material for the speedy and powerful exploitation of a successful breakthrough. There were not enough forces from which units could be brought up to eliminate pockets of resistance not taken, but partially by-passed, during the initial assault, from which to feed the attack from the rear. Furthermore, there were not enough men to protect the flanks of the spearhead unless the units planned for the thrust to the Meuse were employed. The Supreme Command, therefore, insisted upon a quick defeat of the enemy on the front attack to counterbalance the disadvantage of having an insufficient depth; also by the speed of the advance the forming of an enemy defense line on the Meuse was to be prevented.

b. The equipment as to personnel and material of the units was insufficient.

c. An effective deception and containing of the enemy in the front sectors adjoining the attacking armies failed.

IN DETAIL:

a. Already fourteen days after the beginning of the enemy attack against the Roer (which occurred on 16 November) at the beginning of Dec 44, it could be seen that there were available for the offensive fewer divisions, the strength and fighting qualities of which were less than originally estimated. In my opinion, it could also be noticed that owing to the strength of the enemy attacks the forces of our own attack out of the Roer bridgehead toward the south were insufficient (attack of the XII SS Corps against Maastricht–Liège). The Commanding General of this Corps and the OB West reported accordingly on 12 Dec verbally to Hitler. But Hitler persisted in his decision. The attack only meant a frittering away of the forces. It endangered the main thrust owing to the shrinking of personnel and material of the attacking armies. That these forces had to be employed in the center of gravity of the main thrust could be increasingly noticed during the time of the preparation of the offensive.

In the end then, there were fewer divisions at our disposal than previously estimated. Some of them were still in the process of moving up to the front at the beginning of the Offensive. Consequently, the 5 Pz Army had to employ two armored divisions in the very first wave. This meant a weakening of the armored thrust and of the breakthrough wedge. I pointed this out again and again. In the original plan of the WFSt an employment of armored divisions in the first wave had been strictly forbidden following the traditional German principles of leadership.

The 7 Army too was not strong enough to form another attacking force for a thrust into the region of Luxembourg besides fulfilling its originally assigned task: protection of the long southern flank of the two main attack armies. The 7 Army lacked mobile troops which it was not capable of creating out of its own forces. The High Command informed us prior to the beginning of the attack that these were not available. The river-crossing equipment and engineering forces with which the Army was equipped were completely insufficient. Despite all imaginable makeshift devices conceived by the officers and the troops it was nearly impossible to create the prerequisites for the attack which necessitated an immediate crossing of the river from the beginning. Thus the effective solution of both tasks was endangered. But the actions of the southern wing of the 5 Pz Army depended on a decisive way on the advance of the 7 Army. The bringing forward of the enemy's reserves from the area Rheims–Chalons by way of Charleville–Sedan could be expected with certainty. It did not appear certain that the 7 Army would be able to repulse or even prevent the attacks of these army forces against the southern wing of the Fifth Pz Army. Considering the forces available to the Seventh Army the Supreme Command should have contained itself with giving it only the one mission – protection of the southern flank of the main attack armies.

But the lack of manpower had a further grave consequence. It made impossible the formation of a center of gravity for the attack. The latter had been envisaged in the original plan, but was not put into effect, especially in the sector of the 6 Pz Army owing to the lack of manpower and in spite of the makeshifts which the Army tried to employ. Several units were partially, or even completely, missing at the beginning of the attack. Field Marshal Model's plan of helping out the attacking armies by reinforcing them with troops extracted from the adjacent front sectors of the Heeresgruppe was not possible on the desired scale. The Army urged repeatedly the removal of the center of gravity of the attack to the center of the attacking portions of the Heeresgruppe, that is, to the sector of our own army. This request was based on the assumption that it was to be expected with certainty, that the armies on the wings would be attacked in the flank and that this attack would lead to the tying down of forces required for the main attack. But neither of these requests were complied with until 11 Dec nor was the request for the giving up of a secondary thrust by the XII SS Corps.

b. Not all units had their full fighting powers as far as men, materials, and morale were concerned, which are the prerequisites for an action of such far-reaching consequence. The preparation of the forces envisaged for the attack had to be altered in October. This was even more important during November, because on 16 Nov the battle on the Roer broke out. During the second half of the month the crises in the Lorraine and Alsace took place.

The main shortages, which would affect the operations unfavorably, were: lack of relief, training, and rest for units; lack of materials; insufficient mobility of the advance guards, artillery, and bridge equipment; insufficient tonnage at the front and with the supply units; insufficient equipment and mobility of the maintenance services of the armed troops; and the lacking assault gun formations.

Hitler had been informed in detail about this verbally by Field Marshal Model on 2 Dec and once more on 11 Dec, when all generals who took part in the attack were present at Hitler's field headquarters to receive instructions. Field Marshal Model emphasized on this occasion that the battle on the Roer, which had begun on 16 Nov and was still in full swing, was taking a heavy toll of materials, the refurnishing of which was possible only at the expense of the armies envisaged for the attack as far as his Heeresgruppe was concerned. The Supreme Command replied that enemy units, employed in or behind the front could be regarded as similarly exhausted as the German troops and that the difficulties of the enemy's supply services were increasing, his tactical reserve was melting away and that this would lessen the resistance which he would be able to offer to our forces on the offensive. The tactical reserve of the enemy was estimated according to Schramm at three to six large units. The estimate of the enemy forces was probably the reason why the speed of the Offensive was calculated in the most favorable case by the Supreme Command. The latter presumed that on the first day bridgeheads across the Meuse could be established. The Army did not give the information leading to this optimistic estimate of the total situation of the enemy.

c. A pinning down, and with it at the same time, a deception of the enemy in the other parts of the western front did not take place owing to the lack of forces and ammunition. Our own units were weakened to such an extent by the preceding engagements that everybody was glad when he had some rest and was not being attacked by the enemy. This enabled the enemy to withdraw reserves from the remaining western front in order to employ them against the threatened part of the front.

SUMMARIZING

The essential requirements of the original plan for 'a decisive attack in the West' were missing. The resistance in the original decision as regards the objective of the attack as well as organization and plan of commitment of the forces must therefore be regarded as a mistake. The German Supreme Command, not knowing the conditions on the front, and showing increasingly misguided obstinacy in its decisions, could not summon up the necessary mental flexibility to adjust itself to the altered situation.

The decision was entirely with Hitler. OB West and Field Marshal Model had clearly given their points of view, which were to serve as basis for this decision and which culminated in the so-called 'small term solution'.

It is easy, after the event, to reproach the high military leaders with the fact that by the assumption and retention of their commands they also were partly to blame for the inadequate conduct of the war. All military leadership must, by nature, be authoritarian. Success is a combination of the decision made by the Supreme Commander after responsible consideration of all possibilities, of his military skill, and of his gift to turn his decision into the actual victory of the troops he leads. History estimates those successes highest which, thanks to these qualities, have been gained against an enemy far superior in strength. If in the preparation and the execution of the offensive, mistakes were made which frustrated an evidently possible success the Offensive as such still cannot be termed a 'crime' as it has been described in the press with a marked tendency. Nobody will deny the highest commanders in the Ardennes Offensive, I believe, fulfilled their tasks in good faith of success. And even if this Offensive did not bring about the decision and the turning point hoped for by the Supreme Command, but only a gaining of time one still cannot deny the same leaders the reasonable belief that they considered that in this gaining of time there was a possibility of political change favorable for Germany. When I try to put myself in our enemy's place I cannot believe that, for instance, prior to the Invasion of France in 1944 they were absolutely 100 per cent sure of their success. Also a comparison with the situation prior to the attack in the West in 1940 also occurs to me. Then the highest military leaders were skeptical and they were wrong!

Thus, prior to the Offensive in the Ardennes in 1944 a smaller number of units became available than had been originally figured on, which necessitated a change of plan just as the correctly timed transition to the defensive and withdrawal to the lines of departure became necessary when the development of the situation did not permit the continuation of the Offensive.

In my opinion the following reasons are decisive for the failure of the Offensive:

The Enemy:

a. Reacted more quickly than was expected by the German Supreme Command to the attack launched on 16 Dec.

b. Made an over-all decision in his countermeasures and

c. Had, after the weather cleared, unlimited air supremacy.

On the German Side:

d. The Supreme Command did not transfer in time the center of gravity from the sector of the 6 SS Pz Army to the 5 Pz Army which would have been required to:

(1) exploit the success about to be achieved by the Fifth Army.

(2) and to adopt the so-called small term solution after all. The latter recommended itself, after the 6 Pz Army had been stuck soon after the beginning of the attack; the 5 Army however made good headway.

e. The advance of the 5 Pz Army was decisively influenced by the small initial successes of the two armies in its flanks.

f. The course of the operations was not halted early enough after it had become hopeless and a new decision was necessary.

In Detail:

a. The enemy acted more quickly than was expected by the German leadership.

The first reports coming in from the front sectors (American) which had been attacked, about the strength and the depth of the penetrations, showed that the German attack was more than 'an attack with limited objective'. On the evening of the first day of the attack the enemy also observed approximately the extension in width of the entire attack because on the adjoining German front sectors as well as on the remaining German Western front, almost complete quietness prevailed. Still remaining unknown factors for him were the strength and direction of the total attack. The enemy was thus in a position to withdraw forces from the front sectors not attacked, without the danger of having to give up in consequence important areas for which he had just been fighting and which he might eventually require as a starting point for his further operations. The attacks on the entire remaining front were, therefore, immediately stopped.

Further, the tactical reserves made available to support the threatened, front sectors were of considerable strength. The First Army and the VIII Corps, which had been attacked, apparently disposed of only tactical reserves that were available everywhere as the operations of the enemy showed. The First Army and the VIII Corps had the task to withdraw fighting delaying actions until the arrival of reserves should make possible a successful defense which would serve as the foundation of the subsequently envisaged countermeasures.

During the first few days, the spearheads of the two armored corps of the 5 Pz Army only came up against those forces in the tactical area we had expected would be there. This was proved by the units to which we found captured prisoners belonged. The enemy withdrew in the face of superior German pressure. The withdrawal was apparently unprepared, as areas suitable for defence were not held. The narrow German spearheads were therefore less exposed to counterattacks after the breakthrough of the foremost line of security than had been expected. The apprehensions on the German side in respect of the effect of such powerful counterattacks did also not materialize.

On the whole the delaying action of the withdrawing American Army was a success. It slowed down the German advance, though it could not prevent the pursuing German spearheads from coming within 4 km from the Meuse near Dinant without any major engagements. But the resistance by delaying actions gained the time needed to bring up their tactical reserves at the correct moment.

b. The enemy had already made a total resolution with the immediate cession of all his attacks on these front sectors not attacked. This resulted in an extraordinary massing of forces against the German attack. Moreover, he brought his strategical reserves and the forces withdrawn from the front sectors to the points of penetration to decide their commitment only, as soon as direction and strength of the German attacks became more distinct. In this connection he decided to keep the Meuse with corresponding bridgeheads in order to be able to assemble there. Partial reserve elements were not brought up to the withdrawing First Army as this would have meant a dispersal of the forces. Another fact deserving notice is that the reserves were sent in to the threatened points of penetration before it could possibly be known how the German command would respond to the course of the offensive. The German Supreme Command was, after all, faced with an entirely different situation owing to the deep penetration of the 5 Pz Army, the repulse of the breakthrough by the 6 Pz Army, and the strong defence confronting the Seventh Army.

On the American side the situation was presumably estimated as follows (20 Dec 1944):

Whereas the breakthrough of the German 6 SS Pz Army could be repelled and the defense against the Seventh Army was successful, the German 6 Pz Army succeeded in forcing a breakthrough and in advancing far to the west. Of the large German units, which were immediately available, only two to three SS Panzer Divisions and the few divisions of the OKW reserve had not been committed. Their employment with the 6 Pz Army with the aim to renew the attempt at a breakthrough was improbable. From the German point of view this would not have been very promising and also because of the difficulties for the employment of armored forces.

The 5 Pz Army, which had penetrated far to the West, could continue its attack to the west with the aim to reach the Meuse and then turn to the north. It would then have been the task of the 5 Pz Army to turn northward east of the Meuse so that the left wing would be protected by the Meuse in order to penetrate into the deep flank of the forces opposing the German 6 Pz Army and thus enable the 6 Pz Army to renew its attack under more favorable conditions. The final aim would be the close operation of the 5 Pz Army with the 6 SS Pz Army in the area of Liège.

Or the 5 Pz Army would pivot southward near Bastogne in order to roll up the forces located in front of the Seventh Army, in conjunction with the latter, and, advancing by way of Arlon–Luxembourg, to encircle the forces standing to the west of the Moselle. This solution would mean that the German Command would forego any considerable strategic success. The thrust toward the south, or rather the southeast, would have to be launched with an entirely unprotected right flank. The danger to it from the American strategical reserves assembled in the vicinity of Rheims – the presence of which was known to the German General Staff – would make a thrust of the 5 Pz Army to the south less likely.

The Americans when taking their measures have, therefore, to take into consideration the possibility that the 5 Pz Army continues its advance to the west. A strategical threat had already ceased to exist because the wedge, though far advanced westwards, does not possess sufficient width for a strategical success and is not strong enough and protected in its flanks.

From this follows, that the American counterattack can be launched in time before the 5 Pz Army is across the Meuse. The success of an attack against the southern flank of this Army is the more probable as the Seventh Army is mainly forced into the defense and is still holding Bastogne. It is then essential to contain the northern and southern flanks of the German attack wedge so as to prevent its extension. A frontal (passive) defense against the 5 Pz Army was intentionally avoided.

The military–political leadership of the enemy also made a total decision. The unified repulse of the attack and the counterattacks were put under a single command. The First American Army was temporarily subordinated to the British.

However, it is beyond comprehension that the British armies did not launch the expected large-scale attack, the preparation of which was in full swing. If the British forces had launched a large-scale attack during the time the German Offensive was being prepared further German forces would have been exhausted, which would have forced us to use up more forces and more material. If they had started this large-scale attack soon after the beginning of the German attack in the Ardennes their attack across the Roer would have carried them as far as the Rhine, and at the same time favorable conditions for the annihilation of the entire Heeresgruppe B to the west of the Rhine would have been obtained.

c. The activity of the enemy air force was decisive. It controlled the supply routes, railways and roads completely. The efficiency of the railways sank and was only a fraction of the original one. There was not enough room for road transportation. Continuous breakdowns by air attacks increased this lack, which industry could not make up any more to an adequate extent. That and the almost complete breakdown of the railways resulted in requirements on the transportation, which neither the far distances nor the quantities available allowed. The delays which occurred and the non-arrival of the urgently required supplies have decisively and unfavorably influenced the operations. The bringing up of fuel was likewise affected. And further, the non-arrival of the fuel caused the following: A quick transfer of the reserves immediately available and of those available later on was not possible. The conduct of battle of the artillery suffered especially from the point of view of the formation of artillery strong points and the bringing up of the artillery and mortar elements which were at first kept in the lines of departure.

In the same way the air superiority, too, had a bad immediate effect on the fighting forces. When the fair weather set in all troop movements, positioning, and other movements on the battlefield had to put up with all the difficulties caused by the almost complete lack of our own air force and the superiority of the enemy air force.

d. When the attack of the 6 Pz Army had failed, whilst that of the 5 Pz Army had been successful and had widened to a breakthrough, it was necessary in my opinion to transfer the center of gravity from the 6 to the 5 Pz Army.

That should have been done immediately because we were already beaten as far as time was concerned. All the suggestions made by the Army and the Heeresgruppe with regard to this were disregarded. The direct instruction of Hitler's personal aide-de-camp, who was at the time in the sector of the army, was also useless. The Army reported that it was advancing to the Meuse on the southern part of its attack sector along good roads and that the LVIII Pz Corps was in the deep flank of the LXVI Army Corps and the left wing of the 6 Pz Army still resisting the enemy units. Bringing up of reinforcements, however, was urgently necessary.

According to the opinion of the Army there were available for this shifting of the center of gravity: the forces assembled in the sector of the XII SS Army Corps for the second thrust; the reserves of the 6 SS Pz Army which had to discontinue its attacks and the reserves brought up in the depth of the Heeresgruppe.

I never found out when the plan of a secondary thrust by the XII SS Army Corps was given up. When on 18 or 19 Dec the available units were supposed to be started off there was a lack of fuel. Moreover, the 3 Pz Gren Div was diverted and subordinated to the 6 Pz Army. The 6 Pz Army was ordered to discontinue immediately its attacks and to transfer forces to the 5 Pz Army. The 2 and 12 SS Pz Divs, brought up to the 6 Pz Army at a later date, arrived at a time when the 5 Pz Army had already been forced into the defense; in other words, too late.

Lucid information as to manner and strength of the reserves of the OKW was not received. The subordination of reserve elements, which were ready to be employed immediately, did not take place either. This fact remained although the army had decided, with the full consent of the Supreme Command, to advance ruthlessly to the Meuse and to have the gained terrain and the large enemy strong points mopped up by rear portions. The shifting of the center of gravity to the sector of the 5 Pz Army, as was later envisaged by the Supreme Command, could not take effect any more. The consequence of the non-arrival and the late arrival of the reserves respectively, was, that the enemy had in the meantime reinforced the entire area to such an extent that neither the capture of Bastogne nor complete success for the thrust to the Meuse could be achieved. Perhaps the Chief of the WFSt had already been informed of the enemy countermeasures and wanted to avoid too strong a concentration of forces in the salient which was already projecting far to the west.[17] Perhaps the risks involved in a battle of annihilation which had been proposed by the Army to the east of the Meuse (it was now a question of 'the small term solution') appeared too great, after the defense in front of the 6 Pz Army and the Seventh Army proved to be strong and Bastogne and St. Vith were still held by the enemy. Perhaps it was being considered to discontinue the Offensive. Certainly, the Supreme Command was not capable of making a quick decision when there was still some possibility of carrying out the offensive successfully, although in a different way from that originally intended. The question as to whether the forces were sufficient for an Offensive of the type Field Marshal Model had suggested, the so-called 'small term solution' – a thrust to the Meuse and a turn to the north after establishing bridgeheads to the west of the Meuse – I answer in the affirmative, in spite of the dwindling of men and materials prior to the Offensive. It goes without saying, that employment and composition of the forces would have to be altered.

e. The insignificance of the initial successes of the armies adjoining the 5 Pz Army added decisively to the failure. The steadily lengthening flanks of the spearhead consumed forces which had to be diverted from the main thrust to the west, for the protection of the two flanks. As a consequence the fierce defense of St. Vith and the repulse of the attacks by way of the roads Hotton–Marche, the Army was compressed into the southern part of the sector assigned to it for movement and attack. The vigor of the attack was thus allowed until it became stuck for want of forces.

The Seventh Army was too weak to carry out the protection of its flanks as it moved offensively for any length. It had safeguarded only the deep flank of the 5 Pz Army, sacrificing its weak forces in heavy fighting to tie down enemy forces. If the right wing of the Seventh Army had succeeded in gaining ground farther to the west, Bastogne would have lost its crucial importance. It would have been sufficient to encircle the town. The front which ran south of Bastogne, in an east–westerly direction, was a constant incitement to the enemy to attack the German forces in the rear and to establish contact with the garrison of Bastogne. Owing to the defence of St. Vith the Army was pressed further to the south than was desirable because there was no support on the right.

f. When on 23 Dec the 2 Pz Div, which had advanced to the Meuse, was driven back and was partially destroyed it could be seen that the offensive had failed. There were hardly any reserves available and those coming up had to be employed to bolster up our own defense. An immediate withdrawal was necessary in order to prevent a large consumption of forces. The decision to retreat behind the West Wall was made too late. It was forced upon us by the enemy superiority in forces and we paid for this hesitation with considerable casualties and losses in forces and material.

Reviewing the results of the ill-fated Offensive: The counterattack of the Anglo-American forces was launched too early to achieve the total annihilation of the German Offensive forces, which might have been quite possible. It was only a 'common victory', since the attacker, although badly damaged, was able to withdraw to the line of departure. The Allies had to stop their attacks along the whole western front to achieve this; they had to reconquer terrain which they had already had to fight for once before.

The fortress of Germany got a breathing spell. The home front which had been attacked constantly by the enemy air forces was relieved for a while. However, sacrifices and costs, it is true, were so large that it seems doubtful whether the Offensive was really a gain. The last German reserves were badly damaged, they were lacking in effectiveness for continuation of the war in the West as well as in the East. The quick success of the Red Army stood in causal coherence with the Offensive in the Ardennes which possibly accelerated the end of the war, in which case the gaining of time in the West must be regarded as a false conclusion. The reaction on the morale and in consequence upon the total attitude of the troops and the nation probably accelerated the breakdown of the armed forces and the country.

Leadership

1. The limited personal initiative of many officers of all ranks had already been described. Efficiency, based on the ability to make decisions independently, which had brought the German Army very great successes in Poland, France, and the East in 1941, had almost completely disappeared. Even the most experienced of our higher leaders had been forced to comply strictly with the wording of the order issued from Hitler's headquarters, and even in matters of minor tactical significance – the hand of this headquarters interfered often – in fact – as far down as the divisions.

The German leading staff, which in earlier days had been so cheerful in accepting responsibility, had been crippled ever since Stalingrad and became more and more merely a mechanical commanding body – subject to the smallest details of the so-called 'Führer's orders' which originated from a headquarters far from the fighting front. This brought about the death of the German art of flexible command.

Every leader, as well as the troop commanders and their assistants, has to thoroughly weigh the questions of space, time, the available forces, and the effective use of the latest types of weapons at hand. Naturally, it is impossible to lay down hard and fast rules as to which of the above elements is of primary importance! In every operation which may be undertaken, the problems of terrain, the strength of the enemy and his state of morale must be taken into consideration – also critical is how and where the new weapons are to be brought into use. Then there is the question of what defense may be offered, and many other factors, that are all so variable that their mutual relationship must all be taken into consideration in conjunction with the aim of the operation itself.

In this regard, the Germans had proved that certain chronological conceptions cannot be dispensed with. When I see in Schramm's report that the 'German Armed Forces Operational Command' hoped, in the beginning of the 'Ardennes Offensive', to reach the Maas river on the eve of the second day of the attack, the only comment I can make is that the 'German Armed Forces Operational Command' was not properly acquainted with the front line facts. Our Army's reports on the most favorable timing of the attack emphasized that the spearheads could only reach there on the fourth day; this, however, represented the optimum, considering the following: they would have to do their very best, their fighting ability would have to be maximized and the difficulties of the terrain, particularly during this season, would have to be taken into consideration. With examination of these factors in the light of experiences gained, time may be calculated quite accurately. The more experiences the combat leaders have had – thus the more sound are their calculations bound to be.

3. The element of time is of paramount importance in war. A speedy execution of orders allotted to one, the ability of any officer to make decisions and have them carried out independently, a clear mind able to detect the right moment which can be exploited to increase the chances of success, great personal activity and a flexibility in command up to the crucial and decisive moment, these factors are all essential in warfare. Operations designed to deny the enemy an ultimate success require the same flexibility of mind and speed of action.

The element of operational flexibility has become a weapon, and when used in compliance with the knowledge gained from experience, and the latest technical possibilities offered, it becomes a weapon of prime importance.

4. The 'Ardennes Offensive' confirmed that the element of surprise is a principle of warfare to which all other principles are to be considered *secondary* to ensure success. Disadvantages, which may possibly occur, *are all to be put up with.* The fact that the disadvantages occurring during the course of the 'Ardennes Offensive' became very great for the troops and their commanders – as was stated often by different troop commanders – is to be regarded as a consequence of the fact that the Wehrmacht was in its sixth year of fighting! This could be seen in the sinking of the standard of efficiency of the officers and troops, as well as in the shortage of equipment and gear.

It is possible that in wars of the future the element of surprise will play a decisive role, because the advances being made in every field of technology seem to make possible the use of new weapons, exploiting techniques hitherto unknown, which following other concepts of time and space will be independent of terrain and weather conditions. Their effect will likely increase in importance.

5. The 'Ardennes Offensive' likewise taught us that the surprise of the enemy is not only to be born out of strict secrecy, of camouflage and deception, of the availability of new weapons, or in the carrying out with great speed of operations, but that the nature of the terrain chosen also plays a decisive part. The enemy least expected a German attack in the Eifel or through the

Ardennes. Since in wars of the future the decision must be brought by coordination between the air force and the airborne troops, and fast armored units, the latter having been dropped partially or entirely from the air, the difficulties arising from the nature of the terrain can be surmounted relatively easily in comparison with present day performances. And thus – great possibilities arise when the branches of the service work together by making the right choice in matters of terrain to preserve the element of surprise.

6. The German principles of leadership for the commitment and use of armored troops have again and again proved highly efficient. The fact that in these operations a constant pressing towards and over the Maas was necessary which consequently stretched out the flanks to a great length, which, at first could be occupied but weakly, was not at all unusual. For the attacker this does not represent anything to be afraid of. This tactic used by the armored units proved very efficient and formed the basis in the successes achieved in Poland, France, and Russia. These principles of leadership were later on adopted by General Patton from the Third Army in the breakthrough near Avranches where they yielded good results.

Experience had taught that such an exposure of flanks is also liable to happen in the ranks of the defending force, and in many cases become even more inconvenient to the enemy than they are to the attacker because he will have prepared himself to meet the risk. A risk of this sort, which can be anticipated, is diminished if one's reconnaissance is doing an efficient job and works in collaboration with the troops on the ground. We were, it must be admitted, really blind during the 'Ardennes Offensive'. If this had not been true we would have detected the assembling of armored forces north of the line Marche–Vielsalm against the northern flank as well as the bringing up of forces to the line of Bastogne–St. Hubert which were not seen at the time. Operational and tactical air force formations in cooperation with airborne troops will in the future of course not be able to completely diminish such risks as an exposure of flanks and the problem of unsecured flanks in the preliminary stages of an attack, as such areas will naturally be much greater in extent in any future conflict.

7. Many examples can be seen in the course of the 'Ardennes Offensive' where the operational and tactical air forces along with airborne troops including the airborne infantry formations, worked in close cooperation with the fast mobile armored units according to the principles of warfare of that time.

Although the Wehrmacht still had several thousand airborne infantry troops at its disposal, it was not able to commit them any longer with a certainty that they would achieve success. Their commitment in the combat area around St. Vith and around Bastogne would have undoubtedly changed the aspect of the conflict to a certain extent. However, this does not mean that they would have ensured success completely for 'Heeresgruppe B' as the forces were simply not strong enough for this in any case.

The 'weapons' which I brought up have become the weapons which brought the ultimate decision; the 'German Infantry' had become inferior in strength to the enemy force in 1945, since only the weapons mentioned could have solved the problems of time and space and thereby exploit every success without delay. An example follows with reference to the commitment of airborne (parachute) troops ahead of the front of the 5 Panzer Army:

1. Dropped close to the front: on 17 December: St Vith

                                                        Houffalize

                                                        Bastogne

Forces: for each a reinforced battalion

2. Dropped close to the front: on 18 or 19 Dec: Libramont
Forces: one reinforced battalion.

3. Dropped further away from the front: on 18 or 19 Dec: Namur
Forces: one reinforced battalion

Gedinne ⎫   Dinant: one reinforced battalion
         ⎬ Forces: for each one
Houx   ⎭ reinforced battalion.   Givet: two reinforced battalions

Missions allotted them: keeping open the narrow passes, such as bridges, barricading of traffic points; a covering of the flanks toward the north (St. Vith), toward the south (Bastogne and Givet), toward the southwest (Libramont).

8. It is a principle of leadership that any attack must be developed in the depth, otherwise it is doomed to failure unless extraordinarily favorable conditions are prevailing, or the enemy is already staggering. The late war confirmed in many instances on the German side that the conception 'depth' does not necessarily have to mean only the occupation by troops in the depth, but also and of the same importance is the concept of material 'depth'.[18] The necessity for this material depth increases when operations develop rapidly and the sectors are large. The extent of material depth is of course dependent on the losses of equipment, which is to be expected in any operation.

9. Before the war, it was taught that motor fuel is merely a means of transportation. During the course of the late war it has been proved that it has actually become a weapon with which to fight. This does not only mean that a sufficient supply of motor fuel must be available, but also that a tactical officer must have it at his disposal at the right place and at the decisive moment. The conception that tactics are the skill of a troop commander, that his weapons are to be brought up to the combat zone to serve their purpose at the right moment and at the right spot — I deem in this respect motor fuel as a 'weapon' to fight with.

Seeing that the conception of 'greatest possible cumulative effect' signifies smooth working cooperation between all types of weapons, it follows naturally that the form of organization chosen for the supply units is of the very highest moment, and that it cannot possibly be considered as separate.

10. Just as the concept of time cannot be dispensed with, the chances of having success are also jeopardized if other factors are overlooked. In military operations, circumstances must be taken as they come, but not as we had wished they would come. In my opinion, Schramm was very well aware of the contrast between the logical work of the military staff calling for a sense of responsibility, and the attitude and judgment of Hitler himself.

The cause and effect are clear. The only types of officers qualified as assistants to the actual leaders are those who have had *adequate* experience in the *practice* of commanding troops. They must have been with troops in order to comprehend difficult situations, assess and issue the necessary orders with decisions which must be constantly and repeatedly checked. Further, after they have been assigned to such positions, their previous tasks should be taken over by someone else, so that they will not be in danger of being sent back to them!

My assignment to the operational situation of the 'Western Front' in the beginning of September 1944 – at the taking over of the 5 Panzer Army by the 'German Armed Forces Operational Command' (I had just come from the 'Eastern Front' and was not acquainted with the situation on the 'Western Front' as it was after the Invasion started) – revealed to me, with frightening clarity, that Hitler's military advisors were totally ignorant of the facts at the front line.

Since weapons and their application will bring about a basic change in methods of combat and in the techniques of same which – in the future – will be subject to continuous changes, assistants of actual leaders who know their job well and how to act under given circumstances, will be all the more in demand. They must know when and how to revise their techniques from time to time and replace them altogether with new ones when necessary.

Combat Technique – Equipping of the Troops

1. No matter what fast armored panzer formations will look like in the future, they will comprise a *great number* of tanks. Its armored force must form a compact concentrative body able to withstand the full force of attack, with its tanks. All other portions of armored formations should have only one task – namely – to assist the concentrative body wherever and whenever it can. The main support of the tank forces must in the first place be the *Infantry*. I believe that the reason for the fact that the German armored formations started to fail in their efforts now and then after 1942, was that after this time the formations were not furnished with the same number of tanks as before. This phase in the war also proved that the zenith of power had been reached by the armored

units. But I am rather of the opinion that the essential elements of armored formations, fire power, armor, speed in action, mobility and flexibility, all of which are of the essence of armored warfare, cannot be over-emphasized.

2. Reconnaissance vehicles on wheels or half tracks are already out of date as they can be used only on good roads or suitable terrain. They must be equipped with caterpillar tracks completely, must be able to wade through swampland or flooded regions, and be amphibious. Only if these requirements are met can the command expect good results from its reconnaissance.

3. The troops who took part in the 'Ardennes Offensive' were greatly handicapped on account of the failure of their engineering detachments, and the limited mobility of the available engineers. With regard to the organization of the fast troops of the 'Wehrmacht', each battalion of the armored infantry formations, of the armored troops, of the heavy antiaircraft artillery forces, and of the armored reconnaissance formations, had its own engineer platoon, the strength, composition, equipment, and mobility of which had to have the ability to meet the requirements which their tasks called for. They were of decisive importance in the support of their respective units in all engineer technical problems, and were simultaneously a relief of the divisions' own engineer battalions as well as to the 'Heeres' engineer units.

4. The high standard of training of the German tank crews in driving, firing, and radio signal functions, as was maintained up till the end of the war, was an essential contribution in the commitment and use of this weapon. Troops whose duties are training must have the necessary time, tank equipment, motor fuel, and suitable terrain to use tanks. Where firing is possible, ammunition, and any other essentials, are necessary to carry out their tasks efficiently.

In the same fashion, the training in cooperation between the tank weapon and the riflemen fighting alongside of it, and the artillery which supports both, demands special attention. Otherwise close cooperation cannot be achieved during fighting of a rapidly developing nature during which the situation changes often and rapidly, as was the case in 1945 when assault gun units 'suffered' under the infantry as the latter had not been trained to fight in co-operation with the assault gun batteries at this stage of the war.

5. Marching along the main road through Houffalize, which had been plowed up by enemy air raids and deserted by its civilian population, was very difficult during the general advance in the 'Ardennes Offensive', owing to the fact that an adequate force was not available to construct and maintain the roads in good condition. A strong bomber formation dropped patterns of bombs on two separate occasions on the curving road south of the town, consequently blocking it at one place for over twenty-four hours as it was impossible to make a detour on either side. As to whether this bombing mission was carried out on purpose or accidentally, I do not know. The bombing of such points, it seems to me, is very effective in the stopping of moving columns.

During the German retreat in 1945, I was time and again deeply impressed by the heavy damage inflicted by the bombing attack on the road near Dasburg. Although the bridge itself was not hit, the roads leading to it were so hopelessly blocked by twisted chassis of smashed tanks and other vehicles that it took the troops a long time to bring it back to a state where it could be used again.

6. The complaints appearing frequently in German reports during the Ardennes Offensive with regard to the inadequate traffic regulating service compel me to state the following: The military traffic regulating service is a direct aid to the command; the regulating of traffic is of great importance in warfare. Victory and defeat often depend on a frictionless and speedy carrying out of a marching operation, as well as an efficient functioning of the troops of this service. Many examples proving this are to be found in the 'Ardennes Offensive' – here is one:

The bringing up of the Panzer Lehr Division on 16 December east of the Our. This was not solely due to the shortcomings of the traffic regulating service, however, but as much to the troops themselves who were not energetic enough; the following serious disadvantages resulted:

The following up of the heavy guns and the main body of the artillery force of the 18 'Volks Grenadier Division', as well as most of the 'Führer-Begleit Brigade' under Oberst Remer. These forces were to be brought up for the support in the battle of St. Vith. This was a direct result of the inadequacies in the traffic regulating east of Schönberg. When portions of the 6 SS Panzer Army started using these same roads, the difficulties increased further. Other disadvantages resulting, were the following:

An inadequate regulating of traffic during the marching on the southern wing of the 6 SS Panzer Army near Losheimergraben. A considerable combat force of the army had to wait here more than one day doing nothing, while they were urgently needed on the front.

The bringing up later of the 'OKW' reserves – particularly with regard to the transfer of the 9 Panzer Division and the 3 and 15 Panzer Grenadier Divisions from the northern wing of the 'Heeresgruppe' B to the 5 Panzer Army – which was not merely a result of the shortage of fuel, but also of the inadequate regulating of traffic in the general movement from north to south and likewise in the similar movement from east to west going on at the same time, and these delayed notably the process.

According to what I observed after having been taken prisoner, the regulating of traffic of the Allied armies was very well organized; the discipline of the drivers themselves and their respect for the traffic regulating service was much better than we ever had even before the war.

The fact that the traffic regulating services must also be trained in radio communication and intelligence had already been mentioned; the continuous reports of a traffic regulating unit on a bridge over the Maas, regarding the course of a large scale troop movement (the locality, time, and strength of the troops concerned, were all included in these reports), which were tapped by our forces, furnished us with vital information on decisions of the bringing up of reserves out of the depth of the western areas.

Answers to Questionnaire of 9 April 1945

Q. What connections did you have with your divisions, with the headquarters of Army Group B, and with the neighboring units? Were special liaison officers and their staffs of Army Group B, or of 'OB' West present?

A. A running communication by radio was maintained with the superior 'Heeresgruppe' B, which was disrupted for short periods now and then, lasting at the longest one half day during which telephone was used. During the time that the General Staff of the Army was in La Roche, and later – in Mont le Ban – contact was made by directional transmission on the short wave band. This worked satisfactorily.

There were nearly always teleprinters at hand. Furthermore, from the start of the 'Ardennes Offensive', a liaison officer from Field Marshal Model was present at the General Staff headquarters of the Army, who – at that time – had his own radio connections with the Field Marshal.

Finally, Hitler sent his two adjutants to me on 24 December, to get first hand information on the situation. During those days we had several telephone conversations with the deputy of 'Generaloberst' Jodl of the 'German Armed Forces Operational Command'. OB West did not have a liaison officer at my staff headquarters. We had regular radio communications with the neighboring armies, and in many instances also contact by telephone, the lines of which went over the 'Heeresgruppe' switchboard. Telephone and radio communications were maintained at all times with the subordinate corps.

Q. When did you first hear that the LXVI Corps had cut off two regiments from the American 106 Division in the Schnee-Eifel? Did these regiments put up a stronger resistance than you had expected?

A. After Schönberg was taken in the morning of 17 December and particularly after reaching the Walleroder mill in the afternoon of this same day, it was certain that those American troops still in their positions between the pene-tration points Roth–Auw–towards Schönberg and near Bleialf, were in grave danger of envelopment because the attacker had possession of the roads. When the combat group on the left of the 18 Volks Grenadier Division was nearing Schönberg in the late morning of 18 December, it was established that the encirclement had succeeded. It was then, however, not yet known that two regiments were concerned. The resistance of these troops was not as strong as we had previously expected.

Q. What reports did you manage to tap, that were being sent from the American Headquarters to the two regiments which had been cut off? Did you have any difficulties in the maintenance of your signal communications during this period? We have been informed that the Germans were successful during this period in disturbing the American radio signal network. Were these disturbances caused by personnel under your command? If this was not the case, where was this caused?

A. As far as I can remember – we tapped radio messages from the two regiments which had been cut off, which called urgently for support, and which said that an envelopment was threatening. I cannot recall details at this time. We did not have any inconvenience in the transmission of reports at this time, which were due to the enemy's interference. The XLVII Panzer Corps, on 17 December, listened in on a radio conversation to the effect that the 101 Parachute Division at Rheims had first been alerted, and then sent in to attack Bastogne.

I never heard of any jamming from the German side.

Q. The Germans listened in on conversations with good information, from the American Headquarters in Rheims. Did they understand what they heard, that the Allies had decided on a plan?

A. Our signal reconnaissance functioned efficiently and speedily. The transmission of reports on the enemy of our reconnaissance from the German Armed Forces Operational Command to the Army was carried out without friction and rapidly. I do not remember whether or not the Army Command could really conclude out of these reports as to whether the Allies knew anything about our planned offensive or not.

An officer of the 18 Volks Grenadier Division who had been taken prisoner by the Americans had – at this time – a report of his corps containing information regarding the Operation 'Greif', which was taken away from him. From this we could conclude that the Allies had at least some idea about the offensive and its aim towards the Maas.

Q. What reports did you get about the American reinforcements being brought up to the zone around St. Vith? Had it been planned to bypass St. Vith, or did you consider it as a main object of the attack?

A. The strengthening of the area around St. Vith by the 7 American Armored Division was often discussed over the radio, and later this information was confirmed by prisoners who fell in the hands of the 'Führer-Begleit Brigade'. The taking of St. Vith was of the same importance to the advance of the right wing of my Army, as it was for the attack of the left wing of the 6 Panzer Army. Details with regard to this may be found in the earlier account.

Q. After the first four days, it was clearly evident that the center of gravity of the attack had been shifted to the 5 Panzer Army. It is possible that the attack might have been much more successful if portions of the 6 Panzer Army had been transferred to the 5 Panzer Army, and if reserves of the 'OKW' had been transferred at a much earlier date than was actually the case. Was a rivalry between the SS and the Wehrmacht to blame for this delay? What facts could be relied upon?

A. It is not right to assume that the center of gravity had actually been shifted after the first four days. This shifting of the focal point had been decided for 22 December if possible, by the 'German Armed Forces Operational Command', and was ordered to have been carried out by this date. This was actually never brought into effect because the forces envisaged for this purpose arrived much too late. They did not arrive at the Army area until the Allied resistance ahead of the LVIII Panzer Corps and the XLVII Panzer Corps had stiffened to such an extent near Bastogne that the advance had practically been brought to a standstill. Their commitment was not in the attack toward the Maas, for it was already too late, but merely as a tactical force.

I do not doubt, however, that the 5 Panzer Army would have reached the Maas and taken the elevated region around Marche – as is pointed out in the question – if the attack had developed in depth at the right moment Bastogne could also have been taken if the center of gravity had been shifted at the right time, and before this town had a chance to receive reinforcements from the air and the ground.

A rivalry did actually exist between the SS and the Wehrmacht! It, however, did not have any influence on the neighborly intercourse between the two attacking armies. As to whether Hitler had any influence on this feeling of rivalry, and just how much it affected the delay, I am at a loss to know.

Q. The 116 Panzer Division had reached Salle, west of Bastogne and was only a short distance away from the road linking Marche and Bastogne, but on the evening of 19 December an order had been issued that the advance was to be halted in this direction, and that the forces concerned here were to push out northeast of Houffalize.

Did you know that the 116 Panzer Division, although not in its own sector, was practically standing in open terrain? Was it you who gave orders that the advance be halted in this direction? Was it the 116 Panzer Division which captured the medical battalion of the 101st American Airborne Division in this area during the night of 20 December? Had you been informed regarding this fact? The presence of supply and medical installations should have been sufficient evidence that rearward positions were concerned here.

A. During the night of 20 December, the 116 Panzer Division reported to the LVIII Panzer Corps that the Ourthe bridge five kilometers west of Bastogne had been destroyed. To repair it by the Division's own engineers would have taken at least until the evening of 20 December. The Corps itself had no engineers available for this purpose. It had, therefore, to make a decision of sending in all its divisions, if and where necessary over the crossroads northwest of Flamierge against Champlon. We had to reckon with the demolishing of the bridge near Ortheuville in case the Division should be sent in along the road. We would also have to figure with traffic bottlenecks if the 116 Panzer Division in the sector of the XLVII Panzer Corps, were to get its troops mingled with those of the 2 Panzer Division, which was also moving at this time. Houffalize had in the meantime been taken by rearward portions of the 116 Panzer Division. The enemy was here – in contrast to his troops in the area of Bastogne – retreating in a westerly direction. It now became a matter to take full advantage of this weak point in order to win more terrain in a westerly direction as speedily as possible. The Division, therefore, in accordance with an order from the Army, held up by the LVIII Panzer Corps, was then committed through Houffalize against Samree early on the night of 20 December.

The comment of the Commander of the 116 Panzer Division, in his report about his decision, is justified, because he – at that time – did not have an over-all view of the situation and consequently did not write the report from this point of view.[19]

I had been informed about the medical battalion which had been taken prisoner. This was nothing extraordinary, however, for the armored divisions, after breaking through, had to reckon with the fact that they would pierce into enemy territory to such an extent that the rearward sectors would also be reached where the enemy had his medical installations, etc. As far as I remember – the 2 Panzer Division captured the units concerned.

Q. Oberst Lauchert said that, after the 2 Panzer Division had taken Noville on 20 December, he had asked permission to pursue the Americans withdrawing in the direction of Bastogne, which, we assume, was because he expected to take this town during one of these days. His request was not approved. Was it assumed that he took the situation too optimistically, or was it thought that an advance to the west by the 2 Panzer Division was wiser?

A. I do not know. I turned down the request because this division had not been allotted the task of capturing Bastogne. It had to stick more to its own objective of attack, namely, the Maas river.

Q. The American Commanders of Bastogne knew that it would have been impossible for them to hold out in this town during the first phase of the siege if it had been attacked from different sides simultaneously. Why was this not done?

A. According to my opinion at that time, it was possible to take Bastogne on

18 and 19 December by attacking it from the southwest or the west with the Panzer Lehr Division. However, for this it would have been necessary:

a. To send in a strong reconnaissance by the Division, against Bastogne, which could deliver effective results,

b. The Division would have to keep strong reserves available in order to employ them according to what the reports of the reconnaissance would tell.

The Division Commander, however, did not realize the actual situation, or his judgment was not correct. This opportunity which is seldom granted a Panzer Division, was not taken advantage of either speedily enough or with enough force.[20]

Q. Did you participate in the writing of the note to surrender Bastogne? Were you informed that a note of this nature had been presented?

A. I did not order either the writing or sending of a note of this kind. The Commanding General of the XLVII Panzer Corps discussed this subject with me several times and expressed this intention. I said that the sending of this note would be justified only if we had the necessary forces to force the surrender in the event that it should be turned down. The forces assembled by the 21 December, particularly those of the artillery, were in my opinion too weak, so that I do not recall having given the permission to send this type of note during these days.

Q. On 26 December the Führer-Begleit Brigade received order not to continue its attack against Hotton, after which it was sent to Bastogne for the purpose of surrounding the city once more. Was it thought that the situation around Hotton was hopeless, or was there at this time no forces at hand to close the breach again?

A. I reckon that the attack of the Führer-Begleit Brigade in the area of Hotton served as a relief for the 116 Panzer Division, and also that it could bring the elevated region around Marche into our hands. I thought the attack had reasonable chances of being successful. An order originally emanating from the Führer himself, but handed on by Field Marshal Model, which resulted during the course of a conversation on the phone with Hitler when it proved necessary to ring him up on some point, compelled us to send in the Brigade at Bastogne as it was the only formation available at the time.

Q. On 1 January 1945, you said to the Commanding General of the 116 Panzer Division, in Roy, 'this year is not beginning good for us', after which you gave order to clean out Bastogne as it was a matter of the greatest importance. Did you do this on your own initiative, or was it done in accordance with orders from your superiors? Was this order issued with the hope of bringing the offensive to an early end, or with the realization that the offensive would soon change into a defensive and that Bastogne would then become an inconvenient thorn? According to the information we have Hitler said as late as 24 December that Bastogne was to remain untouched.

A. The remarks may very well have some truth in them. I had realized a long time that the offensive was bound to fail, and thought it wiser to draw the troops back to a safer position. During the last week, everything I did was characterized by this opinion and my chief of staff also acted accordingly. The many failures in the carrying out of my orders inspired me to make the remark stated in your question. The order to clean out Bastogne was issued by Field Marshal Model, which, as far as I remember, in turn was done in compliance with a strict and urgent order from the Führer himself.

Q. The 116 Panzer Division was withdrawn from the LVIII Panzer Corps on 17 December, and then sent to the XLVII Panzer Corps. Was this done on account of the breakthrough which had occurred earlier on the bridge in Dasburg in the direction of Heinerscheid? Did the 116 Panzer Division meet resistance which it had not expected in the sector of the LVIII Panzer Corps? Which unit actually captured the bridge at Dasburg? What resistance was encountered there? While making a detour around Ouren, did the 116 Panzer Division encounter resistance before crossing the Our, or while it was in the process of crossing?

A. When the 116 Panzer Division had built a small bridgehead over the Our near Ouren during the forenoon of 17 December, the following were the reasons for the decision to bring up the Division over the bridge in Dasburg to the western bank of the Our:

a. The bridge at Ouren was relatively weak. It was in need of recon-struction which – if the circumstances were favorable – could be carried out by the evening of 17 December.

b. The roads leading to the bridge at Ouren were covered by a thick layer of mud so that only those vehicles completely on tracks were able to advance.

c. The bridges at Dasburg had been constructed by two Panzer Divisions which completed it at 1600 hours on 16 December, so that it was not a difficult matter for the 116 Panzer Division to cross the stream here.

The bridge at Dasburg was used by the Division only to get its troops on the western bank of the Our as soon as possible. The fact that it had to move through the sector of the XLVII Panzer Corps in order to do this, was reckoned with beforehand. Permission to use the bridge had been given by the Army upon a request made by the LVIII Panzer Corps. The Division was not sub-ordinated to the XLVII Panzer Corps. The reconnaissance battalion of the 116 Panzer Division was set in march through Dasburg in the evening of 16 December. In cooperation with portions of the 560 Volksgrenadier Division, the battalion captured Heinerscheid, and reached Asselborn as early as 17 December.

Q. What support did you have from your air force?

A. We were, and remained 'blind'! The enemy had an unlimited air superiority both by day and night. We had no support whatsoever from our own air force. In my opinion, the one sole air attack against Bastogne was of no significance.

Q. Was the weather of any assistance to you during your operations?

A. Up till 22 December, the weather was of a decisive assistance in our movements and fighting.

Q. What disadvantages resulted from the bad roads in your operation?

A. It was not as much the bad roads, as the bad condition that the vehicles were in and the difficulty in driving them, which caused friction wherever troops moved off the main paved roads. The trucks could not be used on open terrain, i.e. they did not have complete tracks. The vehicles suitable for use on open terrain – i.e. vehicles on half tracks or with more than two axles, which had surmounted even worse difficulties on the roads in the East than were existent here – were not allowed off the main roads by their drivers for fear that, in case damage should be done to them, parts could not be acquired to repair them. The condition of these roads in winter was therefore a headache, but not to the extent that the ensuing difficulties became of decisive importance.

Q. Report all changes you were ordered to make in the plans you received from Army Group B after the attack had begun.

A. Hitler ordered that Bastogne had to be taken. This order was to the effect that Field Marshal Model ordered me to send in the Führer-Begleit Brigade in the area of Bastogne. This order meant that the original plan would have to be abandoned insofar as the Brigade would be committed in the focal point of the attack and its troops were first class troops.

Q. When were you at first sure that the objective of the attack would not be reached?

A. As of 20 December I doubted very much as to whether the object of the Heeresgruppe – a forward push up to the Maas by setting up bridgeheads – would be reached. We had already taken beatings at this time. The neighboring armies had only minor preliminary successes, and strong portions of them had been pressed back into the defense. After 24 December it was certain that we would not reach our objective.

Notes

1. For background see Donald G. Brownlow, *Panzer Baron*, Christopher Publishing Company, 1975; also 'Hitler's Last Gamble', in B.H. Liddell Hart's *The German Generals Talk*, Quill, New York, 1948, and 'Battle of the Ardennes', in *Decisive Battles of World War II: The German View*, G.P. Putnam's Sons, New York.

2. 'An Interview with Gen. Pz. Hasso von Manteuffel: Fifth Panzer Army, Nov 44–Jan 45', ETHINT-46, 29 and 31 October 1945. Documentation regarding the actions of this army are voluminous: Generalmajor Carl Wagener, 'Fifth Panzer Army, 2 Nov 44–16 Jan 45', B-235; Generalmajor Carl Wagener, 'Fifth Panzer Army: Additional Questions', A-961, 18 October 1945; Richard Metz, 'Fifth Panzer Army Artillery', B-393, and Karl Burdach, 'Fifth Panzer Army Artillery', B-761, 1948. It should further be noted that the document recited in this volume is only half of von Manteuffel's original manuscript; MS B-151 contains the preparations and organization of the army.

3. Von Manteuffel, ETHINT-46, *op. cit.*

4. The load capacity of the bridge columns: Bridge column 25 m up to 16 tons; Engineer column 50 m up to 70 tons; or four large ferries up to 70 tons capacity. Motor transport columns 55 m for loads up to Panzer IV inclusive (therefore not suitable for Panzer V).

5. 1129 VG Regiment. Note that von Manteuffel frequently confuses 1130 Regiment with 1129 Regiment in the narrative.

6. This was 244 StuG Brigade, attached to 18 VG Division.

7. Von Manteuffel is probably referring to the 3rd FJ Div of 6 Pz Army, which was not well advanced. However, in fairness it should be noted that 1 SS Pz Div had broken through American lines just north of the army boundary and was the most advanced German unit on the evening of 17 December.

8. The 112th Regiment of the 28th Division was on the east side of the Our River.

9. Probably parts of the 9 SS Pz Div, which was searching for free road space that led west.

10. Von Manteuffel is confused on this point. The weather cleared the following day.

11. And also from the divisional commander, Bayerlein, taking ill-advised civilian advice.

12. Kampfgruppe von Fallois was the reinforced reconnaissance battalion of Panzer Lehr Division.

13. Kampfgruppe Kunkel was the reinforced reconnaissance battalion of 26 VG Division.

14. Von Manteuffel's memory is probably wrong regarding the date of this event.

15. Again, von Manteuffel is confused on dates; the resupply missions came on 23 and 24 December.

16. Strength of at least a reinforced regiment, however.

17. Jodl does not admit giving up the Antwerp goal before Hitler's reconciliation on 28 December.

18. Material in this case is armor, artillery, bridging equipment and so forth.

19. In the report of the 116 Paner Division commander, General von Waldenberg, he indicates that this decision 'was fatal to the initiative of the division.'

20. Again, von Manteuffel seems to blame General Bayerlein for his lack of initiative.

4

The Ardennes Offensive: Seventh Army

BY GENERAL DER PANZERTRUPPEN
ERICH BRANDENBERGER

Introduction

Compared to Dietrich and von Manteuffel, General Erich Brandenberger was the least favored of General Model's three army commanders. He was too methodical for the hard-driving Model, who had once derided him as 'a typical product of the general staff system' and as having 'the features of a scientist.' But regardless of Model's sarcasm, Brandenberger brought considerable experience to his post. He entered Russia from the starting gun in 1941 as commander of the 8th Panzer Division, which was frequently the spearhead of General Erich Manstein's LVI Panzer Corps. He was promoted to General der Panzertruppen in August 1943, and led the XXIX Army Corps for a year before being chosen to command the Seventh Army in the Ardennes.

General von Manteuffel, head of the Fifth Panzer Army, which was to be on his right, thought better of the bespectacled Brandenberger. He described him to John Toland as a 'vigorous son of a Silesian school master.' He was 'indifferent to danger, brusque and a product of the German Staff School.'[1] The Americans who came into contact with General Brandenberger also formed a favorable impression:

> I talked the next day at Freising with General Brandenberger, who had commanded the Seventh Army in the Ardennes, and left him a brief to be answered in writing. Like General Westphal, General Brandenberger quickly saw the purpose of our historical activity. In my brief conversation with him, I was highly impressed by this officer's intelligence and knowledge of what had taken place in the units under his control. The manuscripts which he prepared were very detailed accounts of the operations in which he engaged … Brandenberger's general appearance (graying hair with a tendency to baldness and shell-rimmed glasses which interrupt the roundness of his face) is that of a man in his middle or late fifties … He gives the impression of being a careful, steady worker, rather than a flashy brilliant one.[2]

But General Model's denunciation of the paunchy commander obviously carried over to Hitler, who, although personally selecting Brandenberger, was disinclined to provide him with the wherewithal necessary for the success of his mission. He was charged with blocking the left flank of the offensive from the feared U.S. General George Patton and his Third Army. Originally, the OKW plan had allocated Seventh Army the use of six infantry divisions and one panzer division for the task. But when the shoe pinched the flow of troops to the west, it was Brandenberger whose order of battle suffered. His army of four mostly inexperienced divisions entered the fray as more of a reinforced corps than an army. And in spite of General von Manteuffel's nearly continuous appeals, a panzer formation for his Volksgrenadier army was not forthcoming. But if Brandenberger's forces received least attention, his account of his army's operations is perhaps the most detailed of the three. The ETO Historical Section editor of manuscript A-876 described it as 'a model report'.

Danny S. Parker

Seventh Army in the Ardennes Offensive

Events Leading Up to the Offensive

The Initial Situation

I. THE EVOLUTION OF OUR SITUATION

In the course of the withdrawal of the German Army in the West toward the frontier of the homeland, the remnants of the Seventh German Army reached the sector of the West Wall between Geilenkirchen and Wallendorf in the second week of September 44. By the subordination of the LXXX Inf Corps on the right wing of our southern neighbor, First Army, the Seventh Army sector was extended on 17 Sep 44 as far as south of Trier.

At this time there was a direct enemy threat to both wings of the army, in the Aachen sector, and southwest of Bitburg. In both of these sectors the enemy had pushed forward and breached the West Wall. He clearly intended to continue his large-scale offensive toward and across the Rhine. Whereas it was possible by prompt action on the left wing of the Army to wipe out part of the enemy forces at Wallendorf, where they had broken through, and to drive the rest back westwards over the frontier, it was possible only to seal off the breach made at Aachen by the relatively stronger enemy forces. All our attempts here to retake the forward line of the West Wall came to naught. However, Seventh Army (having transferred the sector from Geilenkirchen to east of Stolberg to Fifth Pz Army on 22 Oct 44) was able, despite the loss of Aachen and the Aachen sector, to prevent the strategic penetration attempted by the enemy in the direction of Cologne and Düsseldorf. And a brief consideration of the state of the beaten Western Army and the difficulties of supply and replacement will give the reader an idea of the extraordinary performance of the German troops in achieving such a defensive success.

The German formations arriving in the West Wall in mid-September 44 were all battle groups having only a few hundred men each and a scattering of artillery pieces and heavy weapons as armament. The security forces of the Home Army occupying the Wall and the Army (Heeres) and Luftwaffe fortress battalions arriving from Germany were now merged with these battle groups. These replacement units suffered either from incomplete training, as in the case of the Luftwaffe units, the naval retrainees and the soldiers who had been taken out of school before finishing their courses. Otherwise they had ear or stomach ailments or were otherwise not completely fit. Desperate attempts were made to obtain equipment and weapons, but the urgency of the danger meant that many units were a patchwork of diverse equipment and personnel. This can be fully understood if one realizes that in a single unit there might be men having 100 different APO numbers, while in a single artillery regiment there might be four different types of foreign weapons. The grave disadvantages of such a situation are evident. Furthermore, some units had to be reorganized and reconstituted while heavy fighting was in progress (e.g., at Aachen and in the Hürtgen Forest), or else units which have been occupying quiet sectors of the front (e.g., the Eifel) had to be committed in some very active sector during or immediately after their reconstitution. Such was the fate of 344 Inf Div and 353 Inf Div.

Such conditions, which made tremendous demands on both officers and men, were unavoidable, although the Supreme Command was anxious above all to ensure that newly constituted or rehabilitated reserve or panzer divisions be committed in active sectors only as a last resort. The Supreme Command had decided quite some time ago that the 'new' panzer and infantry divisions should be welded into an assault army for the purpose of mounting a fresh and decisive operation.

However, the violence of the fighting at the frontier, both at Aachen and in Lorraine, forced us to modify this rule in many instances. During the battles of Aachen, for example, we had to commit a total of five volks grenadier divisions (12 VGD, 47 VGD, 183 VGD, 246 VGD, and 272 VGD), one airborne division (3 FJ Div), and four panzer-type divisions (9 Pz Div, 116 Pz Div, 3 Pz Gren Div, and later 15 Pz Gren Div), in order to prevent a strategic breakthrough eastward across the Roer, which would have upset the whole plan for a counteroffensive. In Lorraine also, we were occasionally obliged to employ single divisions and panzer-type units undergoing reconstitution (e.g., Pz Lehr Div and 11 Pz Div) in order to stabilize the situation. And although portions of these infantry divisions and almost all of the panzer-type units could be used in the December 44 offensive, it cannot be denied that their commitment seriously hampered their rehabilitation and the preservation of their fighting power for the offensive.

After the penetration at Wallendorf had been eliminated during the second half of September 44, the situation on the Eifel Front between Monschau and Trier remained comparatively quiet with the exception of small, local engagements. In October and November 44, newly-arrived volks grenadier divisions were committed here, to relieve the West Wall divisions mentioned above for employment in Lorraine and Aachen, and also to replace the panzer-type units still engaged in fighting and due for a rest. These volks grenadier divisions were supposed to utilize their time on this relatively peaceful front to continue their training and to acquire fighting experience gradually.

The left flank of Seventh Army was constantly endangered by the situation in Army Group G's sector, since an enemy penetration through the Orscholz switch line or in the Saar would undoubtedly have had the result of opening the Moselle 'Door'. Therefore, security measures had to be maintained constantly in the area south of Trier.

This description of our situation makes it clear that Seventh Army never had time, from the moment it occupied the West Wall until the offensive began, to prepare adequately and to organize for the great attack. But it shows, nevertheless, that Seventh Army contrived, in the most difficult circumstances, to fulfill the necessary strategic conditions for the mounting of the offensive. The fact that certain of the units earmarked for the attack had to be used beforehand was a necessary evil.

II. ESTIMATE OF THE ENEMY SITUATION

It may be left to the judgment of posterity whether it was the Allied supply situation, or the psychological effect of the West Wall, or the increasing resistance of the German troops on the western frontier, which produced the 'West Wall Miracle'. The fact remains that, against all expectations, the apparently overwhelming advance of the Allied tank armies was halted. During the frontier battles which now developed, it became clear that the enemy had two main centers of gravity: the wide Aachen sector (First U.S. Army) and the Lorraine area (Third U.S. Army). The more important of the two was the area of Aachen, which could be identified in November 44 as the Ninth U.S. Army sector; here it seemed that all the reserves at the disposal of the Allies had been almost magically assembled. The strategic objectives of the enemy were plain: in the north, a breakthrough across the Cologne–Düsseldorf line into the Ruhr; in the south, the conquest of the Saar. The loss of the two important industrial regions of western Germany would have a decisive influence on the course of the war. And from these two offensives, corresponding operations against the interior of the Reich were to be expected. Obviously, the Allies' estimate of German war potential and the German leadership was this: after the decisive defeat of our armies in the Battle of France and after the heavy defensive battles on the Eastern Front, a large-scale German offensive need no longer be expected. The Allies estimated that our available reserves were – at most – sufficient for only local counterattacks. The Allies saw this latter view apparently confirmed by the location of the area chosen for the reconstitution of the Sixth Pz Army. They took the risk of holding the 160-kilometer front between the Hürtgen Forest and the northern flank of Third Army, southeast of Luxembourg. Here they had only two or three divisions in the line and with an armored division thoroughly subdivided into little 'fire departments', located behind the line.[4] Moreover, these divisions were the exhausted Hürtgen Forest divisions, at that time being rehabilitated and brought up to strength. This soft spot in the enemy front and the apparent estimate of the situation made by the enemy were certainly the determining factors which induced the Supreme Command to mount the planned offensive.

From 22 Oct 44 on, Seventh Army was in control of the sector east of Stolberg as far as Nittle, south of Trier. Enemy dispositions in this sector led us to expect heavy attacks in the Hürtgen Forest sooner or later, attacks which would have a direct bearing on the enemy goal of a breakthrough across the Roer in the direction of Cologne and Düsseldorf. There were two other possible threats: a double envelopment across the Sauer and the Moselle, or, alternatively, a push from the sector of First U.S. Army against the southern flank of our Seventh Army. The greatest threat was undoubtedly to the right wing of Seventh Army, since the results of our reconnaissance indicated that the enemy's reserves were assembling in the Aachen–Liège area. For a while we were disturbed by the possibility that the 4 U.S. Armd Div and 6 U.S. Armd Div were still opposite our left wing. In this connection it is interesting to recall that the oblique maneuver of the above-mentioned 9 U.S. Armd Div was interpreted by Seventh Army as a northward displacement of 4 U.S. Armd Div or of 6 U.S. Armd Div. The American attempt to simulate the presence of 75 U.S. Inf Div in the area of Luxembourg must be regarded as a failure; from this area we received notice of the presence of nothing more than a fairly large number of tanks, and Seventh Army considered this report to be based on the location in Luxembourg of American tank workshops.

Seventh Army was dependent upon the Supreme Command for intelligence concerning the enemy's strategic reserves. This intelligence indicated that a limited number of such forces were located near Paris and Metz. It was also presumed that one or two new divisions were already on the way from the United States or England, and due consideration was given to the possibility that these fresh formations would eventually be committed at Aachen.

III. APPRECIATION OF THE TERRAIN

It was only natural that in our estimate of the enemy situation and in our suppositions regarding the enemy's estimate of our own position the very difficult terrain in the Eifel and in the Ardennes – especially in winter – should play an important role. Both of these mountainous and heavily wooded districts possess only limited networks of rather poor roads. The gradients and the numerous sharp curves and hairpin turns make motorized traffic difficult, especially in the presence of snow and ice. In addition, the majority of the wider and better roads on both sides of the frontiers between Germany and Luxembourg and Germany and Belgium run north and south, in a direction unfavorable for an offensive from either side. In the northern portion of the American 'undefended' sector there tower the heights of the Schnee-Eifel, partly in American, partly in German hands. Further south, the boundary between the fronts was formed first of all by the Our river, then by the Sauer, and finally by the Moselle. Even in peace time the comparatively narrow but high-banked Our forms a considerable barrier to traffic when the snows began to melt or when ice forms on it.

It is true, to be sure, that none of these obstacles impeded the progress of the German Army in its forward march of 1940, but it must be borne in mind that our attack took place in the month of May and that the German Army at the time was infinitely stronger than its opponent. Above all, in 1940 Germany enjoyed complete air supremacy, whereas in 1944 this lay, to a still greater degree, on the side of the Allies.[5]

So far as the terrain was concerned, the heavily wooded slopes of the Schnee-Eifel favored a German attack only with regard to concealment and camouflage. And this advantage was more or less offset by the Allies' possession of almost limitless facilities for air reconnaissance.

Preparations for the Offensive

I. THE FIRST INDICATIONS

Before Seventh Army learned of the plan for the Ardennes Offensive, the following signs indicated that the Supreme Command intended a completely new operation:

About the end of October 44, the Ia of the Operations Section of the Wehrmachtführungsstab, Obst i.G. Wilhelm Meyer-Detring, appeared at Seventh Army Headquarters at Camp Falke some six kilometers east of Münstereifel. He expressed the somewhat astonishing desire to look over the terrain of the Schnee-Eifel. In a short time he and the army chief of staff started by car to the LXVI Inf Corps and, on arrival at his destination, he went to an observation post on Calvary Mountain (immediately west of Prüm), where he was able to scan the surrounding landscape minutely.

Simultaneously, Seventh Army was ordered to reconnoiter positions for an army command post in the vicinity of Daun, and another near Wittlich, and to prepare them for occupation. This was not an easy task because most of the villages there were filled with refugees, conscripted labor, and supply installations. However, Army Group B was very insistent and declared itself in favor of the position previously reconnoitered, with Manderscheid as an alternate location. (This town later became the command post of Fifth Pz Army.) The southern command post was prepared on the outskirts of Wittlich.

At the beginning of November 44, the Commanding General of Seventh Army personally received from Field Marshal Model an order to designate on a map sketch a line which would offer the best defensive potentialities between Givet and Grevenmacher. The element of antitank defence was to be weighted heavily in the selection of this line. Further, he was to calculate the strength required for such a defense.

The Commanding General of Seventh Army, after careful consideration, proposed a line which would have its right wing leaning on the Meuse and the Semois; this line would also rest on hills and minor obstacles along the general line from Givet to Grevenmacher. The strength required, according to his calculations, would be six infantry divisions and from one to two panzer divisions.

The following divisions were withdrawn from the front:

At the end of Oct 44:   2 SS Pz Div, relieved by 18 Volks Gren Div.
Beginning of Nov 44:   2 Pz Div, relieved by 26 Volks Gren Div.
On 10 Nov 44:   36 Volks Gren Div, relieved by 212 Volks Gren Div.
On 15 Nov 44:   347 Inf Div, relieved by 272 Volks Gren Div.

Additional volks grenadier divisions, as well as several volks artillery corps, volks projector brigades, and other Army (Heeres) formations were announced as due to arrive. Rehabilitation and assembly areas were to be reconnoitered in the Eifel for all of these units.

II. THE FIRST BRIEFING AND THE FIRST PREPARATIONS

On 6 Nov 44, the chiefs of staff of Seventh Army, Sixth Pz Army (Gen Krämer), and Fifth Pz Army (Gen Gause), were called for a consultation with the Chief of Staff of Army Group B (Gen Krebs) at the headquarters of Army Group B, south of Krefeld. Here, after having been sworn to absolute secrecy, they were acquainted with the plan of the offensive. Gen Krebs handed each a message which read as follows:

'The German war potential enables us, by summoning all our powers of organization and by straining every nerve, to form an offensive force by rehabilitating and completely reconstituting the twelve panzer and panzer grenadier divisions at present employed on the Western Front, as well as some twenty volks grenadier divisions and two Fallschirmjäger divisions. With the aid of these forces, the last that Germany is able to collect, the Führer intends to mount a decisive offensive. Since such an operation would offer no prospect of a decisive success on the vast Eastern Front, and since a similar operation on the Italian Front could not be of decisive strategic significance, he has resolved to unleash his attack from the West Wall. The success of this operation will depend fundamentally upon the degree of surprise achieved. Therefore, the time and place for this offensive will be such as to completely deceive the enemy. Considering the situation, the terrain, and the weather, the enemy will be least likely to expect such an attack shortly before Christmas, from the Eifel, and against a front only thinly held by him. The objective of the offensive will be Antwerp, in order to rob the Allies of this very important supply port and to drive a wedge between the British and the American forces. After achieving the objective, we will anni-hilate the British and American forces then surrounded in the area of Aachen (Aix-la-Chapelle)–Liège–north of Brussels. In the air, the operation will be supported by several thousand of the best and most modern German fight-ers, which will secure – at least temporarily – supremacy in the air. The most important factors will be first – SURPRISE, and next – SPEED!'

Each chief of staff was thereupon handed a map, on which had been indicated the mission of his army, together with an estimate of the forces which would be available for the operation.

Each army received only the following information about the units on its flanks: the boundary lines, their zones of attack, and their missions. For example, Seventh Army learned only that at the beginning of the attack its right neighbor would be 26 Volks Gren Div, under Fifth Pz Army, north of the line Stolzemburg–Wiltz–St. Hubert–Givet.

On the basis of their instructions, the armies were to consider the missions assigned to each of them and to make the necessary preparations. In the meantime, only the commanding general of each army, his chief of staff, his Ia, and one other officer of the army staff were to be made aware of the secret.

The primary mission assigned to the army at this briefing was the protection of the south flank of strong German armored forces along the line Bastogne–Namur to Brussels–Antwerp. In order to defend this flank, the army would have to advance at least to the approximate line Givet–Libramont–Marte-lange–Mersch–Wasserbillig. For the accomplishment of this mission, it was proposed to assign to the army three corps staffs, six infantry divisions, one panzer-type division – presumably 25 Pz Gren Div – from two to three volks artillery corps, from one to two battalions of Army (Heeres) artillery, two volks projector brigades, from one to two artillery brigades (assault guns, self-pro-pelled), one engineer brigade, one Organization Todt brigade, and six bridge columns. Preparations for the offensive were to be completed by the end of November 44. The decision as to when the corps and division staffs, as well as the other members of the army staff, would be briefed was to be made in each case by Army Group Headquarters.

III. SECRECY PRECAUTIONS

From the very beginning, the following precautions were ordered:

a. The strategic concentration, and all preparations for it, were to be so arranged that they could be interpreted as the strengthening of German forces in the Eifel area to repel an Allied offensive on both sides of the Schnee-Eifel, an offensive which the Supreme Command had reason to suspect the Allies of planning.

b. Radio traffic was to continue without any changes whatever.

c. Reconnaissance patrols were not to be increased.

d. No reconnaissance beyond the former limits (especially by officers wearing panzer-type uniform or by members of new divisions) was to be permitted.

e. Seventh Army would continue to control the same sector as before, and would direct the movements of the new units arriving in the assembly areas, including those of the two new panzer armies.

These two panzer armies were to conceal themselves as completely as possible; later they received special names for the sake of secrecy.

f. All movements into the assembly area were to be carried out in darkness. During daylight there was to be no abnormal activity in this area. Special staffs and units were to be chosen to enforce this precaution.

g. The construction of rear area fortifications by public effort, was to continue as before. The gauleiters, even though they were defense commissioners of the Reich, and their assistants and subordinates, were to be kept as completely in the dark as the service command (Wehrkreis) staffs, the fortress engineer staffs, and the other home defense agencies.

h. The name of every single individual initiated into the plan of the offensive was to be entered on a special list. Each person whose name appeared thereon had to sign an oath to observe absolute secrecy about the project, on pain of the severest punishment.

i. All sketches, diagrams, maps, and written orders were to be registered, and a check was to be made daily to see that none were missing. Furthermore, these documents were to be under the surveillance – day and night – of one of the initiated officers.

j. Special precautions were to be taken to prevent any eavesdropping on staff conferences or map exercises.

k. An order was circulated, directing the withdrawal from the front line of Alsatians, Luxemburgers, Lorrainians, Belgians, and other undependable elements, in order to prevent any of these from going over to the enemy.

l. During the training period before the offensive, only the word 'counterattack' was to be used.

m. Each headquarters was to use a different code-name for the operation (for example, Seventh Army called it 'Winter Storm').

Further secrecy measures ordered for the strategic concentration will be mentioned later.

All of these precautions were adopted with the object of preserving completely the element of surprise. As an example of what might happen if the secret were betrayed, the initiated officers were reminded of the German Somme Offensive in 1918, when the enemy received advance warning from deserters. Naturally, the maintenance of such secrecy hampered preparations, for much information could not be written down, and no clerks or cartographers could be used. Therefore, all of the preliminary work had to be done by a small circle of initiates.

IV. INITIAL PLANNING

Under the conditions outlined, the Army began its preparations for the concentration and the operation. First of all, attack zones, immediate objectives, routes of advance, crossing sites, and reconnaissance and operational objectives were selected and submitted to the army group for approval. Because the Seventh Army was quite uncertain as to the size of the forces which the army group would allot to it for the operation, Seventh Army submitted only a very modest estimate of its requirements in troops and material:

    a. One panzer or panzer grenadier division, for commitment on the right flank of the attack.

    b. Six infantry divisions.

    c. From two to three volks artillery corps and the same number of volks projector brigades.

    d. From two to three artillery brigades (assault guns, self-propelled), or heavy tank destroyer battalions.

    e. At least four Army (Heeres) engineer or bridge construction battalions and from six to eight bridge columns, including one for the erection of a bridge for tanks.

    f. The Army also asked that several divisions be placed in reserve behind its left wing.

The army was promised:

    a. 25 Pz Gren Div, which, although still committed under Army Group G, was to be withdrawn and rested very soon.

    b. Four volks grenadier divisions in the assault line, and from two to three in reserve.

    c. Three volks artillery corps and one Army (Heeres) artillery battalion.

    d. Two volks projector brigades.

    e. Two artillery brigades (assault guns, self-propelled), and from one to two heavy tank destroyer battalions.

f. One engineer brigade [47th] comprising two battalions; one Organization Todt brigade, likewise of two battalions.

g. Six bridge columns, with 100 large rubber pontoons.

All the preparations now begun by the army were based on the above figures, which, in its opinion, represented the minimum forces required for the successful accomplishment of its mission.

The first outline of the army attack plan was as follows: Four volks grenadier divisions, controlled by two corps (LXXXV Inf Corps on the right; LXXX Inf Corps on the left) will attack abreast in the sector Vianden–Wallendorf–Echternach and smash through the enemy front, destroying him in the process.

a. Immediate objective of the right corps will be the ridge line and the road from Diekirch to Hosingen. This corps will take this objective before the end of the first day of attack, and it will continue to advance straight westward, committing – if necessary – its advance reserves in order to seize the crossings over the Clerf and Sauer. 25 Panzer Gren Div, initially in army reserve behind the right corps, will then – if possible during the night following the first day of the attack – be moved across the tank bridge set up in the meantime at Wallendorf. 25 Panzer Gren Div will next push straight ahead through Ettelbrück, Harlange and south of St. Hubert, in a westerly direction, in order to maintain contact with the left flank of Fifth Pz Army and to protect – by aggressive action – the southern attack flank in the sector Gedinne–Neufchâteau. At this time, the Staff of LIII Inf Corps will be placed in control of operations on the right wing. The divisions of LXXXV Inf Corps will then turn southwest from the Wiltz–Diekirch area, in order to go over to the defensive, en masse, along the approximate line Neufchâteau–Martelange–Mersch. This will be done so that tactical centers of gravity can be established in accordance with the enemy situation and the anticipated enemy movements along the roads leading north and northeast. Advance elements will push forward rapidly to the Semois sector to reconnoiter, to deny the crossing sites to the enemy, and to stop (or at least delay) the enemy advance.

b. The Seventh Army main effort, assigned to the right corps, will be completed by the attachment of two volks projector brigades, two volks artillery corps, one artillery brigade (assault guns, self-propelled) and one heavy tank destroyer battalion.

c. The left corps (LXXX Inf Corps) will attack with two volks grenadier divisions across the Sauer in the Wallendorf–Echternach sector and then, turning soon thereafter to the south and the south-west, will quickly seize the known enemy artillery area of Medernach–Christnach–Altrier. Then it will go over to mobile defense along the Wasserbillig–Mersch line, and send strong advance elements into the area north of Luxembourg.

When the plan was first drafted at the beginning of November 44, the left attack wing of Seventh Army was expected to extend only as far as Bollendorf.

This limitation would have permitted a more concentrated attack. Very soon, however, Hitler demanded that the attack front should extend as far as Echternach. He was under the impression that a German bridgehead still existed there, and that it could be used during the first stage of the offensive. The report announcing the withdrawal from this bridgehead apparently went astray on its way to Hitler, so that on the 'Führer Map' the bridgehead still appeared.

Another oft-repeated demand of the Supreme Command was that Seventh Army should push as far south as possible, so as to gain sufficient freedom of movement for a delaying action in the event of strong enemy attacks against the southern flank of the German offensive. This demand was not entirely consistent with the Supreme Command's basic concept: if the Americans follow their customary methods, it is likely that they will send their main forces to the Meuse rather than make any important assault on the flanks of the offensive. Hitler was firmly persuaded that the internal difficulties inherent in a combined Allied Command would delay the countermeasures and that the Allied leaders, dwelling too much on the factor of security, would initially concentrate on trying to halt the German offensive at the Meuse.

Seventh Army, in contrast to this, was firmly convinced that the German operation would evoke a speedy reaction from the enemy. Since it was highly probable that the Franco-Belgian area contained no large reserves, the possibility had to be considered that all available enemy troops in the area of Metz and perhaps also in the sector opposite Army Group G would be brought up for offensive action against the southern flank of the attacking German armies. And for that, the roads leading north through Luxembourg and Arlon would be considered first. Seventh Army estimated that strong enemy forces would arrive in the Arlon area north of Luxembourg not earlier than the fourth day of the attack. The fact that these forces would probably be commanded by General Patton made it quite likely that the enemy would direct a heavy punch against the deep flank of the German forces scheduled to be in the vicinity of Bastogne. In the Battle of France, Patton had given proof of his extraordinary skill in armored warfare, which he conducted according to the fundamental German conception.

On the basis of this concept of enemy action, the Commanding General of Seventh Army emphasized again and again during discussions with army group the need for placing sufficient forces at his disposal for the protection of the southern flank of the attacking forces, stressing that this was a prerequisite for the success of the operation. He emphasized above all the need for highly mobile units furnished with antitank weapons and heavy artillery, so that a flexible and active resistance could be offered to the enemy along the 100-kilometer front. Basing his supply estimates on the same concept, he strongly urged that a generous supply of ammunition be furnished, since the heavy defensive battles to be expected would consume much greater quantities of ammunition than would the mobile warfare of the two panzer armies. But his requests were answered with vague promises that a number of units would be placed behind the left wing of the attack by army group or High Command West (OB West). Consequently, these would be available for temporary use in the southern zone of the attack. The requests of Seventh Army for ample supplies of ammunition, as well as for adequate supplies of other equipment, unfortunately remained unheeded.

V. MAP EXERCISES AND CONFERENCES, PROBLEMS INVOLVED

With the consent of Army Group B, the commanding generals of the corps assigned to Seventh Army (LXXIV Inf Corps, LXVI Inf Corps, LXXX Inf Corps, and LXXXV Inf Corps) were briefed on 16 Nov 44. (I am not quite sure of the date, as I am writing entirely from memory.) LIII Inf Corps, later to be assigned to Seventh Army, had not yet come up. For the time being, no other members of corps staffs were to be told the secret, but Army Group B permitted us to inform the following additional members of our staff: Ic, Oberquartiermeister, Signal Officer, Artillery Officer, and Engineer Officer.

Although the concentration of the units earmarked for the offensive was by this time well under way, it became clear that the date first set for the start of the great attack – about the end of November – could not be reached.

a. Fifth Pz Army, which was to hand over control in the Aachen sector to Fifteenth Army, could not yet be freed owing to the heavy defensive fighting in the third Battle of Aachen still in progress. It was only in the second half of November that Fifth Pz Army (under the code-name, Feldjägerkommando z.b.V.) could be sent to Manderscheid. Sixth Pz Army (under the code-name, Auffrischungsstab 16) had already proceeded to Schlenderhan, near Quadrant; this name was designed to conceal from the enemy its presumable dimensions.

Seventh Army controlled the assembly of all units (except SS panzer-type units); it controlled their movement, billeting, supply, camouflage, etc.

Seventh Army furnished both panzer armies with all information culled from the enemy news services and gathered the results of reconnaissance for the sectors in which they were to attack.

On 29 Nov 44, map exercises were carried out at Seventh Army Headquarters with the Commanding Generals and Chiefs of Staff of the three corps assigned to the army for the offensive, in the presence of the Commanding General of the army group, Field Marshal Model, during which the execution of the first phase and the expected course of the attack in the first day were discussed. In this discussion, the following important points came up for consideration:

a. **Should the attack be started at night or in the daytime?**

The overwhelming majority of those taking part in the discussion expressed opposition to a night attack, justifying their view with the observation that the state of training of the troops was far below that required by the peculiarly arduous conditions of a night attack.

b. Should there be an artillery preparation or not?

On this question, opinions differed, as might have been expected in view of the different nature of the situation in the various sectors. Seventh Army was all for an attack *without* such a preparation, not only so that the element of surprise might be maintained, but also because the scarcity of worthwhile targets would result in a considerable wastage of valuable ammunition. Army Group B later permitted us to ignore the wish of the Supreme Command for an artillery preparation lasting half an hour, but insisted that measures taken by Seventh Army be uniform throughout the Army.

c. The first river crossings.

Carefully executed reconnaissance had shown that one bridge column would be required for each crossing of the Our (swollen by melting snows and jammed with ice packs), and two per crossing of the Sauer. One vehicular bridge and one or two footbridges would be required for each division, as well as a tank bridge, later to be utilized as the main supply bridge. Crossing sites on the two rivers were to be at Roth, Gentingen, Wallendorf, Bollendorf, and Echternach. The military bridges soon to be constructed over the streams would in the meantime be replaced by improvised bridges, so as to have the equipment available for the construction of bridges over the Sauer at Ettelbrueck and over the Clerf at Kautenbach, and for other crossings. Material for the erection of the improvised bridges was to be placed in readiness conveniently near the banks of the streams and carefully camouflaged, and only after the attack had begun was it to be moved to the river banks and set in place. The reconnaissance of fords was going on currently. The presence of bridging materials in the vicinity of the streams was to be explained by the argument that enemy air attacks were to be expected and that the material was destined for the repair of bridges damaged by expected enemy air attacks.

d. Destruction of the enemy's artillery.

All of the enemy gun positions in the army's attack zone had been precisely located by our artillery reconnaissance. It was presumed that many of the located positions were, in reality, alternate positions. Numerous army artillery batteries had been observed in the Altrier–Christnach area. It was to be feared that their highly-skilled gun crews, familiar as they were with the terrain, would wreak havoc on the bridge positions while our troops were moving across the Our and the Sauer. It would be important, therefore, to pin down these crews as much as possible at the beginning of the attack and then to force them to move to other positions to avoid counterbattery fire.

e. The creation of a manpower reserve.

The Supreme Command had already ordered the constitution of a 'Führer Reserve'; in addition, it was now ordered that companies should attack with a strength of only eighty men each, the remainder being transferred to the field reinforcement battalions.

At the beginning of December 44, after the division commanders had been briefed, map exercises were held at corps headquarters, at which time the questions of the leadership of the offensive, organization, support, camouflage, etc., were fully discussed.

The Commanding General of Seventh Army and his Chief of Staff were present at several conferences at Army Group Headquarters, at which the progress of the preparations was reported and necessary alterations in the plan for the strategic concentration were announced.

VI. THE INFLUENCE OF OTHER FRONTS

As a result of the situation in the area of Aachen and in Alsace-Lorraine, several divisions could not be withdrawn from combat for rehabilitation and reconstitution, as planned. On the contrary, the situation was such that a number of divisions already withdrawn for the reception of reinforcements had to be recommitted. 116 Pz Div, for example, had to remain in the line in the Hürtgen Forest during almost the whole of November 44; 272 Volks Gren Div, 3 FJ Div, and 47 Volks Gren Div – against all expectations – had to be temporarily committed in an emergency. All these divisions, particularly 47 Volks Gren Div, suffered heavy losses in the fighting.

Pz Lehr Div was now placed at the disposal of Army Group G to lead a counterattack in the area of Zabern.

Seventh Army was particularly affected by these alterations in the original plan, for 25 Pz Gren Div could not be released by Army Group G to participate in the offensive. As a substitute, 5 FJ Div, recently completely reconstituted from Luftwaffe personnel, was assigned to Seventh Army. In training and in the quality of its officers – both junior and senior – this division displayed notable deficiencies. But as it was an especially large division, with a comparatively high number of weapons, including an assault gun battalion, there was nothing else to do but to assign this division the main effort, i.e., the thrust on the right flank of the army.

At this time, only three more volks grenadier divisions were expected to be made available to Seventh Army, although – to be sure – two more were to be brought up later as High Command West reserves. All other supporting arms were sharply reduced as well, so that, in comparison with the strength originally promised, Seventh Army had been considerably weakened.

Strategic Concentration for the Offensive

I. GENERAL FEATURES OF THE CONCENTRATION

The main body of the units which would launch the offensive arrived in, or began moving to, the assembly area during November 44. Individual divisions (for example, 212, 272, 277, 18, and 26 Volks Gren Divs) were committed to replace the panzer divisions slated for reorganization, and the West Wall divisions previously committed but now to be reorganized. The other divisions were assembled in the areas selected by Seventh Army. These areas had been so chosen as to place each division immediately to the rear of its attack zone. Volks grenadier divisions were located nearer the line of departure and motorized divisions further to the rear. The entire area bounded by the West Wall, the Moselle, and the Rhine was now jammed with troops. Despite the excellent concealment afforded by the terrain in the Eifel, the strict regulation of all traffic along the roads, and the deceptive measures already mentioned, it seemed scarcely possible that all of this movement could remain hidden from the vigilant eyes of enemy reconnaissance and observation. However, to conceal every move still more, all supplies for the offensive (ammunition, POL, food etc.) were brought up during the hours of darkness (even moonlight being avoided) and placed as far forward as possible. Since the railroads could bring the main part of these supplies only as far as the Rhine, motor transport had to finish the job. Unfortunately, the roads in this area were filled with sharp curves and hairpin turns, and there was almost a continuous succession of steep hills. Furthermore, the local citizens – in a fervor of enthusiasm – had, under the leadership and supervision of the gauleiters, innocently set up road blocks at the entrance and exit to every small village, along the paths of likely enemy approach. Even worse, owing to some mistake by the political functionaries, these road blocks were often so narrow that our heavy tanks (Mark V and Mark VI) simply could not pass through them. It was only with the greatest effort that the gauleiters of Cologne and Trier, as Defense Commissioners of the Reich, could be induced to have these bottlenecks widened or removed.

To be sure, *rumors* did circulate among the population and in Party circles to the effect that an offensive was being prepared; this was to be expected because the magnitude of the troop movements could not be completely concealed from the population. The marvel is therefore all the greater that we finally *did* achieve a tactical surprise!

As of 1 Dec 44, the Supreme Command had ordered that all reconnaissance of the attack zones was to cease, in order to prevent anyone from being taken prisoner or from deserting to the enemy. At the beginning of December 44, the SS panzer-type units of Sixth Pz Army arrived in their assembly area of Cologne–Bonn–Münstereifel–Düren–Bergheim; and, simultaneously, the divisions previously committed in the Fifteenth Army area (12 Volks Gren Div, 3 FJ Div, and 47 Volks Gren Div) began to arrive in the area of Zülpich-Gemünd–Schleiden. The Oberquartiermeister section of Sixth Pz Army was transferred to Seventh Army with the mission of supplying the assault units. On 10 Dec 44, Fifth and Sixth Pz armies finally took over control in their attack zones. Simultaneously, Seventh Army Headquarters moved from Camp Falke, 6 kilometers east of Münstereifel, while Sixth Pz Army was arriving at Wittlich.

Seventh Army's extreme right wing, the Hürtgen Forest Front from Düren to Lammersdorf, was turned over to Fifteenth Army.

II. THE STRATEGIC CONCENTRATION OF SEVENTH ARMY

Seventh Army's strategic concentration was greatly simplified by the inavailability of many of the units earmarked for the offensive. After 352 Volks Gren Div (Commander: Obst, later Genmaj, Schmidt) had released 353 Inf Div on the right wing of LXXX Inf Corps for commitment in the Hürtgen Forest, two assault divisions (352 Volks Gren Div and 212 Volks Gren Div) were in the front line. All they had to do, therefore, was to link up later on in their attack zones. 276 Volks Gren Div (Commander: Gen Möhring), which was intended for later use on the right assault flank of LXXX Inf Corps, had already been moved to the area southeast of Wittlich on both sides of the Moselle. 5 FJ Div (Commander: Obst, later Genmaj, Heilmann), which was to replace 25 Pz Gren Div, arrived about the beginning of December 44 in the area east and southeast of Bitburg. Other units which had arrived were the two volks artillery corps, one Army (Heeres) artillery battalion (120 mm), one volks projector brigade, and one incomplete bridge column (to be used only for unit assemblage of equipment). Still missing were one projector brigade, the engineer brigade, the Organization Todt brigade, and all the other bridge columns. The self-propelled assault gun companies at first assigned had been cancelled again.

Most of the supplies had been collected in various dumps, with the notable exception of all engineer and ferrying equipment. Stock piling of supplies immediately behind the line of departure was not to be accomplished until about four to six days before the start of the attack. In this regard, it was forbidden to move supplies by truck nearer than ten kilometers to the front, so that the enemy would not become aware of the increased motor traffic during the hours of darkness. For this reason, all supplies had to be transferred at the edge of this limit to horse transport, or else be manhandled further by bearer columns (as, for example, ammunition to the firing positions). Seventh Army had set up listening posts in the forward line, whose duty it was to exercise surveillance and report any excessive noise from our truck motors. Thanks to the results collected by these listening posts, it was found possible to draw in the perimeter of this forbidden area to five kilometers.

By the end of November 44, Seventh Army had issued attacks orders to the corps:

Attack Order

Seventh Army will cross the Our and Sauer rivers on X-Day, smash its way through the enemy front in the Vianden–Echternach sector and, with its strong right wing, will defend the south flank of Fifth Pz Army by advancing to the Gedinne–Libramont–Martelange–Mersch–Wasserbillig line. The Seventh

Army mission will then change to one of mobile defense. Advance elements will proceed as far as the Semois sector and the area north of Luxembourg, in order to reconnoiter, to deny the main roads and river crossings, and to delay the advance of the enemy forces toward the blocking line. Therefore:

a. At 0530 hours on X-Day, LXXXV Inf Corps (with 5 FJ Div on the right and 352 Volks Gren Div on the left) will cross the Our and breach the enemy front in the sector Vianden–Wallendorf (exclusive). It will drive west and turn south to the Gedinne–Libramont–Martelange–Mersch line, where it will – en masse – go over to the defensive. By the use of mobile advance elements, it will maintain contact with the south flank of Fifth Panzer Army, which will be driving through Bastogne on the north. LXXXV Inf Corps will continue its advance beyond the blocking line as far as the Semois sector, where the main crossings will be denied to the enemy.

b. LXXX Inf Corps (with 276 Volks Gren Div on the right and 212 Volks Gren Div on the left) will jump off at 0530 hrs on X-Day and cross the Sauer, smash its way through the enemy front in the Wallendorf–Echternach sector. LXXX Inf Corps will drive forward to the Mersch–Wasserbillig line and then will – en masse – go over to the defensive. LXXX Inf Corps will advance mobile elements as far forward as Luxembourg, with the same mission as the corresponding elements of LXXXV Inf Corps, except that LXXX Inf Corps will delay the enemy advance to the *north* or *northeast* through Luxembourg. Thus, the enemy artillery area of Medernach–Christnach–Altrier will be reached as quickly as possible. In order to deceive the enemy, assault detachments will cross the river south of Echternach as well.

c. LIII Inf Corps will be initially in army reserve. It will be prepared to take command (during the course of the operation) of either the right wing or the center of the Seventh Army zone.

d. Boundary Lines:

Between Fifth Pz Army and Seventh Army:

Kyllburg (Fifth)–Neuerburg (Fifth)–Stolzemburg (Fifth)–Wiltz (Seventh)–Bastogne (Fifth)–St. Hubert (Seventh)–Gedinne (Seventh).

Between LXXXV and LXXX Inf Corps:

Speicher (LXXX)–Kruchten (LXXXV)–Wallendorf (LXXX)–Ermsdorf (LXXX)–Mersch (LXXX).

Between Seventh Army and First Army:

Nittel (Seventh)–Luxembourg (First).

LXXXV Inf Corps and LXXX Inf Corps had issued their attack orders to their divisions at the beginning of December. Simultaneously, the division commanders and their chiefs of staff had been initiated into the plan, as with the other initiates, under the injunction of strictest secrecy.

Since their arrival in the assembly area, divisions had undergone an active training program, with emphasis on remedying – by mid-December 44 – the serious inadequacies of unit training and of combined-arms training. Special attention was given to river crossings; practice crossings were made on the Saar, the Kyll, the Prüm. These practice sessions were explained to the troops and the local population as being preparation for counterattacks in the event of an enemy breakthrough in the Eifel.

X-Day was designated by a very special enciphered message four days in advance. Therefore, movement into the forward assembly areas was to be completed during the first two nights of the last four days preceding the attack, and only in the night before the actual attack were the jump-off positions to be occupied. Since on 9 Dec 44, 12 Dec 44 was finally set as the great date, it follows that the two subsequent nights were to be those for the final assembly. All these movements had been thoroughly scrutinized and checked in every minute detail. One of the greatest difficulties was that of avoiding, at all costs, any collision of one unit with another, for 2 Pz Div and Pz Lehr Div had to march from the rear assembly area, across the Seventh Army rear, to the forward assembly area. Withdrawal of the divisions scheduled for reconstitution and their assembly after reorganization in the proper attack zones had been very thoroughly planned. These movements were facilitated by prior reconnaissance executed by special detachments, and by the issuance of detailed instructions. Another particular difficulty was the movement of guns and mortars into their firing positions. Since no motor vehicle could move closer than five kilometers to the front, all guns had to be manhandled or towed by horse power for this distance.

Once emplaced, guns were camouflaged as thoroughly as possible. The wheels of the guns and motor vehicles had previously been wrapped with straw and rags, so as to diminish incidental noise; to a certain extent, 'noise-camouflage' was secured each night by having planes fly low above the moving vehicles to drown the sound of their motors. In order to foil the enemy air reconnaissance, guns were dug in to the maximum extent possible. Tanks were well concealed by the construction of deep, well-camouflaged emplacements.

No artillery registration was permitted. Firing data, therefore, had to be obtained by calculation or by liaison with the batteries of the divisions which had been occupying the position.

Seventh Army was obliged to transfer a considerable part of its relatively ample transport facilities to the newly constituted Sixth Pz Army, so that we now had only the minimum necessary for our supply requirements. Therefore, the motor transport of the volks artillery corps and volks projector brigades had to be fully utilized in the movement to the forward assembly area.

Seventh Army's left wing, behind which one regiment of 212 Volks Gren Div had been placed as security against a threat emanating from the Orscholz switch line, was to be uncovered recklessly, so as to enable 212 Volks Gren Div to be held ready as closely integrated as possible in its attack zone of

Bollendorf–Echternach. Therefore, the entire front between Wintersdorf and Nittel was defended only by 999 Penal Bn, one fortress machine gun battalion, and six immobile guns.[6] As a reserve south of Trier stood the Seventh Army Service School (strength, one weak battalion). Even this minor reorganization was permitted only during the last night or two.

On 12 Dec 44, the engineer brigade finally arrived. It consisted of two battalions, which had been trained only in obstacle construction and had no training in military bridge construction. The arrival of the Organization Todt brigade and of the bridge columns was delayed by the difficult transportation situation on the west side of the Rhine. Seventh Army tried to move them up with the motor transport of the volks artillery corps, but by 17 Dec 44 had succeeded in bringing up only one more column, conveyed irregularly in single vehicles as available.

Since X-Day (originally 12 Dec 44) was postponed from day to day because of the weather conditions, Seventh Army still hoped that sufficient stream-crossing material would be brought up. When, on 14 Dec 44, the attack was finally set for 16 Dec 44, Seventh Army protested vehemently to Army Group B that the shortage of engineer equipment stream-crossing material would seriously threaten the accomplishment of the Army's mission.

On 11 and 12 Dec 44 all Army, corps, and division commanders of the units to participate in the offensive were summoned to the Staff Headquarters of High Command West, at Ziegenberg near Bad Nauheim, where Adolf Hitler impressed on them the vital importance of the offensive. On this occasion, the Commanding General of Seventh Army seized the opportunity to express Seventh Army's viewpoint to Genobst Jodl, and emphasize its fears that the lack of engineer equipment and troops would jeopardize the attainment of its mission. Genobst Jodl promised further assistance, just as Army Group B had done. But, actually, on the day the attack began the catastrophic nature of Seventh Army's engineer situation had not been remedied one iota. The Organization Todt brigade did not come up until 17 or 18 Dec 44, and one or two additional bridge columns arrived only shortly before Christmas.

Antiaircraft defense in the army was provided by a flak brigade (two regiments) of III Flak Corps (Commanding General: Gen Pickert). During the concentration, most of the antiaircraft guns were placed forward, at the Moselle and Kyll bridges, as protection for the troops and equipment moving through these defiles; but, at the beginning of the offensive their center of gravity was shifted to the right wing so that they could protect the highly important Our and Sauer crossing sites and, incidentally, their own assembly and artillery area. At the main crossings were placed batteries which could instantly move to the western bank when required. Single batteries were attached to the elements. 5 FJ Div had its own integral flak battalion; the volks grenadier divisions each had one battery (20 mm and 37 mm). Single batteries (20 mm and 37 mm) were placed along the routes of advance and main supply routes to defend the open stretches and the defiles. (The above details have been checked and confirmed by Gen Pickert, Commanding General of III Flak Corps. Allendorf, June 46.)

Although Army Group B had directed that *a very brief artillery preparation* be made simultaneously along the entire army front, Seventh Army left this matter to the discretion of the various corps, since conditions in each zone would depend upon the width of the river and the distance between the enemy positions and the line of departure. Seventh Army ordered that any artillery preparation and all fire support be directed only against known targets (such as pockets of resistance, bivouac areas, etc.), with the main concentration to be on located enemy batteries. The most advanced assault groups were to take advantage of this preparation to work their way through No Man's Land and across the first streams. But an order from higher headquarters forbade them to pass the most forward line of combat outposts before 0530 hrs.

As favorable results had been obtained from experiments in the use of searchlights to illuminate enemy territory, several searchlight batteries were assembled, mainly on the high plateau of Ferschweiler, with the object of blinding the enemy and lighting up the targets when the preparation began. About fifty heavy searchlights were available for this purpose.

Because of the postponement of X-Day (originally 12 Dec 44) to await a period of bad flying weather, all movement into the forward assembly area was halted. To be sure, most of the preparations had already been completed, e.g., the emplacement of guns and mortars, the bringing forward of the improvised bridge material, the insertion of staffs for the relief of units in the forward line, etc. This delay entailed a certain danger of betraying the project. Nevertheless the careful scrutiny from the air of our positions by the enemy revealed nothing to him of significance, so that we could still count on achieving surprise. The troops themselves were told of the offensive only one day in advance.

With the exception of the severe difficulties in the assembly of engineer troops and equipment, all preparations for the attack had been carried out according to plan with comparative smoothness. In the night of 15/16 Dec 44, our forces were disposed as follows:

a.   On the right, **LXXXV Inf Corps:**
     Gen Inf Kniess
     C of S: Obst i.G. Lassen
     CP: Burg
(1) With, on its right: **5 FJ Div**
     Sector: Vianden – east of Bettel
     Cmdr: Gen Heilmann
     Ia: Maj Passlik

CP: a bunker north of Roth

Composition: 13, 14, and 15 FJ Inf Regts

              assault gun bn (about 20 SP assault guns) [11 StuG Brig.]

              one flak bn

              one mortar bn

              one arty regt (two bns: one mobile, one immobile)

              one engr bn

              one AT bn

              three reinforcement bns

Total strength: about 20,000 men

(2) And, on its left: **352 Volks Gren Div**

Sector: Gentingen – Wallendorf (exclusive)

Cmdr: Obst Schmidt until 25 Dec 44, then Genmaj Batzing

Ia: Maj i.G. Schneider

CP: Hüttingen

Composition: as for other volks grenadier divisions, incl one battery of 6

              SP assault guns*

(3) And, as **corps troops:**

one volks arty corps (five bns)

one volks proj brig

one obsn bn

b.   On the left, **LXXX Inf Corps:**

Gen Inf Dr. Beyer

C of S: Obst i.G. Goestlin

CP: Wolsfelder Burg

(1) With, on its right: **276 Volks Gren Div**

Sector: Wallendorf – Bollendorf (both inclusive)

Cmdr: Genmaj Möhring, KIA 18 Dec 44, then Obst Dempwolff

Ia: Maj i.G. Wittmann

CP: Schankweiler

Composition: as for other volks grenadier divisions, except no battery of

              SP assault guns, until one arrived at the end of the month.

(2) And, as **corps troops:**

one volks arty corps (five bns)

one arty bn (120 mm)

one volks proj brig

c.   Under army control:

LIII Inf Corps HQ, located at Föhren.

one engr brig, controlled at the crossing sites by the Army Engr Off

one flak brig, especially instructed in cooperation

---

* Jagdpanzer 38t 'Hetzer'.

d.   Simultaneously arriving in the army rear area:
(1) In High Command West reserve: **9 Volks Gren Div**
     Assembly area: vicinity of Wittlich
     Cmdr: Genmaj Kolb
     Ia: Obstlt i.G. ?
     Composition: as for other volks genadier divisions, incl one battery of 11
                   SP assault guns
(2) In High Command Wehrmacht reserve: **79 Volks Gren Div**
     Assembly area: northwest of Wittlich
     Cmdr: Obst Weber until 30 Dec 44, then Obst Hummel
     Ia: Obstlt i.G. Henneberg
     Composition: as for other volks grenadier divisions, incl one battery of 11
                   SP assault guns
(3) In High Command Wehrmacht reserve: **Führer Gren Brig**
     Assembly area: vicinity of Bitburg
     Cmdr: Obst Kahler until 25 Dec 44, then Obst Kühn, until 27 Dec 44,
            then Obst Meder
     Composition: one pz gren bn, incl one hv armd car co
                   one bicycle bn
                   one rcn bn
                   one pz bn (25 Mk IVs & Vs)
                   one battery of 20 SP assault guns
                   one engr bn
                   one reinforcement bn
(4) Later, one artillery battalion of a volks artillery corps moved up.

Thus, the total strength of the army at the beginning of the attack (exclusive
of the strategic reserves of the higher commands) was:
    24 inf bns
     6 engr bns
    30 self-propelled assault guns (approx)
    25 arty bns (319 guns)
     2 proj brigs (108 projs)
     2 obsn bns
     6 flak bns
     6 field reinforcement bns
On 15 Dec 44 Seventh Army was advised that X-Day would be 16 Dec 44.
Therefore, the operations section of the army staff moved during the night of
15/16 Dec 44 to the forward command post at Dockendorf. The main command post simultaneously moved to Eisenschmidt.

The Offensive

The First Two Days

I. 16 DEC 44

At 0530 hrs on 16 Dec 44, Seventh Army started its part of the attack, according to plan. The form of artillery support differed between the two attacking corps. In the case of LXXXV Inf Corps a ten-minute artillery preparation was laid down, under cover of which the assault companies stole forward as far as the combat outposts – in certain instances, beyond these as far as the point where they would be just out of range of stray shells emanating from the enemy's most advanced artillery positions – and began the task of crossing the streams. The fire plan foresaw a gradually increasing intensity of fire, directed so that it would reach its highest concentration of ferocity shortly before the breakthrough of the enemy's strongpoints. It was provided that known enemy artillery positions, presumably manned, receive the main concentration, along with his assembly areas.

On the other hand, LXXX Inf Corps, whose assault waves had a much greater distance to go before reaching their point of breakthrough, dispensed with any artillery preparation so as not to alert the enemy. Its spearhead troops jumped off from their line of departure and silently crossed the Sauer under cover of darkness. It was only when they had achieved a breakthrough that their artillery support would come into play, at which time its targets would be the same as in the other corps. For dealing with the enemy batteries further ahead in the area of Altrier, a 120 mm artillery battalion had been subordinated to LXXX Inf Corps.

Seventh Army was of the opinion – an opinion later confirmed – that, with so few worthwhile targets present, the effect of the artillery fire would be very dubious, especially since the accuracy of our guns had been diminished by digging them in to ground level and by camouflaging them.

Insofar as it had been possible to use them near the front, the guns of the infantry regiments, the guns of the flak battalions, impressed with the necessity for full collaboration, and also the heavy infantry weapons had been included in the fire plan.

The searchlights proved of great assistance, making the enemy area as bright as day and blinding his gun crews while our own troops remained shrouded in darkness. This eased the task of the attacking infantry.

Each of the divisions attacking had formed two attack groups which sent their best shock companies against the enemy resistance nests to their front. These companies were supported by detachments carrying bridge-building equipment. Such shock companies were used along the entire attack front of Seventh Army:

    a. In the sector of 5 FJ Div, east of Vianden by 14 FJ Inf Regt, and at
       Roth by 13 FJ Inf Regt.
    b. In the sector of 352 Volks Gren Div, at Gentingen by 915 Inf Regt,
       and at Ammeldingen by 916 Inf Regt.
    c. In the sector of 276 Volks Gren Div, south-east of Wallendorf by 986
       Inf Regt, and at Bollendorf by 987 Inf Regt.
    d. In the sector of 212 Volks Gren Div, at Weiterbach by 423 Inf Regt,
       and east of Echternach by 320 Inf Regt.

In the main, the jump-off of the attacking spearheads began smoothly and according to plan, with scarcely any losses. The element of surprise seemed to have been completely achieved along the entire front. The degree of resistance which the advancing attack groups met on the western bank of the river varied for the different groups. The weakest defense was encountered by the right wing of 5 FJ Div, which succeeded in taking Vianden and after a short battle fought around single strongpoints – mainly in the vicinity of Vianden Castle – and in establishing a bridgehead some two to three kilometers in depth west of Roth. This offered sufficient protection to start bridging the stream at once. And this was where the first snags appeared. The conveyance of the building material proved to be a lengthy affair as a result of the bad roads, the steep grades, and the hairpin turns on the way.

Through a local failure of the lower echelons and the unsatisfactory way in which the boundary had been drawn between 5 FJ Div and 352 Volks Gren Div, the initial surprise was not properly exploited to take the enemy strongpoint at Föhren. Heavy mortar fire skilfully directed from an excellent observation post, was emerging from this point against the bridge position at Roth. The erection of the bridge by the poorly trained bridge columns took a long time; only on 17 Dec 44 was the bridge complete – after the enemy strongpoint at Fouhren had been taken by 15 FJ Inf Regt in coordination with elements of the 352 Volks Gren Div.

The attack group on the right, 14 FJ Inf Regt, was able to sweep through Vianden and take considerable territory. On the afternoon of 16 Dec 44, it attained its immediate objective, the ridge line and road Diekirch–Hosingen– vicinity of Hoscheid. To the rear, local battles took place against American groups fighting valiantly in the area of Putscheid and Weiler. The bringing up of the reserve regiments (15 FJ Inf Regt) whose task it was to mop up these resistance nests, was in progress.

352 Volks Gren Div, likewise exploiting skilfully the element of surprise, had considerable success. The attack group on the right, 915 Inf Regt, moving forward energetically against an enemy stoutly defending himself in well-fortified positions, had attained by the afternoon of the first day the heights around Bastendorf and Longsdorf, its initial objectives. Here, too, enemy

groups were resisting, and these were attacked by 914 Inf Regt, which had been brought up for that purpose. For the moment, these two places remained in the hands of the enemy. The Army had ordered that in general such nests of resistance were to be by-passed and left to be disposed of by the reserves coming up later.

The attack group on the left (916 Inf Regt) had encountered very stubborn resistance on the heights west and northwest of Wallendorf, where it became involved in very bloody fighting in its attempt to free the division's left flank, north of the Sauer.

During the day of 16 Dec 44, enemy resistance on the right wing of the division notably stiffened, so that before the advance elements could push on to the Sauer sector of Michelau–Ettelbrück they had to be reformed again. In the building of the bridges over the river in the division zone even more trouble was met than had been encountered by 5 FJ Div. Here also the enemy was accurately placing his mortar shells with the assistance of excellent observation posts on the heights, and the task of erecting the bridges was made more difficult by the fast current of the stream and the softness of the river bottom. At this point, we lost a good deal of construction material and suffered many casualties.

Along the entire front of LXXX Inf Corps, enemy resistance was notably stronger, more concentrated, and tougher, despite the achievement of surprise. The elements of 4 U.S. Inf Div employed here defended themselves in skilfully constructed strongpoints which utilized the favorable configuration of the terrain to great advantage. These American troops made a much more formidable impression on us than did those in the sector of 28 U.S. Inf Div. Furthermore, American artillery in the Medernach–Altrier sector, which we had known to be very strong, lent very efficient support to the defenders after midday of 16 Dec 44, and very greatly hindered the work of erecting the bridges, not only on the left wing but in the entire sector of the corps.

The 276 Volks Gren Div, even as early as the moment when the infantry was to cross the river, encountered unexpectedly serious resistance, mainly from machine guns and mortars emplaced on the heights west of Wallendorf, in the triangle of the Our and Sauer rivers. As a result of this hammering at its right flank, the division was unable to attain its initial objective. But while the right wing of the right attack group was thus halted, the left wing was able to take Bigelbach by the evening of 16 Dec 44. The attack group on the left, by taking possession of the heights on the western bank of the river, southwest of Dillingen, and by pushing into the valley of the Schwarzen Ernz, was able to build a small bridgehead across the Sauer. The third regiment of 276 Volks Gren Div was still moving to the assembly area during the night prior to the attack, so that it was not available for the first day of the offensive. It may have been this, as well as the unexpectedly large number of enemy strongpoints encountered, that split the division and diminished its weight and penetrating power. In this case, the inadequate training of the newly constituted division made itself painfully felt.

212 Volks Gren Div, aided by surprise, had attacked energetically and quickly crossed the river. However, the relatively strong enemy forces occupying Echternach, the difficult nature of the terrain, and – later on – heavy American artillery fire, made their mission an arduous one.

Despite these drawbacks, the well-trained and well-led troops on the right flank (423 Inf Regt) managed to seize the heights above Berdorf and to penetrate into the village itself. Here, heavy and bitter fighting developed, but our troops succeeded in holding the place even though the enemy made a heavy counter-attack with tank support, an attack which we succeeded in defeating with only close range antitank weapons (panzerfausts, rocket-launchers, etc.), knocking out a number of enemy tanks in the process.

The left attack group (320 Inf Regt) succeeded in pressing forward on both sides of Echternach. They reached as far as Roudenhaff, two kilometers further south, to the southern fringe of the wood north of Dickweiler and the heights just west and south of Girsterklaus. Inside this bridgehead, enemy strongpoints were still holding out, principally at Birkelt and Echternach; the fire from here, directed by artillery observers against the Sauer crossings, had a very damaging effect. Due to these enemy actions and the aforementioned lack of engineer strength and material, not a single bridge had been completed at the end of the first day.

The third regiment of the division (316 Inf Regt) had been placed in Seventh Army reserve, so that neither the division nor the corps had any control over its employment.

On the evening of 16 Dec 44, Seventh Army was satisfied with the tactical successes achieved. If it was true that the goals reached – above all in the center and on the left wing of the army – were not all that had been planned and expected, it was also true that the penetration of the enemy front, especially on the strategically important right wing of the army, had succeeded. Our estimate of the enemy had been fully confirmed. Seventh Army had always expected that enemy resistance would be strengthened by early commitment of his rearward reserves. It was now a matter of making the breakthrough a thorough one before the enemy had a chance to bring up stronger reserves, and, with our main effort definitely on the right wing of the army, of winning more ground to the West. If – by chance – the left wing of the army should not make such good progress as we hoped, this would not be terribly serious, so long as it 'fixed' enemy forces by drawing them into combat with itself, if possible.

It was of decisive importance for the continuation of the battle plan, however, that the artillery, the heavy weapons, and the assault guns of the divisions should be transported to the western bank of the river in order to support adequately the further offensive advance. But the bridge situation was nothing less than catastrophic! In previous calculations, the Army had assumed that it would be possible to erect one 24-ton bridge in each division zone by the night of 16/17 Dec 44 at the latest. But on the basis of the reports received such construction seemed to be decidedly uncertain on the right wing, and impossible in the center and on the left wing. The Army did what it could, so far as material assistance was concerned, without being able to overcome this disadvantage. Its worst fears had been realized. On learning, during the evening of 16 Dec 44, that one Our bridge had been completed at Gemünd on the southern flank of Fifth Pz Army, Seventh Army sought to utilize this for the conveyance across the stream of the assault guns and motorized artillery of 5 FJ Div. Unfortunately, the bridge in question was so heavily occupied by the tanks of Fifth Pz Army that our request was rejected.[7]

However, notwithstanding the difficulty in the matter of bridges, Seventh Army ordered the attack to be pressed on 17 Dec 44 with all available means. LXXXV Inf Corps was ordered to advance across the Clerf and the Sauer and, above all, to seize the crossings at Kautenbach and Ettelbrück. LXXX Inf Corps was ordered to continue its efforts to attain its initial objective, i.e., the enemy artillery position areas. The resistance nests still in existence were to be bypassed and left to the attention of the reserve regiments.

II. 17 DEC 44

These intentions were realized on 17 Dec 44 only on the right wing, where 14 FJ Inf Regt of 5 FJ Div succeeded by quick, sharp attack in seizing the Clerf crossing at Kautenbach and thus opening the way for the further progress of the division through Wiltz to the west. By this action, the primary mission of Seventh Army, protection of the southern flank of Fifth Pz Army and the maintenance of contact with it, was fulfilled.

As a result of the Bridge situation, only during the night of 17 Dec 44 were the advance reserves of 5 FJ Div able to cross the Our in order to push further west out of the Kautenbach bridgehead. The regiments of 5 FJ Div were still mopping-up between the Our and the Clerf, principally in the area of Holzthum and Consthum and along the length of the road from Putscheid to Hoscheid. But the rest of the div now assembled. Artillery was still completely lacking, as were antiaircraft guns, for the bridge of Roth was finished only in the afternoon of 17 Dec 44. It had proved feasible to get single assault guns over the top of a weir near Vianden, but with very great difficulty. It was impossible to ford the Our because of its swollen state at the time. However, the lack of artillery and heavy weapons was not such a serious drawback in this zone, as the enemy was no longer putting up any concentrated resistance.

It was obvious that the German attack on both sides of the boundary between Fifth Pz Army and Seventh Army had struck upon a particularly weak spot, for the southern wing of the neighbor unit on the right had also made good progress and was now, after the capture of the Clerf sector and Drauffelt, fighting abreast of the spearheads of 5 FJ Div. On the other hand, the complete lack of artillery support had a disastrous influence on the situation along the remainder of the army front, so that, except in the 5 FJ Div zone, only minor local successes were achieved.

It is true that 352 Volks Gren Div had finally been able, with the assistance of the newly committed 914 Inf Regt, to take Longsdorf, after it had held out for some time. However, 352 Volks Gren Div made no further progress worthy of mention either in the sector of Bastendorf or in the sector northwest of Wallendorf. Nor did the attempt of the two attack groups to gain contact with each other through the insertion of 914 Inf Regt meet with success. The toughening resistance of the enemy made it clear that he was committing all reserves available locally (engineer troops were now appearing on his side), throwing them into the defensive battle, and fighting desperately to keep open his Sauer bridgeheads at Ettelbrück and Diekirch. And the increasing casualties on our side showed plainly that this tough resistance of the Americans was not to be broken without the aid of artillery and assault guns. As it was expected that the miliary bridge at Gentingen would be ready for traffic by 17 Dec 44, it was hoped that we would be able to get the artillery pieces and heavy weapons of the 352 Volks Gren Division over to the other side in the night of 17/18 Dec 44. But the roads down to the river and up the other side proved to be so steep (some were curved as well), and so slippery because of the weather, that the transfer to the other bank of the river proved to be a slow and wearisome task. The Organization Todt brigade whose assistance had been promised had not yet turned up.

On the right wing of LXXX Inf Corps, 276 Volks Gren Div's right assault group was able to make some local progress and to take the wood north of Beaufort. Nevertheless, the resistance on the right flank, where the enemy was obstinately resisting in the Our–Sauer triangle, could not be crushed. In the direction of Waldbillig, the attack was brought to a halt through a lack of adequate support.

The difficulties of the river crossing were especially great in the case of the 276th Division. The attempts to erect a military bridge at Wallendorf were defeated by the artillery fire of the enemy, with heavy material and personnel losses on our side.

After this fiasco, all of the undamaged bridging equipment and the newly arriving portions of a bridge column were utilized in erection of a bridge alongside the old road bridge. This new bridge was not ready for use until 17 Dec 44, so that the 276 Volks Gren Div was compelled to use the bridges at Gentingen in the zone of its right neighbor, the 352, and at Weilerbach in the 212 Volks Gren Div zone, to get single heavy weapons across to the other side.

In the zone of the 212th Division, attempts to get a bridge thrown across the stream east of Echternach had been broken up by enemy artillery fire. The attempt, too, to continue the work at night under searchlights was a failure. After this, 212 Volks Gren Div had – on its own initiative – repaired a covered-in bridge (already damaged by artillery fire) at Weilerbach, north of Echternach. This, however, was possible only after the enemy strongpoint at Birkelt had been eliminated on 18 Dec 44. Thus, on 18 Dec 44, there was at least one way across the river open to both divisions of the LXXX Inf Corps.

Because of the inadequate support received, 212 Volks Gren Div made little progress on 17 Dec 44; however, Echternach was now completely encircled, so that the American troops heroically fighting there were putting up a losing battle. Several enemy counterattacks against Berdorf were repulsed.

As had been foreseen, the overall position of Seventh Army was a perilous one, owing to the lack of engineer troops and equipment. For this reason, it was a stroke of pure luck that the consequences of this shortage had been felt least of all on the decisive northern wing of the Army. It was now a matter of advancing the right wing with all forces at our disposal, in a westerly direction, and of protecting this movement by advancing southwest through Michelau and Ettelbrück. The situation of LXXX Inf Corps was of lesser significance. Here it was only a matter of getting the attack going again, in order to hold down enemy forces, of eliminating the influence of the enemy artillery where the corps on the right was trying to cross the river, and of delaying the advance of the enemy reserves as much as possible.

It was to be hoped that by 18 Dec 44 – three bridges would be completed with one or two more finished by 19 Dec 44. This would relieve the whole general situation on the western bank of the river. But in the meantime valuable time – the precious moment of surprise – had been lost! The enemy forces opposite our center and our left wing had recovered from the initial shock and had begun to counterattack. Considerable losses on our side had been the result.

LXXXV Inf Corps Drives to its Operational Objective (18–22 Dec 44)

The difficulties met in crossing the river – scarcity of building material, insufficiently trained personnel, and the state of the river itself at the time, not to mention the slopes and turns down to and up from the banks – caused traffic jams at the points of crossing. But one thing we had to be thankful for was that the inclement weather spared us the ordeal of heavy air attacks. During the next few days after 19 Dec 44 the clouds cleared away somewhat, but the moderate raids by enemy planes were adequately dealt with by our antiaircraft defenses, the main force of the enemy's air strength being at this time concentrated on the panzer armies. Losses in personnel at the points where the bridges were being set up were not very great initially. What did constitute a serious disadvantage was the delay in getting the guns and heavy weapons across the streams (due to the narrowness and the poor quality of the roads leading to and from them), and the delay in getting our troops and supplies across.

I. 18 DEC 44

By 18 Dec 44 we had succeeded in getting the main body of 5 FJ Div over to the western bank. In the main, only the large reinforcement battalion of this numerically strong division (20,000 men) was still waiting to cross – about 6,000 men, plus some rear-echelon troops, remained on the eastern bank. During the course of this day, the enemy resistance nests still holding out between the Our and the Clerf were mopped up and 5 FJ Div started to move westward. The leading battalions from the Kautenbach bridgehead, pushing ahead along the highway south of Wiltz through Nocher and Roullingen, went first. Next, the 14 FJ Inf Regt moved by the same route, while 13 FJ Inf Regt proceeded along the road flanking the Sauer to the North, through Hoscheid in the direction of Esch sur la Sûre. 15 FJ Inf Regt, assisted by elements of 352 Volks Gren Div, had taken the strongpoint at Föhren and now had the task of fighting a way clear on the northern flank of the 352 Volks Gren Div, in the direction of Brandenburg.

However, on this day, 352 Volks Gren Div did not succeed in making any noteworthy progress with its right wing, as the artillery was still moving to the western bank of the Our. At this time, the main effort of the division lay on its left wing where – as a prerequisite for its further progress and for the elimination of the obstacle facing the right wing of LXXX Inf Corps – the resistance on the heights west of Wallendorf had to be broken. From these heights the enemy could still sweep the crossings at Gentingen and southeast of Wallendorf with partially directed artillery fire. A coordinated attack by our troops overcame the enemy elements fighting tenaciously in strongly fortified strongpoints, and finally took the heights. Isolated strongpoints and resistance nests were bypassed.

Our neighbor on the right (XLVII Pz Corps) had, on 18 Dec 44, taken Allenborn with two panzer divisions, Niederwampach with Pz Lehr Div, and Oberwampach with 26 Volks Gren Div. Therefore, the mission of Seventh Army, whose right wing had taken the sector of Wiltz on the first day, was now much closer to accomplishment.

II. 19 DEC 44

On 19 Dec 44, 5 FJ Div scored a particularly fine success. While the advance elements of the division pushed ahead to reach Harlange (southeast of Bastogne), the reinforced engineer battalion, which had turned off northward, was able to encircle a strong enemy group (elements of 28 U.S. Inf Div and 9 U.S. Armd Div). Several hundred prisoners were taken, with rich booty. Among the material taken were some 40 Sherman tanks, 20 of which were put in order by the engineer battalion and manned with members of the assault gun brigades, constituting a very welcome addition to the forces of the division. Here on the right wing of the Army the impression had grown that no further resistance of any great significance was to be expected from the enemy in this zone. The main body of 28 U.S. Inf Div and 9 U.S. Armd Div seemed to have been wiped out.

Along the length of the roads running across the area to the south of Bastogne there was only sporadic and incoherent resistance still being offered by isolated enemy groups.

352 Volks Gren Div was able to take Bastendorf with its right assault group and regain contact between it and 915 Inf Regt on the left. This meant that a unified command within the framework of the division was again possible. The continuation of the attack, however, still hung up somewhat, for the artillery and heavy weapons had not yet all arrived. Local attacks on our part alternated with counterattacks by the Americans on heights, in villages, and in woods here and there in the vicinity of Diekirch and north thereof. During one of these battles the Division Commander, Obst Schmidt, was wounded. He remained in command of the division in spite of this, until relieved by Genmaj Batzing.

In the entire zone of LXXXV Inf Corps, no new enemy detachments – with the exception of rear-echelon units (engineer troops) – had appeared. But this did not mean that the enemy troops in front of the left wing of the corps had been beaten. It was therefore imperative to get the attack of 352 Volks Gren Div going again, to wipe out the important enemy bridgehead of Ettelbrück–Diekirch, and to transfer our forces to the other side of the Sauer. Otherwise, enemy reserves might soon come pouring out of the bridgehead in a counterattack against the southern base of the German offensive, or – at least – might be able to strengthen the bridgehead greatly.

Seventh Army, therefore, gave the necessary orders and made an effort to form an artillery center of gravity with portions of the Volks Artillery Corps, the Volks Projector Brigades, and the flak units, so as to lend assistance to 352 Volks Gren Div, whose part of the attack was still hung up.

It had already transpired in the course of the fighting that the practice of trying to bypass isolated enemy nests of resistance was not always successful. The enemy did not simply lay down his arms even if he had been isolated, and he managed to interrupt our lines of supply frequently. In other cases, however, our own tempo of attack flagged considerably; significant numbers of troops were absorbed by security duties in the rear, as there were no reserves available for such duties, although the Army had asked for them to be made available. And again, the half-trained troops were not fully accustomed to the type of warfare being conducted, a type in which tank groups had to be followed by closely-integrated infantry formations for mopping-up purposes.

III. 20 DEC 44

On 20 Dec 44, the development of the situation along the entire front was favorable to LXXXV Inf Corps. Its right neighbor (XLVII Corps) was stalled along the Noville–Bizory–Neffe line, northeast and east of Bastogne, having come up against strong enemy resistance in the shape of 101 U.S. A/B Div, and was regathering its tank forces, in order to advance them past Bastogne – 2 Pz Div on the north and Pz Lehr Div on the south.

However, 5 FJ Div south and southeast of Bastogne had not met with any resistance worth mentioning. Reconnaissance patrols sent out by the division had penetrated west of the road from Bastogne to Martelange, but had discovered no signs whatever of any enemy forces arriving from the south or the southwest. The leading units of the division – 14 FJ Inf Regt on the right and 13 FJ Inf Regt on the left – closed their ranks and managed to advance their forward elements almost to the Berle–Liefrange line. 15 FJ Inf Regt, which at the time found itself in the area of Brandenburg still east of the Sauer, pressed forward to the west and succeeded in taking the Sauer crossing at Michelau.

Both corps and army then paused to weigh the advantages of an attack west of the river Sauer in a southerly direction, with the object of opening the crossing at Ettelbrück from the rear; but decided against such a tactical move, since it was contrary to the idea of keeping the center of gravity of the attack on the right flank. In addition, the difficulties of crossing the river at Michelau were so great that such a push could not have been followed up without sufficient artillery support.

Meanwhile, the attack of 352 Volks Gren Div (after the capture of Bastendorf and the location of the artillery west of the Our) had started moving again. On 20 Dec 44 they succeeded in taking heights of some tactical importance south of Bastendorf, and the left attack group (916 Inf Regt) captured Diekirch. The enemy had succeeded in destroying every one of the bridges over the Sauer between Wallendorf and Diekirch, with the exception of a small bridge west of Reisdorf. However, the bridge at Diekirch was not completely destroyed and the infantry and single heavy weapons could be brought over to the other side. The division closed its ranks, therefore, with strong detachments of 916 Inf Regt pushing west along the southern bank of the Sauer with the mission of opening the crossing at Ettelbrück from the rear. The division command post had been displaced to Bastendorf. Seventh Army now collected a bridge column and, in the night of 20/21 Dec 44, sent it over to the division, which was to have the mission of throwing a bridge over the river at Ettelbrück. The construction was done that night.

There was still no sign of the appearance of enemy reserves moving to attack the Martelange–Ettelbrück line. Owing to the unavailability of any air reconnaissance, we were entirely dependent on the results of ground reconnaissance and radio intelligence. However, there were now signs of the appearance of a new enemy formation in the zone of LXXX Inf Corps; therefore, Seventh Army concluded that the enemy, contrary to our expectations, was about to throw in the first reserves he could lay hands on from the sector of 4 U.S. Inf Div. Our opinion was that tank formations would momentarily appear in an attack against the deeper flank of our offensive, between Neufchâteau and Ettelbrück.

IV. 21 DEC 44

During 21 Dec 44, the situation continued favorable in the attack zone of LXXXV Inf Corps. After its advance elements had previously passed across, 5 FJ Div reached with its forward elements the road from Bastogne to Martelange without any considerable resistance from the enemy. 13 FJ Inf Regt, on the left flank of the division, was therefore ordered to turn inward against Martelange and to prepare itself for defense and the mission of denying the Sauer crossings. The advance detachment and the march group on the right now received the order to press on ahead to Libramont. 15 FJ Inf Regt would follow the division through Wiltz.

According to news received from our neighbor on the right, Bastogne was now surrounded and was being called upon to surrender. Gen Pz Brandenberger, Commanding General of Seventh Army, was now able to link up with the troops of Gen Pz von Lüttwitz' XLVII Pz Corps in Berlé. The latter declared the situation of his corps to be favorable; he expected the early fall of Bastogne. It was true that the most forward elements of his corps – 2 Pz Div – had gotten only midway between La Roche and St. Hubert, although – according to plan – they ought to have reached the Meuse on the fourth day of the offensive (19 Dec 44). However, the enemy in front of this corps appeared to be completely defeated and no enemy reserves of any significance had made their appearance, so that there appeared to be nothing to prevent them from reaching their initial objective, the Meuse. To be sure, at this point the specter of a fuel shortage made its appearance.

Up till now, Seventh Army, in spite of difficulties, had completely fulfilled its mission. It now received an order from Army Group B that, in addition to its mission of protecting the southern flank of the offensive, it would form a front to the north and prevent any escape of the trapped garrison of Bastogne, in the direction of Martelange; Pz Lehr Div and elements of 26 Volks Gren Div would secure the front at Sibret in the direction of Neufchâteau. For assisting in this task, portions of 14 FJ Inf Regt would be used, later to be relieved by 15 FJ Inf Regt.

352 Volks Gren Div finally succeeded in taking Ettelbrück. The bridge over the Sauer was partially destroyed, but could very soon be rendered usable again with the aid of the material and bridging equipment being brought up. The

long and obstinate resistance put up by the enemy at this point seemed finally to have been broken. The division was able to move forward with its advance elements towards its ultimate objective, the Attert sector of Bettborn–Bissen. There it was to pass to the defensive.

Seventh Army now had three main problems:

a. The strengthening of the front south of Bastogne, where – owing to the failure of our troops to take Bastogne – it had to be ready for attacks of enemy reserves moving in from the south and southwest to relieve the town.

b. It had to tackle the problem of the ever-widening gap between the left wing of LXXXV Inf Corps and the right wing of the LXXX Inf Corps, which neither of the two corps was able to fill. This worry could only be eliminated by the rapid advance of 276 Volks Gren Div through Medernach and Cruchten, which, however, in view of the serious situation of the division and of LXXX Inf Corps was not possible.

c. In the event of a further advance by Fifth Pz Army, the protection of its southern flank could only be assured if further troops were assigned to Seventh Army. Seventh Army once again asked Army Group B for the OKW reserves which had arrived in the Bitburg–Wittlich area, a mobile unit to be sent in on the right wing and an infantry division to be used as an army reserve in accordance with the development of the situation.

Seventh Army intended to commit the staff of LIII Inf Corps (under Gen Kav Rothkirch) on its right wing, assigning the mobile unit and 5 FJ Div to it, while LXXXV Inf Corps would confine itself to the control of 352 Volks Gren Div and the new arriving formations.

The front had already become too wide for LXXXV Inf Corps to control adequately. LIII Inf Corps, therefore, received the necessary orders to take over its new zone on 22 Dec 44.

V. 22 DEC 44

This day represented rom a tactical and organizational point of view the turning point in the conduct of the offensive by Seventh Army. On this day, the last offensive successes occurred on the one hand; on the other, a striking change occurred in the enemy situation. The flank attack of Third American Army, under General Patton, began to make itself felt.

In the meantime, we had received no news of what was happening to the right wing of the Army. Lack of air reconnaissance on our part meant that the advance of the American formations remained hidden to our eyes until their forward elements clashed with our own ground reconnaissance. (23 Dec 44!)

The leading elements of 5 FJ Div were able to reach Vaux-les-Rosieres on 22 Dec 44. Motorized patrols pushed on to Libramont–Neufchâteau and beyond without encountering any strong enemy resistance. The regiment on the right of the division (14 FJ Inf Regt) assembled in the Hompré–Hollange area and at the same time blocked, mainly with antitank guns, the road from Bastogne to Martelange between Lutrebois and Assenois, to the north. The regiment on the left (13 FJ Inf Regt) took Martelange with its forward elements after a short battle and tried to establish a bridgehead at this point, so as to be able to send reconnaissance patrols south and southeastward. In the meantime, mopping-up operations were in order. This regiment, therefore, assembled and moved further forward to protect the northern bank of the Sauer on both sides of Martelange and to build up strongpoints with the aid of detachments sent south of the River (Arsdorf, Bilsdorf, Bigonville). The third regiment of the division, 15 FJ Inf Regt, was moving through Wiltz to the west. Division headquarters at this time was at Berlé, with an advance command post in the castle at L'Ossange, one kilometer west of Lutrebois. LIII Inf Corps set up its headquarters in Dahl, four kilometers south of Wiltz, and took over control of only 5 FJ Div at first.

352 Volks Gren Div had moved out of the area of Ettelbrück and started in the direction of its objective, 915 Inf Regt moving through Feulen–Mertzig toward Bettborn–Redingen, 914 Inf Regt moving through Michelbouch–Vichten toward Usseldingen, and 916 Inf Regt moving south through Schieren. The forward elements of the right column reached Pratz, while the main body of the regiment reached the Mertzig–Grosbous area.

Both the other regiments had reached Michelbouch and Schieren and had taken these places against rather weak enemy resistance. At this moment the division was surprised by a blow delivered by the 80 U.S. Inf Div, strengthened by elements of the 10 U.S. Armd Div. Although there was a lack of air reconnaissance, this surprise must also be blamed on our ground reconnaissance, which to a certain extent had failed us. The right flank of the Division was now very gravely threatened. 915 Inf Regt, attached to the division for the attack, did not rise to meet the crisis, although it must be borne in mind that the enemy possessed superiority of numbers and greater mobility. The enemy, moving up rapidly on both sides of the road, now succeeded in completely encircling the forward elements of this regiment in Pratz and the main body of it in Grosbous–Mertzig area. The other regiments of the division could not come to its aid, attacked as they were by the enemy, and they were driven over to the defensive. Incompleteness of training and inefficiency on the part of the lower command had a decisive effect on the outcome of this action. There was no choice but to withdraw the division into a bridgehead at Ettelbrück and to order the encircled 915 Inf Regt to fight its way out to the northeast.

Neither the corps nor the army had any reserves whatever to help the division in this critical situation. The lack of the reserves which the Army had asked for repeatedly was now bitterly felt.

Now LXXXV Inf Corps reached its decisive turning point. With the exception of the capture of Martelange, the corps had failed to reach its objective since the difficulties of crossing the Our and the lack of bridging material had caused a delay of two or three days. Had it not been for this delay, the corps would doubtless have reached the envisaged defense line with time enough to prepare for mobile defense against the expected enemy attack against the German southern flank.

VI. THE MOST URGENT PROBLEM

For Seventh Army, the area between Martelange and Ettelbrück constituted the most urgent problem in the immediate future. Everything depended on preventing the enemy from achieving a breakthrough across the Sauer at this point and striking northward. Such a thrust into the deep flank of Fifth Pz Army would find the most dangerous strategic spot; it would not only imperil the continuation of the offensive, but would also endanger the whole army group.

In acknowledgement of this danger, 79 Volks Gren Div (Cmdr: Obst Weber) and the Führer Gren Brig (Cmdr: Obst Kahler) were released from their reserve status by the OKW and given to Seventh Army to fill its requisition. However, their most forward elements could not be expected to arrive in Hoscheid until 23 Dec 44 at the earliest.

Seventh Army intended on 22 Dec 44 to insert 79 Volks Gren Div in the gap between LXXXV and LIII Inf Corps to clear up the enemy detachments there. The Führer Gren Brig was to be delivered to LIII Inf Corps, for use as a mobile flank defense in the Gedinne–Libramont zone of the army group advance toward the Meuse. The Brigade was ordered, because of the road and bridge conditions and because of the unclarified situation between Martelange and Ettelbrück, to use the route Roth–Hoscheid-Niederschlinder–Heiderscheld– Eschdorf– Harlange.

The Fifth Pz Army on 22 Dec 44 had 2 Pz Div at a point southeast of Marche, with Pz Lehr Div in front of St. Hubert, and was obviously making good progress in its drive toward the far side of the Meuse. However, 5 FJ Div could no longer provide adequate flank protection for the attacking spearheads of the Panzer Army without further support. And, in spite of its intention, Seventh Army could not avoid temporarily committing the Führer Gren Brig in the gap between LXXXV and LIII Inf Corps.

LXXX Inf Corps (18–26 Dec 44)

I. A THANKLESS TASK

A thankless task indeed had fallen to LXXX Inf Corps. This corps, considering the terrain and the enemy situation, had the most difficult portion of the attack to control. Moreover, its striking power had been diminished by the extension of its zone of attack from Bollendorf to Echternach, inclusive. Such an extension, however, was not only necessary, but quite correct from an operational point of view, since the arc formed by the Sauer and the Moselle had always furnished the enemy with the possibility of a large counterattack. Since the additional troops urgently requested by the Army after its attack zone had been extended could not be made available, Seventh Army had decided, despite the fact that its main effort was located on the right wing, to give its best division to LXXX Inf Corps. This was 212 Volks Gren Div under Genmaj Sensfuss, which was best in terms of training, leadership, and fighting experience. The corps could hope to receive no further reserves whatsoever, for these had had to be sent in on the strategically more important wing of the Army. It was compelled, therefore, to try to execute its mission with the rather weak forces at its disposal, even though it was important that it attempted to draw upon itself the fire of as many enemy forces as possible, and thus to tie them down. Heavy losses had been sustained by the divisions of LXXX Inf Corps as early as the first two days of the attack.

II. 18 DEC 44

276 Volks Gren Div was able to take Reisdorf on 18 Dec 44, against an enemy defending himself stoutly. And since its right neighbor, 352 Volks Gren Div, had succeeded in taking the heights west of Wallendorf, the enemy on the right flank of 276 Volks Gren Div had finally been flattened, after he had exerted a decisive influence on the progress of the entire division. In the same vein, conditions for the river crossing were now more favorable. True, only ferries were available, since all of the bridging equipment had been carried off for use in the construction of the military bridge at Bollendorf. Since 276 Volks Gren Div still possessed no bridge of its own, it was compelled, in an effort to get a portion of its artillery and heavy weapons across, to use the bridges of its neighbor at Gentingen and Weilerbach. Both were ready for use on the night of 18/19 Dec 44.

With this assistance, and thanks to the fact that the northern flank was free, the right attack group, 986 Inf Regt, succeeded in taking Eppeldorf, thereby securing elbow room in the direction of Medernach. Meanwhile the left regiment, 987 Inf Regt, succeeded in taking Beaufort and in penetrating into the wood to the west and south. Hopes were now held that the attack on the enemy artillery position areas of Medernech–Christnach could be energetically pursued.

The division commander, Genmaj Möhring, while on a trip through the wood two kilometers east of Beaufort, was killed by enemy machine gun fire issuing from the most forward enemy line. During the next two nights the psychological influence of the death of their commander was perceptible in the attitude of the men. The noticeably diminished fighting spirit of the division could be traced partly to this cause; but it was also connected with the failure of the assault gun company to appear, and with the division's incomplete training. After the division had been temporarily under the command of Obst Schroeder, Artillery Commander of LXXX Inf Corps, Obst Dempwolff assumed command on 22 Dec 44.

Despite the fact that the bridge at Weilerbach was not ready for use until the night of 18 Dec 44, thus rendering it impossible to get the heavy weapons, artillery, and assault guns over to the other side of the stream, 212 Volks Gren Div was able to push southward between the defended villages of Osweiler and Dickweiler with its left attack group, 320 Inf Regt, and to penetrate into the forest of Dewald, northwest of Herborn. However, 423 Inf Regt on the right was still fighting around Berdorf, where the enemy – supported by tanks – continued to fight with especial tenacity. The enemy strongpoint was still holding out at Echternach as well. It is true that a shock company of the third regiment, 316 Inf Regt, had already penetrated into the city on 17 Dec 44, but it did not succeed in clearing out the enemy troops. Nor had it been able to prevent the enemy from bringing up tank reinforcements through Lauterborn into the city.

On 18 Dec 44, the division first identified elements of 10 U.S. Armd Div in its zone. This meant that the first point for the commitment of enemy reserves against the German attack had been decided. Both Army and corps now considered the situation of the division, as a result of this development, to be very critical. Seventh Army thus released the division's 316 Inf Regt, until then envisaged as Army reserve, to be employed as the division saw fit.

III. 19 DEC 44

This date brought with it the greatest success along the entire front for LXXX Inf Corps, after it became possible to convey the mass of the supporting weapons over the bridge at Weilerbach, at last ready, and to commit them in support of the offensive.

276 Volks Gren Div, using its right regiment, had now reached Ermsdorf (two kilometers north of Medernach) and the heights north of Savelborn, Haller, and Waldbillig. On the left wing, a task force of the left regiment forced its way into the valley of the Schwarze Ernz as far as the area of Müllerthal. By a simultaneous attack from the north and the east the left attack group succeeded in penetrating into Christnach. This toughly defended village changed hands several times in the course of the day and at evening was again in the hands of the enemy. But the initial objective had been reached to the extent that the enemy artillery had been compelled to displace to the rear; the cessation of artillery fire against the bridge positions testified to that. On this day, also, the military bridge at Bollendorf was completed, so that the division had at last a crossing of its own. The division command post was now transferred to Beaufort.

On 19 Dec 44, 212 Volks Gren Div succeeded in gaining ground to the south, taking little heed of the enemy strongpoints still holding out to the rear, and in reaching the line: the southern fringe of the wood north of Consdorf–the northern edge of Scheidgen (zone of 423 Inf Regt)–Michelshof (one and a half kilometers southeast of Scheidgen)–the southwest fringe of the forest of Dewald–northwest of Herborn (zone of 320 Inf Regt).

This meant that here we had approached to within four kilometers of the initial objective of the attack – the area of Altrier. In the course of the day's fighting, elements of 423 Inf Regt also succeeded in taking complete possession of Berdorf, and the division reconnaissance battalion managed to destroy the enemy strongpoint at Echternach. Here, four officers and 180 men of the valiant American defenders were taken prisoner. Opposite the enemy strong-points at Osweiler and Dickweiler security forces were left, later to be relieved by elements of 999 Penal Bn. The reserve, 316 Inf Regt, was now moved up behind the center of the Division.

While the attempt to throw a bridge across the river east of Echternach was foiled by enemy artillery fire (aerial spotting!), another bridge was successfully erected at Edingen on 19 Dec 44. In spite of these successes achieved by the division the prospects did not seem completely favorable either to the Army or the corps. Owing to the delay which had intervened as a result of the difficulties of getting our weapons across the streams, valuable time had been frittered away, and the amount of territory gained, to the south, on which the Supreme Command had laid such emphasis, was insufficient. Even if the elements of 4 U.S. Inf Div (originally engaged in their unsupported state) had been seriously weakened by the heavy fighting, the signs were that fresh enemy forces, in addition to the elements of the already identified 10 U.S. Armd Div, would soon arrive.

Another disadvantage which had to be borne was that, as a result of the weather having cleared considerably, the enemy air force came out in strength and greatly worsened the conditions for our troops. The manner in which the five-kilometer gap continued to grow between the 276 Division and its neighbor on the right in the area of Ermsdorf–Diekirch was causing the for-mation great disquiet. Because of the absence of reserves it was now impossible to close this gap.

For the reasons stated, it appeared that the attack of LXXX Inf Corps could be continued only if the division had an opportunity to re-assemble, and if its neighbor on the right should succeed in clearing the area of Ettelbrück. Because of the enemy situation and our total lack of air reconnaissance, a reckless advance of the individual spearheads would invite catastrophe; catastrophe, because heavy counterattacks by the newly-arriving American reserves would fall upon our unprepared and unfavorably-disposed troops. For this reason, LXXX Inf Corps decided that on the following day it would strive to make only local gains, to clean up the area in its rear, and to close its ranks.

IV. 20 DEC 44

On 20 Dec 44, all the attacks made by the different divisions came up against stronger American opposition; the American counteroffensive was beginning. The result was a struggle, involving 276 Volks Gren Div around Savelborn and Christnach and 212 Volks Gren Div around Consdorf and Scheidgen. Battles which raged back and forth, which brought no gains of any significance for us.

Most important, in the 212 Volks Gren Div zone, planned enemy counterattacks, assisted by tanks, started to be felt. During the next few days we were able here to identify definitely all regiments of 5 U.S. Inf Div, while in front of the division on the corps right portions of 80 U.S. Inf Div were identified. Since here was the first recognizable reaction on the part of the enemy against the southern flank of the German offensive, Seventh Army presumed that the main force of the enemy countermeasures would come from the area of Luxembourg, to be thrown against the base of the German offensive in an attempt to achieve a breakthrough across the arc of the Sauer and Moselle rivers. On the other hand, the continued absence of 4 and 6 U.S. Armd Divs, which had to be expected sooner or later, seemed to indicate that the enemy tank reserves had been sent in through Arlon–Neufchâteau in the general direction of Bastogne and to the east.

V. THE TURNING POINT

Thus, the turning point in the battle had arrived for the LXXX Inf Corps. On 21 Dec 44, the enemy attacks increased in ferocity to such an extent that it was clear that in front of the center and the right wing of the corps fresh enemy forces were being employed. The situation on the extreme left wing of 276 Volks Gren Div was so vague that it also constituted a grave threat to the right flank of 212 Volks Gren Div. 423 Inf Regt fighting here was forced to pull back, so as to absorb the force of punches delivered by the enemy against its flanks. However, with the exception of a breach which the enemy made at Michelshof, 212 Volks Gren Div was able to maintain its position. In order to arrange its forces for defensive fighting the division started to move off in the night of 21/22 Dec 44 along the following line: Hill 347 (northeast of Müllerthal)–the hill north of Scheidgen–the fringe of the wood north of Michelshof–the heights south of Rodenhof–Echt–the heights north of Dickweiler–Hill 370 (west of Girsterklaus)–Enberg northeast of Girst. On the left wing of the Division there now stood only strong elements of 999 Penal Bn.

LXXX Inf Corps engaged in heavy fighting also on 22 Dec 44. Along the boundary of the two divisions, in the valley of the Schwarze Ernz north of Müllerthal, the enemy succeeded in making a deep salient, which became during the days following the main point of danger. It imperilled the internal cohesiveness of the corps and the bridge at Bollendorf. As the loss of this bridge would have placed 276 Volks Gren Div in a serious position, Seventh Army ordered the establishment of an auxiliary bridge at Dillingen, which was not completed until 25 Dec 44.

212 Volks Gren Div was now ordered to counterattack to clear up the position along its boundary with 276 Volks Gren Div. Both of these divisions had sustained heavy losses. The companies within them had now an average strength of no more than 30–40 men and the severe weather had caused many frostbite cases among the troops. Besides the reinforcements obtained from the field reinforcement battalions only about 100 men could be supplied to the corps, not nearly enough to even approximately replenish its ranks. The situation south of Bollendorf forced 212 Volks Gren Div to withdraw during the night of 22/23 Dec 44 to the line Kalkesbach–Hill 313 (southwest of Lauterborn)–the hill north of Osweiler.

VI. 23–24 DEC 44

On 23 and 24 Dec 44, all positions in the center and on the left wing of LXXX Inf Corps were successfully defended. Counterattacks by both the inner flanks of the divisions had enabled us to restore the position in the valley of the Schwarze Ernz for the time being, so that the Sauer bridge lying at Bollendorf and shielded by the deeply eroded Sauer valley could still be used. Nevertheless, the threat at this spot remained real, and had a decisive influence on the general situation.

The greatly weakened 276 Volks Gren Div, extended on too wide a front during the preceding fighting, had to be withdrawn to the line of the heights northeast of Eppeldorf–Beaufort–Point 191 (three and a half kilometers west of Berdorf), as a result of the increasing weight of the enemy attacks. This brought into existence a wide, almost completely unsecured, gap between it and its neighbor whose left wing was still located in the bridgehead at Echternach on 23 Dec 44. This gap represented a serious threat to the cohesiveness of the Army front. In spite of this, Seventh Army had to insist on the continuation of the hopeless battle of the corps on the southwest bank of the Sauer, since enemy forces had to be 'fixed' as long as possible. Further reinforcements were not available to LXXX Inf Corps.

VII. 25–26 DEC 44

While the 276 Volks Gren Div was able on the whole to maintain its position on 25 Dec 44, 212 Volks Gren Div was obliged to retire that night to the line of Berdorf–the hill southeast and the hill southwest of Echternach. The forces still located southeast of Echternach were at the same time withdrawn behind the Sauer, only strong combat outposts being left on the southern bank of the river. The next morning an enemy tank attack issued from the woods south of Posselt and penetrated as far as Felsmühle on the Sauer. As a result of this and of renewed strong attacks (from the valley of the Schwarze Ernz) against Berdorf, the bridgehead occupied by 212 Volks Gren Div was further diminished in the night of 25/26 Dec 44. On the following day, it only extended over the hill at Hamm, one and a half kilometers north of Berdorf. In the meantime, contact between the divisions had been lost. 276 Volks Gren Div had likewise been pressed back until it was now occupying a small bridgehead on the heights on the western bank at Dillingen.

As the final mission of LXXX Inf Corps – the fixing of enemy forces – could no longer be fulfilled, Seventh Army decided to withdraw the LXXX Inf Corps in the night of 26/27 Dec 44 to the West Wall. Both the divisions had now lost about one-third of their total and about three-fourths of their *fighting* strength in bloody combat, without reinforcements to make up such losses. Nevertheless, this corps had to remain fully ready for defense in the West Wall as there was a danger of the enemy attempting to smash through the Wall with a subsidiary push. As a result of the critical nature of the situation of LXXXV Inf Corps, the right wing of 276 Volks Gren Div in the West Wall had to be extended as far as Gentingen, so as to build up a security garrison behind the heavily engaged 352 Volks Gren Div.

VIII. THE CORPS SITUATION

Despite the fact that the LXXX Inf Corps had not accomplished its mission, and on 27 Dec 44, had been driven back to its starting position, it must be said that it had fulfilled its thankless task to the best of its abilities. Two and perhaps three large enemy units had been tied down, at heavy cost to the corps. This aided considerably the main effort in the German southern flank. On the other hand, the fact that the corps had still fallen short of its goal had a very damaging influence on the morale of both officers and troops. The belief in final victory and in the infallibility of the Supreme Command had received the heaviest blow yet.

At this time, a subsidiary enemy push across the Sauer against the sparsely-occupied West Wall – in view of our weaknesses in morale, personnel, and material – would have offered favorable prospects of success and would certainly have constituted a very great strategic threat to the whole German Western Front. But, surprisingly enough, enemy pressure now relaxed completely, so that combat outposts were able to secure the last bridgeheads on the southern and western banks of the Sauer. Reconnaissance showed that the enemy obviously had no immediate intention of attacking here. This meant that Seventh Army was now in a position to withdraw 276 Volks Gren Div at the beginning of January 45 for reconstitution.

The Battle of the Army Center
(23 Dec 44–11 Jan 45)

I. 23 DEC 44

The reaction against 352 Volks Gren Div on the left wing of LXXXV Inf Corps on 22 Dec 44 had notably diminished this division's fighting power. 915 Inf Regt, which was encircled in two groups in the area of Grosbous–Mertzig, vainly attempted to smash its way out to the east and northeast. Finally, certain elements of the regiment succeeded in breaking a way out into the woods to the north, and managed to rejoin the division in the Ettelbrück bridgehead on 25 Dec 44. But by this time the regiment had lost the greater part of its heavy weapons and its equipment, as had its supporting artillery battalion. Both the other regiments had also suffered heavy personnel and material losses, so that the whole division possessed only the value of a combat team. The forces at its disposal, however, were sufficient for the occupation of a bridgehead at Ettelbrück on 23 Dec 44 and for securing the Sauer sector east of Ettelbrück southward – and north of Ettelbrück westward. The whole of the area between Arsdorf (eight kilometers northeast of Martelange) and Bourscheid, remained without security.

The enemy, who soon discovered this state of affairs thanks to his air and ground reconnaissance, exploited it at once and sent 80 U.S. Inf Div north against the Heiderscheid–Eschdorf line on the same date. Part of the American division turned inward against the bridgehead at Ettelbrück. When the Commanding General (Gen Kav Rothkirch) of LIII Inf Corps looked out of the window at his headquarters that afternoon, and observed from there (Dahl, five kilometers southwest of Wiltz) that enemy infantry and armored forces were descending the slopes at Heiderscheid and moving northwards into the Sauer Valley, he immediately collected all the forces he could lay his hands on (rear echelon troops of 5 FJ Div and elements of the 47th engineer brigade) in order to build up a security garrison at the Sauer crossings between Esch and Bochholz sur la Sûre which would be ready to blow up the bridges if necessary. Thus, at the last moment, a surprise attack by the enemy in the vicinity of Wiltz was prevented, an attack which would have placed Seventh Army in a very awkward position.

There can be no doubt that in this instance 80 U.S. Inf Div missed a highly favorable opportunity, for a resolute push further north on 23 Dec 44 would likely have met with success.

On receiving a report on the enemy situation from the LIII Inf Corps, Seventh Army hoped that the troop movements reported there referred only to a change-over among our own troops, perhaps part of 352 Volks Gren Div or forward elements of the Führer Gren Brig, so it ordered a check to be made. Unfortunately the investigation disclosed that the enemy was present. In the meantime, the reserve units newly assigned to Seventh Army were on the way to the positions allotted to them:

a. Führer Gren Brig (Cmdr: Obst Kahler), through Roth–Nieder-schlinder–Bourscheid–Heiderscheid–Eschdorf, to LIII Inf Corps.

b. 79 Volks Gren Div (Cmdr: Obst Weber), through Gentingen–into the area of Bourscheid–Burden–Niederfeulen, to LXXXV Inf Corps.

Seventh Army intended to use 79 Volks Gren Div, after its assembly, in an attack southward from the area mentioned, in order to restore the position between LIII and LXXXV Inf Corps and to throw the enemy back on to the defense line envisaged as the operational objective. The march columns now approaching had been seriously delayed as a result of the poor facilities for crossing the Our. These difficulties, together with enemy air attacks, had forced them to disperse thoroughly. Both Seventh Army and its corps pressed them to hasten the tempo of their march forward, especially in the case of the Brigade, and at least to send ahead, into the area they were to occupy, elements capable of putting up a stiff fight. On 23 Dec 44, an advance task force of the Führer Gren Brig (reconnaissance battalion and heavy armored car battalion) reached the area of Eschdorf–Heiderscheid in the morning, and reconnaissance patrols sent on ahead had gotten as far as the area east of Martelange, but all other elements of the Brigade were still astride the Our. This excessive dispersion in depth arose from the different degrees of mobility of the various portions (wheeled vehicles, tracked vehicles, and bicycles). That portion of the Brigade mounted on bicycles, for instance, was still in the vicinity of Bitburg. The most advanced elements now received the blow of the III U.S. Corps in its southern flank and were cut off. The rearward elements were forced to prepare for defense at Eschdorf and Heiderscheid without the support of the other parts still straggling behind (tanks, self-propelled assault guns, artillery, etc.). Meanwhile, the Commander (Obst Kahler), who had moved ahead to the front of his troops to carry out a personal reconnaissance, was seriously wounded. The effect of this was that the fighting value of the newly constituted Brigade was much lessened in this very difficult situation. Furthermore, Maj von Courbière, Commander of the armored car battalion, who now took over control, was not quite up to the task.

Of the 79 Volks Gren Div, only the most forward regiment (208 Inf Regt) had crossed to the east bank of the Sauer. Both of the other regiments, 212 and 226, were still on the way. Before Seventh Army and LXXXV Inf Corps were fully informed on the situation at Heiderscheid, 208 Inf Regt had captured Niederfeulen in the vicinity of the position it was to occupy. Both Seventh Army and the LXXXV Inf Corps now wondered whether to commit the regiment, on the basis of the altered situation in an attack at Niederfeulen and Heiderscheid. The mission would be to free the elements of the Führer Gren Brig encircled there and by simultaneous attack on Eschdorf and Bourscheid in the vicinity of Heiderscheid to attempt an encirclement of the enemy. However, this idea was not adopted because the enemy attacked Niederfeulen and the forces at our disposal were considered too weak to carry out an attack across hilly and wooded territory.

The final decision of LXXXV Inf Corps was to utilize the elements of 79 Volks Gren Div and the Führer Gren Brig (the elements which had now arrived near Bourscheid) for an attack on Heiderscheid in order to restore contact with these elements which had penetrated as far as Eschdorf. For this purpose the Brig was now subordinated to LXXX Inf Corps.

On 23 December 44, Seventh Army moved its advance command post from Dockendorf to Wiltz, a place previously occupied by the staff of 28 American Inf Div. That night, Wiltz was heavily shelled by enemy artillery, causing losses in the Army Staff. But apart from this, the shelling which was kept up all through the next few days disturbed only our supply trains and our signal communications.

II. 24 DEC 44

On this day the German attacks did not achieve their aim of closing the breach made by the enemy at Heiderscheid. But they did have the effect of preventing the further penetration of the enemy northward across the Sauer. By closing up from the rear the enemy had strengthened his forces and was able to hold the ground already won.

The elements of the Führer Gren Brig cut off around Eschdorf on the previous day collected themselves for an attack and attempted in vain to break out of Eschdorf to the east. Moreover, simultaneous attacks by portions of 79 Volks Gren Div, even though supported by tanks and assault guns, were likewise a failure. The panzer units had suffered many technical breakdowns and had been led into difficult terrain. In addition to this, the artillery of 79 Volks Gren Div, as a result of the difficulties it had met with on its march forward (bad roads, lack of bridges, etc.) was not yet in position and could not adequately support the attack. The attack for the most part had been supported by an artillery battalion of 5 FJ Div which had stalled near Hoscheid owing to lack of prime movers. Along with the artillery, still lacking were one and a half regiments of the division and also the assault gun battalion; the progress of these units had likewise been held up by bad weather, bad terrain, and lack of bridges. (The winter conditions slowed down all the various movements along the poor roads leading up and down the gradients, so that the distances covered were in all cases less than had been hoped for.)

In summary, it can be said that the attack, utilizing the element of surprise, had been carried by narrow spearheads as far as the area of Heiderscheid; but the attack groups – weakened by casualties and technical failures – had been counterattacked in their flanks by the enemy from the woods on both sides of the road Bourscheid–Heiderscheid. Our forces had been shot up so badly by enemy tanks and artillery that they had been driven back to their original jump-off positions. Heiderscheid was lost.

In view of the situation in the zone of 5 FJ Div, Seventh Army ordered the Führer Gren Brig to the northern bank of the Sauer for defense on both sides of Esch sur la Sure. Its defense lines were to face south. It was hoped to get the brigade, badly shot up as a result of the situation, gathered together compactly again. True, as a result of its unhappy experience when employed earlier, it had suffered very serious personnel and material losses. To replace the Commander, who had been seriously wounded, Obst Kühn took over control for a period of two days, later to be replaced by Obst Meder.

It was now Seventh Army's task, after the failure of the attempt to close the enemy breach, to seal off the advance of the enemy troops while still holding a widened bridgehead around Bourscheid.

At 2100 hrs on 24 Dec 44, Seventh Army received a flash report that enemy forces had broken through the lines of 352 Volks Gren Div in the sector of Diekirch–Bettendorf and were proceeding northward across the Sauer. Since if the report were true this would be a very serious matter for the entire army, the Commanding General, Gen Pz Brandenberger immediately started off personally to see if the situation was as actually reported. Happily, the report proved to be false, or at least greatly exaggerated. It was true that the Sauer bridgehead at Ettelbrück had been lost, so that 352 Volks Gren Div was now fighting only behind the Sauer, in defense of the Erpeldingen–Diekirch–Bettendorf sector.

III. 25–27 DEC 44

On 25 Dec 44, the Führer Gren Brig was finally attached to LIII Inf Corps, and between the latter and LXXXV Inf Corps a new boundary line (Kautenbach–Heiderscheid– Bettborn) was established.

While LIII Inf Corps was ordered to defend the Sauer, LXXXV was to hold the Sauer bridgehead at Bourscheid and – starting at Burden behind the Sauer – assume a defensive mission. This bridgehead at Bourscheid, including approximately the line from the fringe of the wood north and east of Ringel–Kehmen–Welscheid–Burden, was of vital import for the continuation of the fighting. Hill 500 (west of Bourscheid) commanded the entire Sauer position and was imperative for observation for the artillery. The terrain on the eastern bank of the river rendered very difficult the right choice of artillery positions. The deeply eroded valley of the river presented great obstacles to wheeled traffic, especially under winter conditions, so that the bridgehead had to be hand supplied.

On the newly-formed right wing of LXXXV Inf Corps on either side of Bochholz sur Sûre, elements of the engineer brigade were still occupying the front. In order to release the latter for their proper functions and to shorten the front, Seventh Army ordered a concentrated attack to reduce the Ringel salient. This attack, after the completion of re-assembly by 79 Volks Gren Div, was carried out on the night of 26/27 Dec 44.

This attack, which began under cover of darkness because of enemy control of the air, achieved some initial success and some of our troops penetrated into Ringel, but here the superior power of the enemy artillery halted the attack and forced its abandonment after we had sustained serious losses. For the first time during the offensive a great shortage of artillery ammunition was felt, a shortage which from that moment onward was felt more and more in all enterprises of Seventh Army.

In the zone of 352 Volks Gren Div no enemy attacks of any importance had taken place, so that this division was able to begin its rehabilitation in so far as that was possible. On 25 Dec 44, Genmaj Batzing took over command of the division from Obst Schmidt, who had been wounded, and the division command post was moved to Brandenburg.

IV. 28 DEC 44–11 JAN 45

During the heavy fighting on the right wing of Seventh Army in the area south and southeast of Bastogne, complete quiet reigned in the sector of LXXX Inf Corps, now back in the West Wall. In the sector of LXXXV Inf Corps, too, with the exception of local engagements and continuous artillery duels, comparative quiet reigned. Despite this, Seventh Army considered the situation tense, especially since in the last days of December there were signs of the appearance of 6 U.S. Armd Div in the sector of 352 Volks Gren Div. But when this American division was located southeast of Bastogne on 1 Jan 45, it did not appear that the enemy before the left wing and the center of the Army had any intentions of carrying out an attack. Therefore, our front there was considerably weakened by the withdrawal of mortars and artillery in favor of the LIII Inf Corps sector, where desperate fighting was in progress. LXXXV Inf Corps now had at its disposal, in addition to the divisional artillery, only two or three battalions of supporting artillery and a few mortar batteries.

LXXXV Inf Corps used the period of quiet on its front to prepare itself for defense, to build new positions, and to re-organize its forces. It was able to report at the beginning of January 45 that it was completely prepared for defense. And as the Sauer was always an obstacle, even if not an insuperable one, Seventh Army was not particularly worried about its Sauer front.

Both Seventh Army and LXXXV Inf Corps still cherished the intention of a breakout from the bridgehead at Bourscheid to be achieved by a punch into the eastern flank of III American Corps. The hope was to lighten the strain of the defensive battle being fought by LIII Inf Corps southeast of Bastogne. Therefore, LXXXV Inf Corps planned an attack by 79 Volks Gren Div in the direction of Niederfeulen, since the failure of the attack on 24 Dec 44 had taught them that under such arduous terrain conditions an attack in the direction of Heiderscheid did not appear advisable. But in the end the scarcity of ammunition and the inadequate numbers of troops forced the abandonment of this plan.

Moreover, the various local attacks attempted had shown clearly that the penetrating power of the German formations was not great enough to achieve any worthwhile success against the enemy superiority in men and material.

The Battle of LIII Inf Corps South and Southeast of Bastogne (23 Dec 44–11 Jan 45)

I. THE SITUATION OF THE ARMY RIGHT WING ON 22 DEC 44

The more likely it became that Bastogne would not capitulate, the more clearly did the Army comprehend that this area would finally become the main point of the Battle of the Ardennes, and that here was the decisive point in its attempt to protect the flank of Army Group B.

Even if the first enemy countermeasures on the southern flank of the German offensive in the area north and northeast of Luxembourg had had no decisive effect, Seventh Army was counting on the assault of strong enemy tank forces of Third American Army – through Arlon and Neufchâteau in the direction of Bastogne. The wide north–south roads presented themselves to the enemy eye for the carrying out of such an operation. The attacks preceding this push (which became stronger from 23 Dec 44 onward) against the left wing and the center of the Army sector had forced Seventh Army – despite its estimate of the general situation – to commit its few available reserves in the central portion of the sector to prevent a breakthrough there.

As a result of these developments, at first only 5 FJ Div was assigned to LIII Inf Corps on the right wing of Seventh Army. This division was unusually large and had also sustained very few casualties so far. Having just been formed exclusively from ex-Luftwaffe personnel, it suffered from a weak lower command echelon, insufficient training, a lack of equipment, limited combat experience and relative immobility. Above all these drawbacks, it had very little artillery and not nearly enough motor vehicles. And even if these deficiencies were partly offset by the enthusiasm of the men and by their excellent morale, the fact remains that its fighting power was moderate and no more than that. Seventh Army had sought to increase this division's combat efficiency by assigning to it artillery battalions from a volks artillery corps and by giving it very efficient officers (individually selected) for its higher and lower command.

This division now had the difficult mission of protecting the area between the Neufchâteau–Bastogne road and the Sauer crossing at Lultzhausen (i.e., it had a

30-kilometer front) from the attacks of an enemy greatly superior in numbers and in material. On 22 Dec 44 the most forward elements of the division were located at Vaux-les-Rosières, 14 FJ Inf Regt in the area of Remichampagne–Hollange–Hompré, and 13 FJ Inf Regt on both sides of Martelange. 15 FJ Inf Regt was still moving through Wiltz into the Harlange area. The engineer battalion was defending along the Sauer south of Harlange. Only one battalion of the division's own artillery was available, owing to the shortage of prime movers. For this reason, two or three battalions of a volks artillery corps were now attached. Because of the absence of the promised motor transport, great difficulties were encountered in supply, especially with regard to POL and ammunition. The fighting ability of this 'green' division was also weakened by its great dispersion.

The development of the situation in the center of the Army presented the realization of its intention to strength the Army right wing by committing the Führer Gren Brig.

II. 23 DEC 44

On this day the enemy counterattacks against 5 FJ Div began. Though such attacks had been expected, the results of our own reconnaissance had been so meager, that when the attacks did start they took our forces partly by surprise. At first, the center of gravity of the enemy assault lay on the east of the Neufchâteau–Bastogne road, where the divisional advance detachment and elements of 14 FJ Inf Regt had, after bloody fighting, been thrown back to the Clochimont–Hompré line. Starting from Hompré, the division had built up a defence flank facing west along the Hollange–Strainchamps line.

To the west there stood elements of 26 Volks Gren Div, its right neighbor in the Sibret–Assenois area. Simultaneously, the tank spearheads of 2 Pz Div (XLVII Pz Corps, Fifth Army) at Foy Notre Dame had gotten a few kilometers nearer the Meuse, so that the Army had to reckon with a continuation of the whole offensive over the Meuse to the northwest. This continuation was strongly indicated by the fact that Pz Lehr Div had now turned off, out of the area of St. Hubert, in the direction of Rochefort.

13 FJ Inf Regt was also being attacked east of Martelange, and very bitter fighting developed in the various villages between Arsdorf and Martelange. However, it proved possible to hold the Sauer crossing and the city. Prisoners captured during the fighting indicated that 4 U.S. Armd Div and 26 U.S. Inf Div were nearby.

This was proof that strong forces of Third American Army were taking part in the attack. Its intention could only be a breakthrough to Bastogne and the liberation of the American forces there. It was therefore our task to prevent such an intention from being carried out. We had to face the likelihood that the American forces encircled at Bastogne would make an energetic attempt to break out, most likely in the direction of Assenois, to meet their relief detachment. For this reason, both Army and corps made up their minds to call a halt to any further westward push and to gather together all their available forces to resist the newly-appearing forces of the enemy.

LIII Inf Corps, which had shifted its command post from Dahl to Winseler (west of Wiltz), on the evening of 23 Dec 44, now did all in its power to make a bastion out of the right wing of 5 FJ Div by assigning to it assault guns, antitank weapons, and by rearranging its artillery support. Since Seventh Army clearly realized that in the coming defensive battles everything would depend on the power of its artillery and its antitank defenses, it ordered that those elements of the volks artillery corps still fighting under LXXXV Inf Corps be transferred to LIII Inf Corps, with the exception of one battalion equipped with Russian 122 mm howitzers. For these there was not sufficient ammunition. The 1st Battalion (75 mm antitank guns) was to be moved as speedily as possible over to the right wing of the Army. But all movements were delayed by the lack of fuel and prime movers, by the air situation, and by the icy roads.

III. 24–26 DEC 44

On 24 Dec 44, it was possible to hold the front on the right wing of the division. It was obvious that the enemy was closing up his ranks from the rear. On the other hand, 13 FJ Inf Regt lost Martelange after fierce fighting. But in any case it would have had to be evacuated very soon, as it would hardly have been possible to hold this bastion on the Sauer very long after the repulse of the regiment on the right at Clochimont and Hompré. 13 FJ Inf Regt retired to a line running from Strainchamps to Warnach, so as later to withdraw still further to another from Hollange to Tintange. In the sector adjoining the east, all our forces had been withdrawn already to the northern bank of the Sauer, although at first it was possible to occupy this spot only with weak security forces.

On 25 Dec 44 the Führer Gren Brig, which had also withdrawn to the other bank of the river, was subordinated to LIII Inf Corps in the Kaundorf–Heiderscheid sector. The new boundary between this corps and LXXXV Inf Corps was Kautenbach (LIII)–Heiderscheid (LXXXV)–Bettborn (LXXXV).

On this day the enemy, who had obviously closed up from the river, attacked 5 FJ Div front in great strength. Supported by artillery fire, about 120 enemy tanks, with their main effort in the direction of Clochimont– Hompré, stormed forward. But this attack was repulsed. However, the situation of the division was now very critical. The high losses in personnel and equipment were not to be made up easily, seeing that the reinforcement battalion of the division was making very slow progress along the ice-covered roads. Equipment vans and field kitchens had to be manhandled through the hilly Ardennes country! Furthermore, there was scant prospect that the stronger elements of Fifth Pz

Army could be made available for the defense of the southern front, because they were still being used in a concentrated attack against the encircled defenders of Bastogne without very much success. For this reason, Seventh Army sent in repeated requests for 9 Volks Gren Div, which was in OKW reserve in the area of Bitburg.

It did not surprise the Army in the least when it learned that the 4 U.S. Armd Div had succeeded on 26 Dec 44 in breaking through the defensive front of 5 FJ Div and the encircling ring of 26 Volks Gren Div (Fifth Pz Army) to establish contact with the troops in Bastogne. All attempts to restore the position by closing the front again behind the enemy forces which had stormed through were wrecked by the material superiority and greater fire power of the Americans.

It was now painfully clear to Seventh Army that the offensive had failed. Daily the decision and order of the Supreme Command for the withdrawal to the West Wall was awaited. But instead it was ordered that the ring around the enemy forces be closed again by energetic attacks from both sides and that Bastogne was to be retaken at all costs!

For such a project it would first be necessary to bring up reserves for Fifth Pz Army; in the meantime, the right wing forces of Seventh Army had the job of keeping the enemy corridor as narrow as possible, for which purpose 5 FJ Inf Div had to take up a flank position along the Remoifosse–Hompré line.

The dangerous situation was finally resolved by a decision to assign 9 Volks Gren Div (Cmdr: Genmaj Kolb) to Seventh Army and commit it on the latter's right wing. Every effort was now made to bring this division up as quickly as possible in motor trucks, but the Army was only able to release a given percentage of transport space and fuel for the purpose, enough to move a single battalion at a time. Getting the artillery up and into position caused us particular trouble, for the Raupenschlepper Ost (a caterpillar tractor designed principally for the Eastern Front) fell behind as a result of the weather conditions. For all these reasons, the arrival of the division took a very long time and it had to be committed piecemeal as its elements arrived, a fact which had a disastrous result on its effectiveness.

IV. 27–31 DEC 44

On 27 Dec 44, the situation of LIII Inf Corps grew more critical after 26 U.S. Inf Div succeeded in crossing the Sauer, breaking through the front of the Führer Gren Brig at Kaundorf, and pushing forward to the area of Nothum. The brigade had not set up its defense line along the river, but on the heights north of it, because it did not have sufficient infantry to build up a continuous line. The enemy, therefore, made his way around the isolated strongpoints on the heights on the northern bank of the stream, where the hilly terrain offered ample concealment. They advanced quickly to the north. This highly threatening breakthrough in the rear of 5 FJ Div, which was facing west and southwest, had to be cleared up. This was necessary to prevent the division from being completely cut off from its line of communications, and also to permit the assembly of 9 Volks Gren Div. Seventh Army, therefore, with a heavy heart, decided to utilize the available battalion of 9 Volks Gren Div for a counterattack. In addition to this battalion, LIII Inf Corps committed on its left wing the Engineer Brigade, which had been withdrawn previously (two weak battalions). Both units were subordinated to the Führer Gren Brig for the counterattack.

But the counterattack was a hopeless failure, for the elements of 9 Volks Gren Div – completely inexperienced as they were – were not up to the demands of the role allotted to them. The battalion was almost completely wiped out. Moreover, the psychological effect of this fiasco later spread through the whole of the division. At any rate, it had been possible to momentarily seal off the enemy breach along the line Harlange–Nothum–Buderscheid.

Meanwhile, the enemy had continued to exert strong pressure against the front of 5 FJ Div. Having strengthened his forces by bringing up 35 U.S. Inf Div to the area north of Martelange, he now attacked heavily the center and the left wing of the division. Here, the elements of 15 FJ Inf Regt, arriving fitfully in odd lots, had been committed. By fighting fiercely and tenaciously the division was able to prevent an enemy breakthrough, but it could not avoid losing some ground.

Its neighbor on the other side of the breach, 26 Volks Gren Div, after losing Bastogne now had to give up Sibret, so that the breach made by the enemy widened still further.

On 28 Dec 44, the Führer Escort Brig (Fifth Pz Army) carried out an attack on Sibret from Chenogne which was a failure. While conditions were quieter at this time in the sector of 5 FJ Div, enemy pressure continued strong in the sector of the reinforced Führer Gren Brig, but the enemy achieved no particular success. The elements of 9 Volks Gren Div continued to arrive slowly and be committed piecemeal, for the Führer Gren Brig had suffered very heavy losses and without some additional support would have been incapable of maintaining its defense front.

On 29 Dec 44 heavy attacks were renewed along the entire front of LIII Inf Corps, attacks which forced 5 FJ Inf Div back to the line of Lutrebois–Villiers la bonne Eau–Harlange–Bavigne. This line, which had been prepared with the most modest of means, was to be held at all costs. It had been ordered that on 30 Dec 44 strong forces would be released by the Fifth Pz Army for the purpose of rewelding our broken ring around Bastogne. One task force consisting of 3 Pz Gren Div and the Führer Escort Brig, under the control of XLVII Pz Corps, was to attack eastward through Sibret; a second task force, consisting of 167

Volks Gren Div and strong elements of 1 SS Pz Div, under the control of XXXIX Pz Corps, would move northwest from the area of Lutrebois–Villers la bonne Eau. Therefore, the elements of 5 FJ Div then in the attack zone were temporarily attached to the Fifth Pz Army, without altering the Seventh Army boundaries.

The attack carried out by the eastern force on 30 Dec 44 achieved initial successes and reached the road from Bastogne to Martelange, northwest of Lutrebois. But heavy enemy counterattacks caused it to lose the ground it had gained; and the attack of the western force unfortunately failed also.

Since the main body of 9 Volks Gren Div (some artillery elements were still missing) had come up in the meantime and taken control on 29 Dec 44 in the sector from north of Nothum to Roullingen, it was possible to withdraw the hard-pressed and almost exhausted Führer Gren Brig (without its bicycle battalion) on the night of 29/30 Dec 44. It assembled northwest of Wiltz and began rehabilitating itself so that it could form an Army reserve. 9 Volks Gren Div was at this time engaged in heavy fighting with a greatly superior enemy force attacking from the direction of Wiltz–Winseler. For this reason it had not been possible to withdraw the engineer brigade still in the front line, although Army Group B had repeatedly requested this. From a captured enemy order it became known to us that the commander of 26 or 80 U.S. Inf Div had expressed the wish that his troops take Wiltz within a few days.

On 31 Dec 44, 167 Volks Gren Div (Cmdr: Gen Höcker) was inserted along the boundary between Fifth Pz Army and Seventh Army. Having been temporarily assigned to Seventh Army (LIII Inf Corps), this division defended the Marvie–Lutrebois sector. On its left, 5 FJ Div had the sector, Lutrebois–Harlange–area north of Bavigne. On the left wing of the corps lay the sector of 9 Volks Gren Div (area north of Bavigne–north of Nothum–south of Roullingen–south of Buderscheid–the Sauer river southwest of Goesdorf). LIII Inf Corps had moved its command post from Winseler to Boevange on 29 Dec 44.

The German Supreme Command had not yet abandoned its idea of an attack on Bastogne. It ordered I SS Pz Corps (with 9 and 12 SS Pz Div) to be sent to Fifth Pz Army within the next few days, so as to renew the attack on the city from the east. Such an intention necessitated Seventh Army's right wing remaining in a stationary position with the unaltered mission of protecting the southern flank of Fifth Pz Army. It was now to be expected that the center of gravity of the enemy attack would move further east to the sector of 9 Volks Gren Div, so as to be able to deliver a blow northward through Wiltz at the deep German flank. But since the Führer Gren Brig had been placed at the disposal of the Fifth Pz Army as of 1 Jan 45, Seventh Army had no reserve whatever.

V. 1–8 JAN 45

On 1 Jan 45 Seventh Army moved its command post from Dockendorf to Jucken (six kilometers east of Dasburg), in order to facilitate control of the center of its sector. This was the first day after the start of the offensive when comparative peace reigned over the whole army front. And now it was possible, at least, to withdraw the engineer brigade from the front line at Nothum. This formation, which had practically been wiped out in the fighting, was also transferred to Fifth Pz Army on the orders of Army Group B.

On the following day a serious crisis arose on the right wing of the Army. The enemy, supported by tanks, broke through in the sector of 167 Volks Gren Div and pushed as far as Wardin along the Army boundary. He was obviously trying, by means of simultaneous attacks from the west and the south, to link up his forces in the area west of Wiltz or at the important crossroads of Doncols, so as to cut off and surround the forces in the projection of the arc at Harlange. The unusually heavy artillery fire directed at the crossroads, and into the woods at Doncols, seemed to confirm this intention. This placed 5 FJ Div in a very serious position. True, 167 Volks Gren Div succeeded by counterattacks in narrowing and sealing off the breach made by the enemy, but the threat still remained real. As a reaction, the attacks against 9 Volks Gren Div became stronger.

Seventh Army's request that it be permitted to attempt to rescue 5 FJ Div from the Harlange pocket was rejected, since the Supreme Command was primarily concerned with fixing as many enemy forces here as possible. Therefore, Seventh Army was able to assist the heavily engaged LIII Inf Corps only by committing on the right wing more and more elements of the volks artillery corps and the volks projector brigade, and by bringing up all the personnel and material reinforcements available.

But these measures were of no avail and rendered only temporary assistance. The most keenly felt lack now was the shortage of ammunition, due in its turn to a shortage of transport at home. Seventh Army decided to withdraw 276 Volks Gren Div – a mere combat team – located on the right wing of LXXX Inf Corps in the West Wall and to hand it over to LIII Inf Corps. The division was to be assembled for this purpose in the area north-east of Wiltz.

167 Volks Gren Div was reassigned to Fifth Army on the 2 Jan 45, so that the sector from which the I SS Pz Corps would lead an attack on 4 Jan 45 against Bastogne would be under unified control. The boundary between the armies was to be Grumelscheid–Doncols–Lutrebois (these three towns were to be within Seventh Army's sector).

The staff of LIII Inf Corps had been driven out of Boevange on 31 Dec 44 by enemy artillery fire and had transferred its command post to Encherange (four km northeast of Wiltz). The command post of 5 FJ Div was located in the railroad station at Grumelscheid, while the command post of 9 Volks Gren Div was at Noertrange.

From the 3–5 Jan 45, no strong enemy attacks took place on the front of the LIII Inf Corps. Nevertheless, the troops, unable to find adequate cover and shelter in the frozen ground, suffered severe losses from the continuous enemy artillery fire. Casualties from frostbite and illness were also high. Local fighting took place here and there. It led to a breakthrough in the sector of 5 FJ Div on 4 Jan 45, which, however, was cleared up again. (This was at La Bonne Eau.)

By 4 Jan 45, 276 Volks Gren Div had been completely withdrawn from the West Wall and two days later its main body had been assembled in the area of Wilwerwitz– Kautenbach. Both Army and corps had decided to commit the division, whose combat value was slight, on the weakly-held left flank of the corps along the line Buderscheid–Goesdorf–north of Ringel. By this action, it was intended to narrow the decisive sector of 9 Volks Gren Div, and thus to acquire a reserve.

On 6 Jan 45, however, the enemy carried out a surprise attack from west and south on Goesdorf and forced his way through the village and on to Dahl. This meant a new and deep salient in the front of LIII Inf Corps and the loss of the commanding heights around Dahl. And the salient which had been halted on the fringes of the wood north and east of Dahl as well as east of Goesdorf, meant a considerable lengthening of the front line, a very great handicap in view of our lack of troops. Therefore, Seventh Army ordered the salient to be eliminated by counterattack and the Sauer front to be regained as far as Esch sur la Sûre. For this operation, the Führer Gren Brig, over which the Army had in the meantime regained control, was delivered to LIII Inf Corps and the elements of 276 Volks Gren Div which had arrived were subordinated to it.

True, this use of the Führer Gren Brig was contrary to the intentions of LIII Inf Corps, which desired to send the formation to the threatened spot on its own right wing (Doncols crossroads), and not elsewhere. The attack was to be made by the Führer Gren Brig from the northwest through Dahl to the south, and simultaneously, by the elements of 276 Volks Gren Div from north and east. All available artillery and mortars were collected to support the attack, so that on the morning of 7 Jan 45 108 guns could fire rounds in support of the assault. Under this protecting belt of fire the attacking spearheads succeeded in pressing forward into the northern and eastern outskirts of Dahl. Unfortunately, however, the attack, which could receive no further support because of the ammunition shortage, stalled when it encountered heavy enemy artillery fire. When the enemy counterattacks began, Dahl had to be evacuated and our troops had to withdraw to their jump-off positions.

Seventh Army ordered the attack to be renewed on 8 Jan 45 and gave to LIII Inf Corps a regiment of 79 Volks Gren Div for this purpose. This regiment had the mission of attacking, simultaneously with the attack from the east of the reinforced Führer Gren Brig, in the direction of Goesdorf. But this operation was also a failure because of the strong resistance and counterattacks of the enemy.

There was nothing left for us to do now but go over to the defense along the front with the assistance of 276 Volks Gren Div. The failure of the attacks on Dahl and Goesdorf had driven home to the Army the lesson that the assault power of its troops – as a result of the ammunition, air, and personnel situation – was now slight indeed.

VI. 9–11 JAN 45

On 9 Jan 45 the left wing of 5 FJ Div was breached by the enemy in the region north of Bavigne. Here, the enemy penetrated as far as Berlé, and now stood deep in the rear of the division, whose elements located at Harlange were practically cut off. The crossroads at Doncols were seriously threatened. If this intersection were lost, the last remaining supply route of the division would fall into enemy hands.

Attempts to eliminate this enemy salient did not meet with success, for visibility was so limited in this hilly terrain that the troops could not execute a well-supported and closely integrated attack.

The situation of the right wing of the Army, already difficult, grew worse on 10 Jan 45 when 90 U.S. Inf Div joined the attack against the completely exhausted and fantastically outnumbered 5 FJ Div. In front of the extreme right wing of Seventh Army there now stood three American Infantry Divisions (26, 35, and 90); at the same time, two American Armored Divisions (4 and 6) were attacking from the west.

The breakthrough by the enemy on 11 Jan 45 to the crossroads at Doncols completed the encirclement of 5 FJ Div. The remnants of its widely-scattered elements fought their way through the wooded terrain to the northeast. The combat elements of the division had now been almost completely crushed, the greater part of its equipment had been lost. Only by the immediate commitment of the Führer Gren Brig was it possible to temporarily halt a further enemy advance.

By 10 Jan 45, 167 Volks Gren Div (adjoining on the north) had already been assigned to Seventh Army, and in turn to LIII Inf Corps, to keep the combat sector under a unified command. 1 SS Pz Div was sent to attack southward from the area of Ober- and Niederwampach, with the mission of recapturing the crossroads at Doncols again. It was hoped that this attack would enable 5 FJ Div and 167 Volks Gren Div to smash through to the northeast. Control of the attack of 1 SS Pz Div was taken over by LVIII Pz Corps of Fifth Pz Army, to which 167 Volks Gren Div and 5 FJ Div were also assigned.

Therewith, the battle in the area of Bastogne had come to an end for Seventh Army, and during the night of 12/13 Jan 45 the organized retreat behind the

Wiltz sector was begun. LIII Inf Corps had not been able to fulfil its mission of protecting the southern flank of the front around Bastogne. However, its task had really been an impossible one. With vastly inferior forces, handicapped by a serious shortage of ammunition, and under the most severe fighting conditions, it had nevertheless been able to tie down considerable enemy forces (two armored and four infantry divisions) from 23 Dec 44 until 11 Jan 45 and to prevent a strategic breakthrough by the enemy to the north against the deep flank of Army Group B. This was all that Seventh Army could possibly do.

The Defense of Wiltz, the Clerf and the Sauer; Withdrawal to the West Wall (12–25 Jan 1945)

I. 12–17 JAN 45

From 12 Jan 45 onward, the measures initiated by the Supreme Command for the liquidation of the Ardennes Offensive were put into effect. As it had been decided that the frontal arc reached during the attacks would be given up gradually and under pressure from the enemy, Seventh Army still had to defend behind the Wiltz and the Sauer. Although it was still important to hold the Sauer front in the center of the Seventh Army sector, measures for the withdrawal of the right wing of the Army to the heights between the Wiltz and the Clerf, and behind the Clerf, were put into effect on a modest scale. By 10 Jan 45, the Wiltz position had been prepared for defense by the use of two construction battalions and of all hands available behind the front, and the troops who had prepared it were withdrawn to the next planned defense line. However, these preparations also suffered from the shortage of men and material; for instance, it was possible to dig antitank ditches only with the aid of blasting cartridges, and there was a shortage of these. So these preparations were not to be valued very highly.

Organizationally, a thorough rearrangement was initiated after it had been found necessary to transfer LXXXV Inf Corps to Army Group G on 12 Jan 45 for use in Lorraine. Seventh Army assigned this corps' right division (79 Volks Gren Div) to LIII Inf Corps, and its left division (352 Volks Gren Div) to LXXX Inf Corps. Since LXXX Inf Corps had previously lost 276 Volks Gren Div, its only other division was 212 Volks Gren Div. The new boundary line between the two corps was Biewels, two kilometers north of Vianden (LIII)–Hoscheid (LIII)–westward along the Sauer.

The southward attack of LVIII Inf Corps of Fifth Pz Army, executed by 1 SS Pz Div, did not reach the crossroads at Doncols, so that the situation along the right Army boundary remained tense. However, Army Group B was now able to order a withdrawal, so that the situation could be restored and a coherent front could be built up behind Wiltz. The boundary line between Fifth Pz Army (LVIII Pz Corps) and Seventh Army (LIII Inf Corps) was the line Dasburg

(Fifth)–Draufelt (Seventh)–Grumelscheid (Seventh)–Doncols. With the situation quiet on 13 and 14 Jan 45, the center and the left wing of LIII Inf Corps could be withdrawn behind the Wiltz from the town of that name to the mouth of the Sauer.

In the sector of the LIII Inf Corps, 9, 276, and 79 Volks Gren Divs were situated from right to left behind the Wiltz. The Führer Gren Brig had already been withdrawn from the front and assembled in the vicinity of the Clerf. It had to be ready for transfer to the Eastern Front, and it left at the end of Jan 45.

II. 18–21 JAN 45

On 18 Jan 45, XII U.S. Corps (Third Army) started an attack across the Sauer on both sides of Diekirch northwards. Seventh Army had long known of the transfer of 5 U.S. Inf Div from the area of Echternach to the sector of 352 Volks Gren Div. But as 6 U.S. Armd Div, observed at the same spot at the end of December, had in the meantime been sent to the area around Bastogne, Seventh Army believed that there was little likelihood of a strong enemy attack in the vicinity of Echternach. Consequently, the attack of 5 U.S. Inf Div came as a great surprise. The greatly diminished power of the artillery of 352 Volks Gren Div, which had not yet overcome the psychological effect of the unhappy days just before Christmas, could not hope to stand up to this attack. By the end of the very first day of the American assault, several deep salients had been pushed into our line. The American troops, moving under cover of a thick smoke screen, bypassed the strongpoints of 352 Volks Gren Div, whose machine-gun and mortar crews could not see what was happening. The artillery was also blinded. All it could do was to lay a thin curtain of fire along the souther bank of the Sauer – on account of the scarcity of ammunition, a very thin curtain! A few of the strongpoints on the northern bank of the river held out for a few days longer. The enemy attack inflicted further heavy personnel and material losses on the division and caused the loss of the greater part of its artillery.

The American drive across the Sauer represented an increased threat to the southern flank of LIII Inf Corps and to the entire Fifth Pz Army, parts of which were still fighting east of Bastogne. The attack brought with it the loss of the southern crossings of the Our as well, since once again they lay within the range of the American artillery. All that remained to Seventh Army were the crossings at Vianden and Gemünd. And now there was a danger of the enemy turning in eastward across the Our and against the West Wall, which at the time was secured from Vianden to south of Trier (some 50 kilometers) only by the weakened 212 Volks Gren Div. Army Group B now placed a task force (Pz Gren Regt, reinforced – Graf Kielmannsegg) of 11 Pz Div, which was being rehabilitated behind the Seventh Army front, behind the right wing of LXXX Inf Corps as a security garrison within the West Wall. This regiment could not be sent west of the Our.

To seal off the enemy push, Army Group B sent a combined-arms task force of Pz Lehr Div (Gen Bayerlein), while Seventh Army assigned a regimental group of 79 Volks Gren Div to the right wing of LXXX Inf Corps. Before these troops could take a hand in the fighting, 352 Volks Gren Div was thrown still further back on 19 and 20 Jan 45. The scarcity of ammunition and POL, as well as the weather conditions (a heavy snowstorm raged on 19 Jan 45) had a very disadvantageous influence on the course of the battle.

Seventh Army's situation was all the more difficult, because the whole retreat of LIII Inf Corps eastward depended on Fifth Pz Army. And Fifth Pz Army's difficulties, because it had a large number of tanks, were even greater than those of Seventh Army. The retrograde movement proceeded exceedingly slowly. It was therefore of vital importance that the position of the southern flank be restored.

On 20 Jan 45 the enemy took Brandenberg, until then the command post of 352 Volks Gren Div, the new command post having just been set up in an air raid shelter south of Bauler. With the assistance of elements of Pz Lehr Div and of 79 Volks Gren Div which we had managed to commit on the right wing of 352 Volks Gren Div, it was possible to halt the enemy in the line: two kilometers south of Hoscheid–Landscheid–Walsdorf–Bettel. But he continued his two-pronged attack: 5 U.S. Inf Div south of Hoscheid, 4 U.S. Inf Div south of Vianden.

Thus, elements of Pz Lehr Div were involved in heavy fighting on 21 Jan 45 in the region south of Hoscheid–Landscheid. To control this section, Army Group B ordered XLVII Pz Corps (CG: Gen Pz Frhr Heinrich von Lüttwitz) to move into the army sector and take over Pz Lehr Div and 352 Volks Gren Div. LXXX Inf Corps once again controlled only 212 Volks Gren Div.

III. 22–25 JAN 45

Meanwhile, LIII Inf Corps, on the southern flank of Fifth Pz Army, had withdrawn to the line: the western fringe of the wood south of Boevange–the stream as far as Weidingen, east of Wiltz–the Wiltz sector, so that the loop of the Sauer south of Hoscheid again formed the pivot of the withdrawal movement and for this reason had at all cost to remain in our hands. Enemy pressure against the front of LIII Inf Corps was not at the time particularly strong, so that the situation was not especially threatening.

On 22 Jan 45, LVIII Pz Corps (CG: Gen Pz Krüger), previously the left corps of Fifth Pz Army, was assigned to Seventh Army, for Fifth Pz Army had to take over the sector of Sixth Pz Army. The Corps stood with 340 Volks Gren Div (Cmdr: Genmaj Tolsdorff), 167 Volks Gren Div (Cmdr: Genmaj Höcker), and 5 FJ Div, along the line: Asselborn–east of Boevange. The command post was in the mill north of Dasburg.

Activity in front of XLVII Pz Corps had died down somewhat on 22 Jan 45, but 352 Volks Gren Div had not been able to prevent small breaches in its line. On this day the enemy had sent in particularly strong air formations. For the first time the situation in the air was similar to that which had prevailed in Normandy.

During the next two nights (22/23 and 23/24 Jan 45), the two corps on the right of the army (LVIII Pz Corps and LIII Inf Corps), starting on the right, withdrew behind the Clerf sector. At the same time, 167 Volks Gren Div was withdrawn from the front by LVIII Pz Corps and sent to Fifth Pz Army via Dasburg. This withdrawal behind the Clerf sector proceeded on the whole smoothly and without incidents. In front of the center of Seventh Army the line had been stabilized once again (23–24 Jan 45). It is true that heavy attacks by the enemy continued to take place, but with the exception of local enemy advances we were able to hold.

Seventh Army had moved its command post on 23 Jan 45 from Jucken to Merkeshausen; LVIII Pz Corps, to Ohlscheid; LIII Inf Corps on 22 Jan 45 to a spot three km northeast of Eisenbach; XLVII Pz Corps, on 24 Jan 45 to Baustert; and LXXX Inf Corps (after the release of 352 Volks Gren Div) to Wolsfelder Berg.

On 25 Jan 45 a breakthrough across the Clerf took place on the southern wing of Fifth Pz Army, opposite 26 Volks Gren Div, threatening the northern flank of 340 Volks Gren Div in the region of Urspelt. But 340 Volks Gren Div was able to seal this off with a counterattack. In the sector of 276 Volks Gren Div there also occurred a breakthrough across the Clerf to Pintsch. Very bitter fighting developed around this village, which changed hands several times and finally remained in ours. Here, the enemy sustained heavy losses.

It was now a matter of vital importance to hold the bridgeheads west of the Our until all material had been transferred across this boundary river. And here we were faced with tremendous difficulties, as the deeply eroded Our valley and the icy roads caused enormous traffic jams; the great shortage of gasoline proved to be simply catastrophic. Consequently, withdrawal of the panzer units, the artillery, and the troop columns was terribly slow. The direct result was that the troops defending the bridgeheads were obliged to fight on much longer and sustained greater losses.

IV. WITHDRAWAL INTO THE WEST WALL (UNTIL 31 JAN 45)

As a consequence of the conditions delineated above, on 26 Jan 45 bitter fighting arose along the whole front west of the Our; the fighting was heavy in the LVIII Pz Corps sector astride the Clerf, in the Pintsch–Lellingen area of 276 Volks Gren Div, and at Hoscheid, which was lost to the enemy on the same day. And during the next day, these ferocious bridgehead battles continued, especially in the area of Hosingen–Putscheid–Weiler. Although we lost many men we succeeded in holding the enemy away from the bridge at Dasburg and Gemünd, so that the greater part of our equipment could be brought over to the eastern bank of the Our. As a result of the shortage of gasoline a number of tanks had to be blown up, as we had no vehicles to spare for towing them. However, by 31 Jan 45 all bridgeheads had been withdrawn to the eastern bank of the Our.

Conclusions

I. REASONS FOR THE FAILURE OF THE OFFENSIVE

The Ardennes Offensive, on which the Supreme Command pinned all its hopes, completely failed because the prerequisites for success were lacking from the start:

    a. The prerequisites were:

       (1) Adequate forces.

       (2) Air superiority, or at least equality.

       (3) Adequate supplies of ammunition.

       (4) Adequate supplies of POL.

       (5) Adequate supplies of motor transport.

       (6) Adequate supplies of engineer equipment.

       (7) Adequate supplies of spare parts for tanks and armored vehicles.

    b. As a result of all these shortages, we were not able to overcome the difficulties of the weather and the terrain

    c. The sole advantages which the German forces enjoyed were the element of surprise, and the favorable conditions in the enemy sector. However, both these things were only of help to us at the beginning.

So far as our estimate of the enemy's reaction is concerned, it may be said that the Supreme Command erred when it imagined that the enemy would content himself with a defensive reaction, and that the difficulties inherent in a unified Allied command would cause a certain time lag to intervene before the Allies struck back. These false suppositions had a particularly unhappy effect on the situation of Seventh Army, which was at least three or four divisions too weak to accomplish its mission. If it can be asserted that Seventh Army, on the whole, performed rather well under the circumstances, this was due only to the fact that the offensive never got as far as the Meuse. For, if the flank of the offensive had had to be protected as far as Givet, the forces assigned to Seventh Army would have been hopelessly inadequate. Actually, the remote objective of Antwerp had from the beginning been deemed by Seventh Army to be simply unrealizable: The Suggestion of Army Group B – to limit the mission of the attack to reaching the Meuse – had been regarded by Seventh Army as one which could be realized. Even the Meuse seemed far away to Seventh Army when shortages became omnipresent:

a. Some of the divisions which had been earmarked for the offensive were still engaged on other fronts when the time arrived for the attack to begin; their timely arrival in the west was thus placed in jeopardy and it was not feasible to prepare them for their mission. Again, some of them were involved in defensive battles up to the very last moment, whence they emerged on one day and, on the next, stormed forward in far-flung attack toward the goal. The panzer grenadier division scheduled to assist Seventh Army in its task was never brought up; instead, there was the Führer Grenadier Brigade, a unit with only very moderate combat power, badly led, and unable to achieve anything of note. The stage of training reached by the divisions was not an advanced one, there was a particular lack of experienced noncommissioned officers, and the intermediate leaders were neither so flexible nor so well-schooled that they could hope to rise to the requirements of a trying war of movement.

b. The artillery prime movers were inadequate; the Raupenschlepper Ost was too weak to pull the guns through mud and – later – through snow, up the hilly ground. Part of the artillery had not been intended for anything but the preparation of the attack, and remained behind – immobile – in the jump-off positions. Not a single division had its full complement of assault guns, some of them had none at all, and others no more than three or four. The bridge columns dumped at the Rhine possessed no vehicles of their own for towing purposes; and Seventh Army was forced to undertake the task of towing the heavy vehicles either with its own motor vehicles or by horse power or even with human strength, to their scene of operation wherever it might be; consequently, the artillery was deprived of its prime movers, which it desperately needed to assure its ammunition supply. In any case, when the attack began on 16 Dec 44, only half a bridge column had gotten as far as the vicinity of the stream.

c. As a result of the shortage of POL, difficulties piled one on the other from the moment of initiation of the attack and gradually increased until they became insurmountable.

d. The number of pontoons provided for the first crossings of the Our and the Sauer was completely inadequate: the divisions possessed no more than eight of these; one division had only two large pontoons, and one of these was destroyed by enemy fire when the first crossing attempt was made.

A notable difficulty was that, until the last moment, the troops were completely in the dark as to what they were supposed to achieve, so that the offensive began with insufficient preparation for the very difficult terrain. However, it was not due to lack of foresight on the part of the Army that such a state of affairs existed; it had pointed out on many occasions the deficiencies which still existed. And the employment of two panzer armies in the depth of winter meant very difficult conditions and not inconsiderable risk. Our years of experience on the Eastern Front should certainly have enabled us to anticipate these difficulties.

Seventh Army was not able to prevent the relief of Bastogne, although it recklessly plundered its other sectors in order to give everything to the right wing: men, antitank weapons, artillery, and ammunition. Even during the second part of the offensive it still had to sacrifice, because strong elements of Fifth Army were still located in the area west and northwest of Bastogne and Seventh Army had the mission of covering their withdrawal. Since once again the order for a retreat was given too late and its tempo was much too slow, the few remaining combat units of any ability were frittered away and consumed; in the end all usable Army reserves were gone. Seventh Army contemplated this development – the concentration of all available reserves on the right wing – with growing concern. The enemy counterattack struck first of all at the southern flank of the German offensive and its strategic effect lessened as Fifth Pz Army withdrew nearer and nearer to the Bastogne–Houffalize line.

What would have happened if the American Command had quickly changed the main effort of its mobile forces to a thrust across the Sauer near Diekirch in order to strike the German flank further east; and had next rolled up the West Wall to the north, advancing west – or worse still – east along the Sauer in order to catch the remnants of Fifth Pz and Seventh Army at the Our?

About the beginning of January 45, when Seventh Army was thoroughly involved near Bastogne, such an operation would have found Seventh Army's thinly manned line incapable of any effective resistance, because of its lack of reserves and mobility. Seventh Army had feared such an attack from the beginning, an attack which began only on 20 Jan 45 – when the front had approached the Clerf sector – and which, even then, was not executed with maximum strength. The limitation of this attack can be ascribed to the fact that Seventh Army was fortunately able to concentrate on this vital point, even if its available forces were rather small. This delaying action enabled us once again to get the remainder of the Ardennes Armies back behind the West Wall and, with their support, to build up a new line of defence.

The Seventh Army Staff is not in possession of sufficient data to enable it to predict accurately the success of an Allied operation which largely ignored the German shock troops in the relatively strong Meuse zone; and which delivered a well-planned, powerful, coordinated attack against the southern pivot of the German offensive in order to drive north or northeast across the Sauer. Such an operation might have succeeded in annihilating the Ardennes Armies and in bringing about the speedy collapse of the Western Front.

II. EVALUATION OF SEVENTH ARMY'S ACCOMPLISHMENTS

It may be observed, in conclusion, that Seventh Army, fighting a heavy and long-drawn-out action under the most arduous and unequal conditions succeeded, on the whole, in accomplishing its mission.

SEVENTH ARMY

1. Command Posts on 16 Dec 44:

Seventh Army	Dockendorf
LXXXV Inf Corps	Burg
5 FJ Div	bunker north of Roth
352 Volks Gren Div	Hüttingen
LXXX Inf Corps	Wolsfelder Berg
276 Volks Gren Div	Schankweiler
212 Volks Gren Div	Prümzurley
LIII Inf Corps	Föhren

2. Bridge Sites:

5 FJ Inf Div	Vianden, aux. bridge, 60 tons, ready 28 Dec 44.
	Roth, aux. bridge, 24 tons, ready 17 Dec 44.
352 Volks Gren Div	Gentingen, aux. bridge, 24 tons, ready 17 Dec 44.
276 Volks Gren Div	Bollendorf, military bridge, 24 tons, ready 19 Dec 44, intermittently usable until 24 Dec 44, when it was destroyed.
	Dillingen, aux. bridge, 24 tons, ready 25 Dec 44.
212 Volks Gren Div	east of Echternach, aix. bridge, construction prevented by enemy artillery fire.
	Weilerbach, restored covered bridge, about 40 tons, ready 18 Dec 44.
	Edingen, aux. bridge, 24 tons, ready 19 Dec 44.

ARTILLERY ORGANIZATION – SEVENTH ARMY – 16 Dec 44

Arty CG – Genmaj Paul Riedel

LXXX Inf Corps Arty Cmdr	**LXXXV Volks Arty Cmdr**
212 Volks Arty Regt 　1st Bn; one battery Danish guns, 　　one battery French guns 　　　(190 mm) 2d, 3d, 4th Bn one battery naval guns	352 Volks Arty Regt (four bns)
	Volks Arty Corps (three bns)
276 Volks Arty Regt (four bns)	5 FJ Arty Regt (ultra-mobile task force) 　four bns 　one battery Danish guns
Volks Arty Corps (five bns)	18 Volks Proj Brig (two regts, of three bns each)
8 Volks Proj Brig 　(two regts, of three bns each)	One battery (120 mm)
One battery (120 mm)	Obsn Bn
Obsn Bn	

Reserve: LIII Arty Cmdr

COMMANDERS and STAFF OFFICERS – SEVENTH ARMY UNITS
during the
ARDENNES OFFENSIVE

1. **SEVENTH ARMY:**

CG:	Gen Pz	Brandenberger
C of S:	Obst i.G.	Gersdorff, Frhr von
Ia:	Obstlt i.G.	Voigt-Ruschewey
Ic:	Maj i.G.	Hirche
O Qu:	Obstlt i.G.	Fusenegger
Harko:	Genmaj	Riedel

2. **LXXXV Inf Corps:**

CG:	Gen Inf	Kniess
C of S:	Obstlt i.G.	Lassen
Arko:	Obst	Beisswaenger

3. **LXXX Inf Corps:**

CG:	Gen Inf	Beyer, Dr
C of S:	Obst i.G.	Koestlin
Arko:	Obst	Schroeder

4. **LIII Inf Corps:**

CG:	Gen Kav	Rothkirch, Graf
C of S:	Obst i.G.	Bodenstein
Arko:	?	?

5. **XLVII Pz Corps:**

CG:	Gen Pz	Lüttwitz, Heinrich; Frhr von
C of S:	Obstlt i.G.	Bernstorff, Graf

6. **LVIII Pz Corps:**

CG:	Gen Pz	Krüger, Walter
C of S:	Obst i.G.	Dingler

7. **5 FJ Div:**

Cmdr:	Obst, later Genmaj	Heilmann
Ia:	Maj i.G.	Passlik; after about 22 Dec 44,
	Maj	Georgi

8. **352 Volks Gren Div:**

Cmdr:	Obst	Schmidt; after 25 Dec 44,
	Genmaj	Batzing
Ia:	Maj i.G.	Schneider

9. **276 Volks Gren Div:**

Cmdr:	Genmaj	Möhring (KIA); after 23 Dec 44,
	Obst	Dempwolff
Ia:	Maj i.G.	Wittmann

10. **212 Volks Gren Div:**

Cmdr:	Genlt	Sensfuss
Ia:	Maj i.G.	Koestlin; after about 26 Dec 44,
	Maj i.G.	Edler von Rosenthal

11. **79 Volks Gren Div:**

Cmdr:	Obst	Weber; after about 30 Dec 44,
	Obst	Hummel
Ia:	Obstlt i.G.	Henneberg

12. **9 Volks Gren Div:**

Cmdr:	Genmaj	Kolb
Ia:	?	?

Notes

1. Interview notes in the John Toland Papers at the Library of Congress, Box 37.
2. Hechler, 'The Enemy Side of the Hill', see note 7, Introduction, part one of this book.
3. Information on the Seventh Army is weighty. See also General Erich Brandenberger, 'Questions and Answers on the Ardennes Campaign', A-934, 12 July 1949, and B-447. Also, from Generalmajor Rudolf von Gersdorff, Brandenberger's capable Chief of Staff: 'An Interview with Gen. von Gersdorff: Seventh Army in the Ardennes Offensive', ETHINT-54; 'The Ardennes Offensive', A-909, 8 November 1945; 'Results of the Ardennes Offensive', 3 February 1946; 'Evaluation and Equipment of the Units Attached to the Seventh Army during the Ardennes Offensive', A-932, n.d.' Generalmajor Paul Riedel, 'Seventh Army Artillery', B-594 and B-783; and 'Battles in the Ardennes: Activity of the Artillery of the Seventh Army', B-467, n.d.
4. This was the new U.S. 9th Armored Division, with each of its combat commands separated across the width of the Ardennes front.
5. A much more important reason for the rapid advance through the Ardennes in 1940 is that the Germans did not really have to fight prior to reaching the Meuse River. The few Belgian Chasseurs Ardennais pulled back across the river as had been pre-arranged. For a comparison of the 1940 and 1944 offensives see Magna Bauer's manuscript on file at OCMH.
6. 44th MG Battalion.
7. Panzer Lehr was using this bridge to cross over the Our.

5

Questionnaire on the Ardennes Offensive

BY GENERALFELDMARSCHALL WILHELM KEITEL AND
GENERALOBERST ALFRED JODL

Introduction

With regard to military affairs, no person was closer to Hitler in late 1944 than Generaloberst Alfred Jodl, taciturn head of the German High Command of the Armed forces (OKW) and the Wehrmachtführungsstab, the Armed Forces Operations Staff, which formed Hitler's household military command center. His was acknowledged to be the brain behind the OKW plan for the offensive, which many, such as General von Manteuffel, were inclined to criticize for its lack of realism:

> Keitel, Jodl and Warlimont had never been in the war ... Their lack of fighting experience tended to make them underrate practical difficulties, and encourage Hitler to believe that things could be done that were quite impossible ... I imagined that Hitler must realize that a rapid advance would not be possible under winter conditions, and these limitations, but from what I have heard since, it is clear that Hitler thought the advance could go much quicker than it did. The Meuse could not possibly have been reached on the second or third day as Jodl expected. He and Keitel tended to encourage Hitler's optimistic illusions.[1]

After the war, the Historical Section described their impressions of the chain-smoking head of OKW:

> He was fairly cold, exact, humorless and stiff in posture and personality. I was impressed by his grasp of details; for example, I started to apologize for one question regarding the American attempt to simulate the presence of an extra U.S. division in the south of the VIII Corps sector. Gen. Jodl said, 'Oh, that's all right, I can answer that question with candor; we didn't know anything about a simulated division, but we did know that a few days before the 16th of December you moved fresh troops in the north flank of the VIII Corps [106th Infantry Division].'

As Jodl was executed at Nuremburg in October 1946, the opinions expressed in his interviews constitute an important primary source.[2] After all, in the course of the interrogations he acknowledged that the plan for the operation had evolved from numerous detailed discussions between Hitler and himself. The attack had to be launched in the West 'because the Russians had so many troops that even if we had succeeded in destroying thirty divisions, it would not have made any difference. On the other hand, if we destroyed 30 divisions in the West, it would amount to more than one third of the entire invasion army.' He and Hitler firmly believed that by a successful offensive 'a decisive turning point in the Campaign in the West, and possibly of the entire war could be achieved.'

However, as the preparations for the offensive continued, Jodl had to accept more and more compromises within the framework of the plan, and found himself leaning towards the 'small solutions' proposed by Hitler's generals: 'The venture of the far-flung objective [Antwerp] is unalterable,' he wrote to General Westphal on 1 November, 'although the goal appears to be disproportionate to our available forces.'[3] Just before the attack Jodl confided, 'I was filled with doubt.' When asked, after the war, if the German army could have succeeded in reaching Antwerp had they possessed the reserves which were available in 1940, he replied:

We would have needed many, many more reserves and correspondingly more aircraft, munitions and fuel. We did not have the other factors of superiority on a large scale. If we had had ten more good divisions, we might have thrown you over the Meuse, but how we could have held the big salient thus created, is not clear. Our strategic position would have been worse rather than better.[4]

Generalfeldmarschall Wilhelm Keitel was a very unlikely figure for one of the most powerful military men in Hitler's headquarters. Born near Brunswick, Keitel was neither a Prussian nor rose very far in the field command. During the Great War he served first as an artillery battery commander and later as a staff officer. In 1925 he took his first post-war job, with the Reichswehr Ministry, eventually becoming a colonel with the Organizations Department of the Truppenamt in 1929. Owing to the fact that he was War Minister Werner von Blomberg's son-in-law, his promotions were rapid thereafter: a Major General in 1934, a Leutnant General in 1936 and a General of the Artillery in 1937. His lack of practical military experience was illustrated by the fact that he never commanded a military formation larger than a battalion. However, Hitler made Keitel his head of the OKW in 1938, mainly on Blomberg's recommendation of him as an efficient chef de bureau.

What Hitler saw in Keitel was an unthinking assistant who would blindly obey his bidding. He was an officer of little imagination or intellectual power and willingly sold out the Reichswehr to the National Socialists. Even Hitler was under no illusion as to his capabilities: 'he has the mental capacity of a cinema usher,' he once observed.[5] Others around Keitel saw him as a sycophant and a mouthpiece for Hitler's decisions – 'Lakeitel' (Lackey Keitel), as he was called by those who saw through his title. Although Keitel seldom made any decisions of his own he was a perpetual fixture at Hitler's side, and often lent his signature to important documents. This, perhaps more than anything else, sent Keitel to the gallows along with General Jodl on 16 October 1946.

It was against this backdrop that Keitel and Jodl composed the following answers to a questionnaire regarding the Ardennes Offensive.[6] In particular, their final statement regarding the planning is unapologetic: they believed the best choice had been made in launching the attack in the West. 'I cannot recall being so divided in my feelings towards any other man as I was towards Hitler,' Jodl said at Nuremberg. 'My emotions ranged from reverence and admiration to hatred. His destructive and caustic criticism of so much I held dear – the General Staff, the middle class, the nobility, the Reichswehr, our sense of right and justice – all this repelled me more and more, during the second half of the war.' Major Hechler, who conducted the interviews at Bad Mondorf, observed that:

General Jodl appeared very eager to write full details on the Ardennes Offen-sive . . . [However] he was very much concerned with the impending war crimes trials . . . General Jodl cleared this particular account of the Ardennes Offensive with Field Marshal Keitel, because Keitel was at all times very jumpy about war crimes, and seemed to be scared to answer any question quickly . . . As with all of General Jodl's answers, I believe that great weight can be attached to the strategic considerations he discusses.

With regard to Generalfeldmarschall Keitel, Hechler wrote:

At about 7:30 PM Maj. Büchs came over and General Jodl sought us out and said that Field Marshal Keitel wanted to speak to me. Keitel came over and in between bows and scrapes and other despicable gestures, he said he had read General Jodl's account of the Ardennes Offensive and had countersigned it. It was obvious that this had been done at Jodl's initiative. I asked Keitel if he did not want to take the questions and expand on them with his own account, but he quickly backed away from that one with the plea that Jodl knew twice as much as he did. I took an instant dislike to Keitel, who looked for all the world like a slave who feels he must bow before a tyrant. I felt like telling him to stiffen his backbone like Jodl and quit talking to me in wheedling tones.

But more important than personality, both Keitel and Jodl suffered a deficiency which was harped upon repeatedly by other German commanders: neither had much in the way of first-hand experience with the war. Although both made nominal trips to the fronts, neither stayed long enough to gain more than transient impressions. And neither had ever commanded a large military formation in peacetime, much less during an all out world war. Dietrich accurately identified the source of their optimism: 'they only waged war,' he said, 'on maps.'

Danny S. Parker

Questionnaire on the Ardennes Offensive

Q. What factors influenced the selection of 16 December 1944 as the date for the start of the German Ardennes Offensive?

   a. First Army (V Corps) attack toward Roer River dams?
   b. Threat offered by Third U.S. Army's imminent attack on the Siegfried Line scheduled to start 19 December (How much intelligence did the Germans have of this attack?)
   c. Situation and Russian capabilities on East front?
   d. Military or Political morale considerations?
   e. Weather.

A. The moment for the attack was dictated by circumstances. In our first planning we hoped to launch the attack somewhere between 26 and 28 November (new-moon period). But the arrangement and refresher training of the combat divisions, as also the bringing up of munitions and fuel dragged on into December, as a consequence of Allied air raids.

16 December was, unfortunately, the earliest moment at which an attack could be made. This brought the operation already into a period of improving flying weather. The divisions of the 1st and 2d wave were marched up, the divisions of the 3d wave were just arriving.

Neither the attack of the 1st U.S. Army nor the intended attack of the U.S. 3rd Army, which was unknown to us, had any influence on the choice of the time of attack. On the contrary the attack of the U.S. 5th Corps was just what we wanted; we should have liked it still better if the British Army Group had already started a major attack over the Roer.

The situation on the Eastern Front had no more immediate influence on the moment of attack, except in the general tendency to make the attack as soon as possible in order to use the experience-proven worst flying weather and to release as soon as possible more units for the east.

The morale of the troops played no part in it. The men were certainly inadequately and hurriedly trained and still not sufficiently welded together, but in the mass they were optimistic and full of aggressiveness. On 12 December HQ was moved from Berlin to Ziegenberg, on 13 and 14 The Führer spoke to the Commanding Generals. On 14 December the 16th was fixed as the day for attack.

Q. What, specifically, were the ultimate and intermediate objectives of the offensive in the final orders issued?

A. The objects of the operations were: Breakthrough with the 6th Panzer Army over the Meuse between Liège and Huy with Antwerp as the objective. The 5th Panzer Army had to cross the Meuse between Huy and Dinant and cover the left flank of the 6th Army against Brussels–Charleroi. The 7th Army was to take the line Dinant–Neufchâteau–Luxemburg and secure the deep left flank of the Army Group. The mission of the left wing of the 15th Army was to press forward over the Hohes Venn into the line Monschau–Verviers–Liège, and there intercept a counterattack of the strong enemy forces from the Aachen region into the deep right flank of the Army Group. A later supplementary attack between the Meuse and Geilenkirchen towards the south was desired by Oberbefehlshaber West but not approved and the forces provided for it were brought up behind the main attack as OKW reserves. Secondary objectives were not given, in accordance with our fundamental operational principles.

Q. Was there ever an intention on the part of the German high command, either in the planning phase, or during the course of the offensive when the attacks to the north failed, to swing south and turn the flank of Third U.S. Army?

A. The idea of turning south after the breakthrough, in order to operate against the left flank of the U.S. 3rd Army, was voiced by the Führer before the final decision on the attack, but it was dropped as it lacked an opposite pole. By reaching Antwerp, on the other hand, the entire British Army Group would have been cut off from its connections to the rear. During the course of the Offensive the idea of wheeling south was never again taken up.

Q. What counter-intelligence measures were used to conceal the assembly and preparations for attack of the 6th Panzer and 5th Panzer armies?

A. The directives for the secrecy and masking were particularly carefully drawn and comprised the following:

  a. Whoever knew about our intention had to subscribe a written undertaking.
  b. All preparations were made under the slogan, counterattack into the south flank of a British major attack on the Ruhr.
  c. The moment when the Armies, Corps, Divisions and Regiments might be informed of our real intention was fixed by the OKW.
  d. The Panzer Divisions of the 6th Panzer Army were brought up at the last moment and in night movements.
  e. The new assault divisions might only be brought into the frontline on the very last night. It was forbidden to send out any scouts in advance

from these units. In the last few days no scouts at all might be used. Unreliable soldiers (Alsatians etc.) had to be taken out of the frontline.

f. Artillery and AA could only fire in the same field as before.

g. Troop movements in daytime were forbidden.

h. Our planes could not move to their jumping off place before the first day of the attack.

i. The 6th and 5th Panzer Armies had to retain their existing CPs. The new CPs for the attack might only be occupied by a small operational staff under a cover name.

k. Comprehensive sending of fake radio messages was to preserve the existing organization of the operational staffs in the radio picture.

Q. Planning dates.

a. When was the Ardennes selected as the area in which the offensive would be launched?

b. When was the plan adopted to use offensively the reserves in the West?

A. In the last few days of September.

Q. What was the minimum build-up of forces considered necessary, in the planning stage, for the launching of this offensive? Was this minimum set or exceeded? When was the build-up started and when completed? Were available reinforcements considered sufficient?

A. 25 to 30 Divisions were considered the necessary minimum. This number was considerably exceeded. The troops began to move up at the beginning of November. The first arrivals, the three Volksgrenadier Divisions, were put into the frontline of the attack sector. No changes were made in the manning of the front until the day of the attack. By about 10 December all the forces had been brought up. Assuming always that the attack was a complete surprise for the enemy we considered the reserves at our disposition as sufficient to attain our objective.

Q. What were the available stocks of motor fuel for the two armies, in terms of kilometers, at the start of the offensive? Was the German Command in a position to sustain the drive by drawing on its fuel reserves, in the event that American POL dumps were not captured? How much fuel and other major supply items needed to be captured in order to sustain the offensive? Was there accurate knowledge of the location of the main Allied supply installations (elements of the I SS Panzer Corps penetrated to the southern edge of a 3,300,000 gallon dump near Spa)?

A. There were three supply units of 200 km (8000 tons) with the troops. Another about 20,000 was also ready. With these the objective could be reached without capturing any fuel from the enemy. We had no exact information about U.S. fuel but assumed that near Liège was the head of a pipe line.

Q. If the plan for the offensive could not be realized, how long did the German High Command estimate it would take for the Allies to recover from the spoiling effect of the offensive and mount a new offensive of their own?

A. In the event the object of the offensive was not attained we believed the Allied major attack would be delayed for a minimum of 6 weeks at any rate.

Q. What, if any, important effects in halting the drive had the heavy air attacks of 24–25 December on German lines of communication?

A. The crushing air attacks on transport installations and crossings aimed especially at the middle Rhine Zone, Koblenz–Mainz–Frankfurt, against the valleys of the Moselle, Lahn and Nahe, and against traffic hubs like Giessen, Hanau and Limburg, had grave consequences. The difficult transportation situation which had already been in existence for a long time, could not be improved, in spite of every kind of auxiliary service and repair and restoration work. The Rhine was the end of any through railroad movements on a large scale. West of the Rhine islands of communication functioned on individual rail sectors, so that all movements, especially of supplies, had essentially to be made across country.

Q. Does the enclosed map correctly depict the original plan of the German attack and its subsequent revision? What factors determined the revision of the original plans? When was the revised plan made and when was it put into effect? Why was the II SS Panzer Corps held in reserve until 23 December?

A. My sketch is a fairly accurate reproduction of the plan of attack for the Ardennes offensive. The Corps divisions I cannot any longer reconstruct from memory. As far as I can remember, there were three corps each in the 6th and 5th Panzer Armies, and at least two Corps in the 7th Army. Already on 24 December we were going over to the defensive. No new plan of attack with far-reaching aims was made. The II SS Panzer Corps originally stood as a second attack wave behind the I SS Panzer Corps and was, after a successful break-through, to follow northeast, driving around west of Liège and wheeling against the Meuse south of Maastricht and against the Albert Canal, in order to start the pocketing of the enemy main force in the Aachen area and to cover against an attack from the British and Canadians on the Albert Canal. The Corps was not held back in reserve, but could not follow up the I SS Panzer Corps on account of the completely jammed roads. It was then brought up behind the right wing of the 5th Panzer Army and wheeled in towards the north.

Q. At what date in the counteroffensive did it become evident that it would be impossible to continue forward to the original objectives and that it would be necessary to take up the defensive of that which had been obtained? At what point did it become evident that a retrograde movement from the whole of the Ardennes salient was imperative?

A. It was recognized already on the 18th or 19th of December that we should not succeed in gaining the Maas or crossing it by surprise. A major battle with the U.S. forces south and east of the river was impending. The decision to defend what we had gained was taken about Christmas, the decision to retreat from the Ardennes was made on 14 January, two days after the beginning of the major Russian offensive. At the same time the relinquishing of nine armored units, three infantry divisions and about one-third of the artillery corps and mortar brigades was ordered.

Q. What was the relative importance of St. Vith and Bastogne to the German High Command plan of attack? Did the fact that St. Vith was seized too late add weight to the importance of seizing Bastogne?

A. The significance of St. Vith and Bastogne was realized, yet it was ordered that the first attack waves ought not to stop to wipe out such stubbornly defended key points but leave them for the second wave. The decision for the immediate capture of Bastogne was made as soon as it was realized that we had to reckon with strong enemy counterattacks east and south of the Meuse. The experience of St. Vith had no influence on this decision.

Q. What caused the failure of I SS Panzer Corps in the Monschau–Malmédy area?

A. The main reason for the failure lay in the indescribably bad road conditions. A thaw had set in and the few unpaved roads were soon quagmires. The deployment and development of the I SS Panzer Corps was greatly impeded. The attack of the LXVII AK did not gain enough ground towards the Hohes Venn and this also hampered the free movement of the I SS Panzer Corps towards the west. SS Oberstgruppenführer Sepp Dietrich can give you more exact details.

Q. Was the Allied reaction to the German attack quicker than had been anticipated by the German High Command?

A. The promptness with which the Allies reacted to the German attack did perhaps exceed our expectations. Before anything else however it was the speed of our own movements which lagged far behind expectations.

Q. What methods were employed to gain an accurate knowledge of Allied dispositions in the Ardennes? To what extent were civilian agents depended upon to supply this information?

A. Our picture of the distribution of American forces in the attack sector was essentially derived from tactical reconnaissance, prisoners of war, radio intelligence and our information was, as far as we know, only obtained to a very small degree from agents. Oberst I.G. (Gen. Staff Col.) Buerklin could give you better information, as chief of the Dept. of Foreign Armies, Western Front (Chef der Abteilung Fremde Heere, West).

Q. Did the Germans, mistaking a limited withdrawal for major retreat, believe that on the 24th of December the XVIII U.S. Airborne Corps was in such a weakened condition that it would be possible to break through to Liège?

A. No. We did not have this opinion. A breakthrough in the direction of Liège was not intended.

Q. What knowledge did the Germans have of the faked U.S. troop movements into the VIII U.S. Corps sector in early December?

A. Out of the ordinary troop movements in the U.S. VIII Corps area at the beginning of December were not observed, only a relieving movement on the north wing of the Corps and a reinforcement of artillery at two points, neither of which exercised any influence on our intentions.

Q. In what order of importance would the Germans place the following factors influencing the failure of the German counteroffensive in the Ardennes?

    a. The failure to seize St. Vith in time to prevent the formation of a stout line of defense by the Allies on the northern shoulder of the breakthrough area?

    b. The appearance of good flying weather on or about 24 December, allowing Allied air superiority to be extensively used.

    c. The failure to seize Bastogne.

    d. The failure to seize large stocks of Allied gasoline and supplies.

    e. The ability of the Allied Command to move reinforcements quickly to the threatened area.

    f. The failure of Operation 'GREIF'.

    g. Other factors.

A. The failure of the offensive is to be ascribed to the following reasons, in the order of importance:

    a. Soft roads which made impossible the rapid advance of armored units and hindered a breakthrough in depth into the Meuse area.

    b. Tougher resistance of U.S. troops than expected, especially at St. Vith. (The forces occupying the Schnee-Eifel in our opinion could have held out longer.)

    c. The inadequate training for such an attack of our leaders, subordinate commanders, and troops; in many of the divisions, especially the Armored Divisions.

    d. The widespread shortage of transport, especially heavy tracked prime movers.

    e. The enemy superiority in the air which made itself felt in particular in the major fighting of 24 December.

    f. In the uniform and promptly applied operational measures taken by the Allies.

The rest of the grounds cited in (c), (d) and (f) in the questionnaire did not play much part. Particularly the 'Greif' operation, apart from a few long-range patrols, never came into effect, since the rapid breakthrough on the second day, to the Meuse, which was its condition precedent, did not happen.

Q. What was the significance of the heavily reinforced attacks on 31 December to 4 January on the Bastogne area?

A. The object of the reinforced attacks in the Bastogne area from 31 December was to capture Bastogne itself and so create more favorable conditions for the holding of the ground gained.

Concluding Remarks: We do not believe, with the troops and material then at our disposal, that the Supreme Command could have done anything better as it saw the situation. The operation was fundamentally one of surprise, and to this extent we believe it was a complete success. Perhaps one or other exaggerated measure to insure its secrecy may have hampered the thoroughness of the preparations for the attack. But such things have to be taken for better or worse as solely in complete surprise did the chance of success lie. That this chance could not be exploited lay in the reasons cited.

The criticism, whether it had not been better to have employed our available reserves in the east rather than in the west, we submit to the judgment of history; whether it was a 'crime' to prolong the war by this attack, we leave to the Allied courts. Our own judgment is unchanged and independent of them.

Notes

1. B.H. Liddell Hart, *The German Generals Talk*, Quill, New York, 1948. Actually there was hope within Hitler's headquarters that the Meuse might be reached on the evening of the first day of the assault.

2. See also Generaloberst Alfred Jodl, 'Planning the Ardennes Offensive', ETHINT-50, and 'An Interview with Genobst. Alfred Jodl: Ardennes Offensive', ETHINT-51; and two documents by Herbert Büchs, 'An Interview with Maj. Herbert Büchs: The Ardennes Offensive', ETHINT-34, 1947, and 'The German Ardennes Offensive', A-977, n.d. Büchs was Luftwaffe aide to Jodl during the period. Extensive comparison between the 1940 and 1944 operations can be found in R-44, Magna Bauer, 'Comparison Between the Planning for the Germans' Ardennes Offensive in 1944 and Operation "Gelb" in 1940', April 1950, in OCMH files.

3. *OB West, KTB Anlage 50*, pp. 30–1, 1 November 1944.

4. This, and all other quotations in the section from Jodl, originate from ETHINT-50, *op. cit.*

5. See Richard Brett-Smith, *Hitler's Generals*, Osprey, London, 1976.

6. The source document is MS no. A-928 from the Historical Division of the U.S. Army, dated 12 July 1949. It is on file at the National Archives as part of Record Group 338.

6

The Ardennes Offensive: A Critique

BY GENERAL DER INFANTERIE GÜNTHER BLUMENTRITT

Introduction

It is perhaps the signature of a great battle, that it is fated to be re-fought in the minds of military strategists for years afterwards. The Ardennes Offensive is certainly no exception and the editor can immediately think of three studies in which this has been done.[1] However, perhaps few have as much authority to indulge in such retrospective generaling as Günther Blumentritt.

A professional career soldier, Blumentritt fought on both the western and eastern fronts in the First World War as a platoon, then company and finally battalion leader. After the war he served in a volunteer corps in Munich and Saxony with the 15th Infantry Regiment. Later, in 1920–2, he attended the war college in Stuttgart and Berlin. By 1938 he had been promoted to full colonel and served as an operations officer during the campaigns in Poland and France and then as Chief of Staff of the Fourth Army in Russia during 1941. He was promoted to Generalmajor in 1942 and became Chief of Staff of OB West from 1942–4, working closely with Generalfeldmarschal von Rundstedt. He later returned to a field command with the XII SS Corps in 1944–5, then the 25th Army in Holland and finally the 1st Fallschirmjäger Army until the cessation of hostilities in May 1945.

Commanding the XII SS Corps in December 1944, as part of the Fifteenth Army's Ardennes operations General Blumentritt was to make a thrust (codenamed Operation Spätlese) from his sector north of Aachen towards the Meuse on the third or fourth day of the attack. The plan was for his forces to converge with those of the Sixth Panzer Army around Maastricht. In the end, however, the idea was abandoned due to a pressing need for the assigned German forces in the Eifel. But as will be seen from the account that follows, Blumentritt obviously continued to ponder the German operation. His plan is an interesting commentary on the methods commonly employed by the German general staff.

Danny S. Parker

The Ardennes Offensive: A Critique

I. Introduction

In the annals of war the German Ardennes Offensive of December 1944 will lay claim to special interest. The following reflections grow out of my personal study of this action, based on the evidence now available. Political aspects are not considered, although they should normally be included in every military study. We know that by the end of 1944 the war had long since been lost and that therefore the Ardennes Offensive had no political purport. This study, then, will review only the purely military – strategic and tactical – problems without regard to the fact that the offensive was pointless.

II. The Basic Situation

All of us are cautious when discussing theories with which we cannot agree. It is nevertheless worthwhile to bear in mind the basic principles of breakthrough, for the Ardennes Offensive was intended to be a breakthrough battle. What does military history and experience tell us about breakthrough operations?

1. A tactical break-through piercing the enemy position is a prerequisite to a strategic breakthrough. Not until the enemy position is tactically overrun is it possible to begin strategic exploitation of the situation. It is therefore not enough to pick out, on a map, a beautiful and desirable strategic objective if the base selected for the tactical jump-off is disadvantageous; for then the attack may easily bog down during its initial stages.

2. The jump-off base must be so broad that during the breakthrough the enemy will be unable to converge the preponderance of his artillery fire upon the breakthrough front from both sides. Today, moreover, the power of the air weapon is critical. If the front is too narrow the enemy air force can fall upon the breakthrough area with devastating effect.

3. In every breakthrough the positions most exposed to danger are the flanks of the force attempting the breakthrough. These flanks become longer as the breakthrough wedge advances. The ever-lengthening flanks are sensitive points, because of their covering forces are in the open field, not dug in. Only an adversary with little initiative will fail to press hard against them.

4. Finally, the breakthrough wedge must not be too pointed, lest it be choked off from the sides. It must maintain a certain breadth.

During the 1940 Western Campaign and its great strategic breakthrough toward the Channel to the south, Army Group A's defensive flank along the Somme and Aisne became longer and longer. When the group reached the coast between Calais and Abbeville this flank was about 220 kilometers long.

The front facing south extended approximately along the line Trier–Luxembourg–Sedan–Laon–Amiens–Abbeville. General von Rundstedt, my commander in chief, daily expected a French counteroffensive from the south, toward Sedan, against the 'armpit' of this defensive front. But in the Ardennes Offensive of 1944 we had neither a large number of divisions, as in 1940, nor divisions of their quality and fighting power. Neither did we have the material. In addition we now faced Americans, highly mobile opponents sparked with initiative, who did not let much time pass before unleashing quick offensives against our flanks.[2] And whereas in 1940 we had control of the air, by 1944 it had passed to the Allies.

An action with extended flanks would be dangerous when facing a strong, even if not superior, enemy, because the spearhead is too pointed; the purely defensive cover of both flanks – without dug-in positions – can be penetrated very speedily by enemy counterattacks; and reserves are insufficient.

An action based approximately as in [map 3] would be better. Its spearhead has breadth. The defensive forces are so strong that they attack as well as defend, and thus they push the halting enemy back on his flanks, widen the breakthrough ahead in both directions, and progressively break up the enemy front. Strong reserves follow behind the spearhead and behind both covering wings.

One can easily say, 'Very well, but for such an action very strong forces are needed. You are therefore presenting only a theory.' To this the only answer is, 'Very large forces are indeed needed for a strategic breakthrough like this. If such forces are not or will not be available, such a breakthrough must not be attempted.'

III. Reflections on the Great German Offensive of March 1918

During the fourth year of World War I Germany's strength was declining rapidly. It was the military, not the political leadership that wanted to gather up all Germany's strength once more in a last effort to change the outcome of the war. At that time, however, the situation was far more favorable for us than in 1944. Germany had not been attacked from the air, had suffered no destruction from saturation bombing, and was operating its industries and railroads practically undisturbed. Peace had been concluded in the East, toward the end of 1917. Most of the German eastern divisions could therefore be transferred to the west. Germany's western army was undefeated, intact, and firmly established in strong, deep positions along a closed front. A single infantry division covered from six to either kilometers of frontage at most. The troops were much better and fresher than those of 1944, and by no means tired. Exceptionally strong artillery supported the front, with batteries echeloned in width and depth. Supplies, especially of ammunition, were plentiful. Really abundant quantities of artillery ammunition were available. Reinforced attack

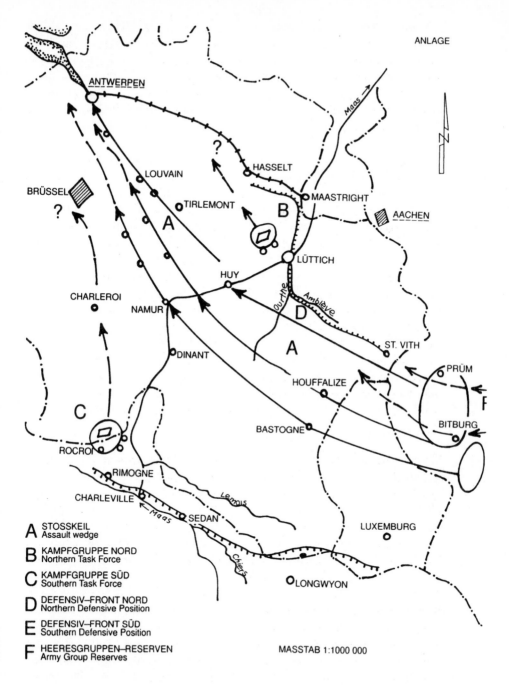

ANLAGE

ANTWERPEN

HASSELT

BRÜSSEL

LOUVAIN

TIRLEMONT

MAASTRIGHT

AACHEN

A

B

LÜTTICH

HUY

CHARLEROI

NAMUR

Ourthe

Amblève

D

A

ST. VITH

DINANT

PRÜM

HOUFFALIZE

F

C

BASTOGNE

BITBURG

ROCROI

RIMOGNE

Lemois

CHARLEVILLE

Maas

SEDAN

LUXEMBURG

Chiers

LONGWYON

A STOSSKEIL
Assault wedge

B KAMPFGRUPPE NORD
Northern Task Force

C KAMPFGRUPPE SÜD
Southern Task Force

D DEFENSIV–FRONT NORD
Northern Defensive Position

E DEFENSIV–FRONT SÜD
Southern Defensive Position

F HEERESGRUPPEN–RESERVEN
Army Group Reserves

MASSTAB 1:1000 000

Blumentritt's diagram of his revised offensive

divisions had been trained systematically for months behind the front. Many reserve divisions followed one another in two and three waves. The attack frontage of a reinforced attack division was only from 2.5 to 4 kilometers. (This was also true of the forces we had available in the 1940 western campaign.) Preparations had begun late in 1917. Everything had been planned in minute detail. Our generals of artillery were experienced in commanding large artillery contingents. The assault army in which I served as regimental adjutant of the 71st Infantry counted not hundreds but a thousand and more guns. This accomplishment on the part of the old Army was quite different from, and more inspiring than, that of the Army of 1944.

The breakthrough was accomplished on 18 March 1918, during very heavy fog. By afternoon my infantry regiment had penetrated to a depth of about twenty kilometers. The attack spent itself, however, a short distance before Amiens, its goal, and we could not make the final ten kilometers. Our forces were strong, but we lacked tanks. All action was by infantry divisions, either on foot or mounted. Counterpressure by French, English, Canadian, and other forces against our flanks and spearheads became stronger and stronger. We were therefore unsuccessful. In addition, we were now handicapped by a huge, curved front in which all our divisions were tied down, without fortifications.

So notwithstanding the greatly favorable situation built up in 1918, this powerful thrust miscarried at the last moment. All hope vanished with it. The disappointment was great. Yet, from the point of view of military history it is interesting to observe under how much more favorable conditions our offensive was launched in 1918 than in 1944.

IV. The Ardennes Offensive

Generals von Rundstedt and Model were far too experienced as officers not to recognize the impossibility of the Ardennes Offensive, for they had served as general staff officers during World War I, including the offensive of March, 1918.

In the fall of 1944 I was appointed deputy commander of the XII SS Corps. Field Marshal Model frequently discussed this offensive with me during his visits to my headquarters near Rückelhoven on the Roer, and he was anything but optimistic about it. Since the offensive had been ordered, he wanted only the so-called 'limited' solution at most; that is, a converging attack on Maastricht, and accordingly against the area around Aachen.

General von Rundstedt, with whom I corresponded, wanted no offensive under any conditions. He wanted to hold the current lines and to keep the panzer and infantry divisions assigned to the Ardennes Offensive as trained and rehabilitated reserves, behind the front, ready for counterattacks. He favored strategic defense.

But the reasons which induced Hitler to insist on the Ardennes Offensive were matters of life and death to him. He wanted to make one more gigantic effort to strengthen our people. Hitler revealed these reasons privately to Field Marshal von Rundstedt when he finally relieved him in March 1945. In no way, however, did the resources available to him match his design. Success was impossible because in almost every aspect the situation was different from that of March 1918.

With respect to the general situation two facts stood out. First, Germany was fighting everywhere in Europe. In the east fighting continued on broad fronts. We were fighting in the southeast and in Italy, while in Norway our forces were tied down and inactive. Secondly, the air war was destroying our industries and railways.

There were many unfavorable aspects in the military situation. The defeated German western army was holding its inadequate positions with difficulty. Many units had suffered heavy casualties; organization was improvised. Training, because of limited time, was insufficient. The troops were willing and aggressive, but tired. Manpower and, to an even greater extent, material were critically short. The offensive did not start during the mild weather that prevailed in France in March, but in December, in the midst of snow, ice, and thaw. In addition, it was started in the central chain of the Eifel Mountains, which have poor highways. Antwerp, the strategic objective, is farther from the Eifel Mountains than Amiens is from St. Quentin, the point of departure in 1918. In addition to fighting the British and French, this time we had to fight the Americans – our strongest and leading adversary. We were short of fuel, ammunition, construction troops, and engineers. There was neither time nor opportunity for training and rehabilitation. The Allied air force dominated the skies. The leadership of the Sixth Panzer Army did not measure up to requirements. We were badly short of reserves, and only inadequate forces were available to cover our flanks, worn-out infantry divisions capable only of defense. The highly-motorized enemy and an aggressive leadership on the American flank carried out effective countermeasures with surprising speed and quickly moved forces into position for a counteroffensive. For security reasons all preparations had to be made in great haste during the last few days before the beginning of the offensive.

Some factors were more favorable in 1944. In 1918 we had very weak political leadership; in 1944 we were under absolute and ruthless command which consolidated all available resources with an iron hand. In 1918 there were signs of revolution in Germany and also in the communications zone; in 1944 there were none. But these two favorable factors were only of qualified value, and they did not outweigh the many disadvantages of the situation.

Accordingly the arguments about the offensive went on for weeks, between Hitler on the one side and Generals von Rundstedt and Model on the other, and ended with the dictator's edict that the offensive would be launched.

V. My Own Plan for the Offensive

1. GENERAL

Although no longer a member of his staff, I shared the opinions of General von Rundstedt in many matters, including the defense of the western front on the best possible line, the abandonment of all energy-consuming frontal salients, the exploitation of terrain tactically favorable for defense, the organization of units and close liaison and tight sectional organization. We further agreed that the infantry reserves thus gained, should be moved to positions near the front for rest, training, and rehabilitation, and that all the troops and training units then stationed in the western military areas should be moved to the front not for pointless attack but for the construction of fortifications and for training close behind the front. I agreed with him also about the alerting of large armored and motorized units – not in the rear but in groups of from two to three tank units each, west of the Rhine and near the front, for rehabilitation and training as strategic reserves for mobile defense.

I am an exponent of thorough training. As early as 1914–1918 we Germans took advantage of every opportunity to train our troops over and over again. Surprisingly enough, the great Napoleon paid scant attention to the training of his army – and he suffered the consequences in 1813–1815. Hitler also did not think much of training. He used to say that a good fighter does not need much training, because soldierly 'spirit' would take its place. But on the basis of my experience, gathered from 1911 to 1945, my advice is, 'Train whenever there is opportunity to train!' And by training I mean, of course, war-oriented training for combat, not useless parade-ground drilling.

Soundly trained troops will not waver when outnumbered. They will handle and care for their weapons much better; they won't 'lose' so many small arms and instruments; they will shoot better; they will drive their vehicles more safely. They will have a feeling of superiority. In short, the right kind of training is half of a victory. In the old army of 1914 and in the Reichswehr of 1920–1933 we held these basic principles in esteem and achieved outstanding results. After 1935, in the new Army, the training period was too short because Hitler thought little of training, and during 1939–1945 there was little time. The consequences were dire.

In the following pages I will present what appears to me to be a more realistic approach to planning for the Ardennes Offensive. Let us assume the problem is before us.

2. CHOOSING THE OBJECTIVE

The smaller French channel ports are not adequate, while the supply routes from Cherbourg or Brest through France to the front are long. The rail network, severely damaged through bombing and sabotage before the invasion, is of little value. The Allies must probably depend on transportation by large-scale motor convoy. The lavishly equipped Anglo-American motorized armies require large quantities of fuel, ammunition, and supplies.

Antwerp, on the other hand, is an efficient port which, along with Rotterdam, played a leading part in Operation Seeloewe in 1940. The seizure of Antwerp would seriously interfere with Allied troop supply, especially that of the British Army Group. The Western Powers would lose a part that is not only large but close to the front. The thrust on Antwerp will endanger also the mouths of the Schelde, which are politically sensitive spots for England. Finally, the seizure of Antwerp will mean for us increased control of the Netherlands. Germany will again occupy an important part of the coast. Questions of prestige need not be considered. The British do not accord them as important a national role as we do.

Antwerp, then, may be regarded as the zone of operations. All other strategic objectives, such as those inside France, are too far away.

3. TACTICAL POINT OF DEPARTURE

On the map it looks feasible enough to penetrate the northern flank of the British Army from the Netherlands with all available forces and then to move on to Antwerp. Moreover, the distance from Holland to Antwerp is short. Even apart from tactical disadvantages, however, two important considerations speak against this course. The possibility of concentrating large masses of troops and moving them to southern Holland is problematical because of transportation difficulties. The completely open terrain of the Netherlands does not permit secrecy and is favorable for espionage activities. In addition, the nature of the terrain, the rivers, canals, and marshy meadows, make rapid advance even more difficult, especially for tanks. The enemy will have time to concentrate all his countermeasures on this watery terrain and prevent German penetration. Furthermore, German supply routes will be unfavorable because they will not lead directly from Germany circuitously. If the offensive miscarries, the German forces will be almost cut off from the Reich and will be left stranded at the river mouths, in a very serious plight. So although in theory, and on a map, an attack from the Netherlands against Antwerp appears to be feasible, it is unworkable in practice.

An attack route from the vicinity of Roermond would also involve a short distance to Antwerp; but it, too, leads across canals, soggy meadows, and open ground. Moreover, such an attack route is too narrow. After fanning out to the south, we will immediately come in contact with the British near Sittard and too close to the Aachen combat area where heavy American and British forces lie.

For the latter reasons the Aachen area also must be ruled out. We will meet powerful resistance there, for three battles have been fought in the area and strong enemy forces are concentrated there.

Instead, the attack will be launched from the Eifel Mountains, south of Aachen. Enemy forces are not strong here. The wooded mountainous area offers cover and permits surprise. In 1914 we detrained at St. Vith as the assembly point. In 1918 we marched back south of the Eifel Mountains. In 1940 our Fourth Army, under Army Group A, used the Eifel Mountains as a staging area. I am therefore well acquainted with the country.

However, for a December attack, with so few trained troops, this area presents as many difficult tactical, transportation, and supply problems. For example, because of fuel shortages the truck and tank drivers we had in the winter of 1944 had received far too little training in driving.

My selection would be the area immediately south of the Hohe Eifel mountains. Any areas farther south would be impracticable for a thrust against Antwerp.

The assembly areas will be located to the south, outside the highest summits (such as the Schwarzer Mann) of the German part of the rugged Eifels. Highways and roads south of the line Prüm–St. Vith–Huy (Maas) are better and more numerous than those to the north.

The first thrusts will be initiated in the north, not against the Hohe Venn but through more favorable terrain.

Cover in the north should be provided in the Ambleve sector, along the lower course of the Ourthe–Albert Canal; in the south, not at the Semois, but south of that river, from Chiers–Maas to Mezieres–Rimogne. Any defensive elongation northward will be out of the question because of the length of this southern flank. Any additional flank protection must be carried out offensively by mobile forces.

To these forces should be added one motorized group of two to three motorized and panzer divisions – first around Rocroi, then according to developments around Charleroi, and finally near Brussels.

4. OUTLINE OF ORGANIZATION

a. The Spearhead. The spearhead will be formed by one panzer army specifically, the Fifth Panzer Army, under General von Manteuffel. It will consist of three consecutive waves:

> First wave: Four panzer divisions.
> Second wave: Two panzer and two motorized infantry divisions.
> Third wave: Four elite infantry divisions

Its mission will be a breakthrough south of St. Vith–Houffalize–Bastogne, and subsequently a strategic thrust via Huy–Namur in the direction of central line Tirlemont–Louvain, against Antwerp.

b. Northern Task Force (Mobile). This will consist of one panzer corps headquarters with one panzer and two motorized infantry divisions.

Its mission will be to follow the right wing of the Fifth Panzer Army northward, echeloned to the rear. Attacking, it will take over mobile flank protection to the north. Therefore it will proceed from area to area, behind the northern wing of the Fifth Panzer Army, according to the situation.

c. **Southern Task Force (Mobile).** This will consist of one panzer corps headquarters with two panzer and two motorized infantry divisions.

Its mission will be to follow the left wing of the Fifth Panzer Army southward, echeloned to the rear – first around Rocroi, then Charleroi, and later Brussels, according to the situation – and to provide offensive protection for the Fifth Panzer Army's left flank.

d. **Defensive Cover.** This will be maintained through three corps, comprising seven infantry divisions, moving north along the Ambleve sector to the lower course of the Ourthe, approximately to Hasselt on the Albert Canal; and through four corps, with twelve infantry divisions and two motorized infantry divisions, moving in the south along a line Chiers–Maas–Mezieres–Rimogne.

e. **Reserves of Army Group B.** These will consist of one panzer corps headquarters with two panzer and one motorized infantry divisions. They will follow in such a manner as to enable them to turn off northward to the Aachen area.

f. **Command.** The entire offensive will be commanded by Army Group B (General Model), under the Commander in Chief West. The Commander in Chief West will make timely preparations to move additional forces from inactive fronts and to assemble them in such a manner that they will be rapidly available for offensive combat.

g. **Concentrations.** All available air forces will be concentrated, notwithstanding the temporary drastic weakening of the eastern, southeastern, and Italian fronts. All available artillery, panzer brigades, chemical units, and other support units will be concentrated behind the breakthrough area. All engineer (bridge and road-building) battalions and regiments from the zone of the interior will be concentrated.

5. CALCULATION OF PANZER FORCES

In the 1940 western campaign we learned that panzer and motorized divisions cannot be moved on a narrow front. Each division needs two or three usable roads; otherwise its mass cannot move effectively and, in addition, it will be too much exposed to air attack. Consequently divisions of these types have to be moved on a wide front and subsequently reassembled for combat. Our problem then was to move, in limited space, eighty-six divisions of Army Group A. The center of the Twelfth and Sixteenth Armies, consisting of seven panzer and two motorized infantry divisions, in three waves, were attached. Two armored divisions advanced with the Fourth Army on the right.

For the action planned now we shall need:

Headquarters:	1 Panzer Corps Headquarters	
Spearhead:	2 Pz Corps Hq with each 2 Pz Divs	– 4 Pz Divs
	2 Pz Corps Hq with each 2 Pz or 2 Inf Divs (motorized)	– 2 Inf Divs (motorized)
	2 Inf Corps Hq with each 2 Inf Divs	– 4 Inf Divs
Northern Group:	1 Pz Corps Hq with each 1 Pz & 2 Inf (motorized) Divs	– 1 Pz-Inf (motorized)
Southern Group:	2 Pz Corps Hq with each 2 Pz or 2 Inf (motorized) Divs	– 2 Pz Divs Inf (motorized)
Defensive Northern Cover:	3 Inf Corps Hq with a total of 7 Infantry Divs	
Defensive Southern Cover:	4 Inf Corps Hq with a total of 12 Infantry Divs	

Reserve:

Army Group B	1 Pz Corps Hq with 2 Pz and 1 Inf Div (motorized)	
	2 Inf Corps Hq with each 3–6 Inf Divs	

The above forces comprise 19 corps headquarters and 47 strong task forces. For defensive northern and southern cover through infantry divisions it is assumed that each division will have no more than a twelve kilometer frontage; only thus can it defend itself. Assault guns must be added for reinforcement.

VI. Concluding Comments

The foregoing reckoning of forces needed might easily be thought utopian, but several considerations should be borne in mind:

Our divisions were far below their authorized strength, both in personnel and material. If we had had, as in 1940, genuine, well-trained divisions at full strength, fewer units would have sufficed. But we did not have them. Two to three of the 1945 divisions would be required to make one full-strength division.

Antwerp, the strategic objective, was about 200 kilometers distant by air. Two very long flanks would have to be supported somehow, and one of them was in the highly active Aachen area. We faced a highly motorized enemy. The

Western Allies could speedily and aggressively draw divisions from other fronts and commit them in depth against our flanks.

The security of an ever longer supply route, through a densely populated and highly industrialized region, requires additional manpower.

Moreover, this action would lead to the final decision in the West. So if the manpower listed above could not be raised, logically the offensive should never have been launched. Unavailability of adequate supplies of fuel, ammunition, and so on constituted additional reasons for not starting it.

It has been the purpose of this study to show that amateurish wishful thinking is not enough. Numbers, precise calculations, and the requirements of the situation must be taken account of. During the second half of the war these scorned general staff matters were not regarded highly by the 'supreme war lord'. But sound military operations cannot be put into execution through 'fanatical faith' alone.

Notes

1. John Strawson, *The Battle for the Ardennes*, Charles Scribner's Sons, 1972; Peter Elstob, *Hitler's Last Offensive*, Macmillan and Company, 1971; Trevor N. Depuy, *Options of Command*, Hippocrene Books, 1984.
2. This point is arguable. Certainly Patton could be expected to respond in such a fashion, but other Allied commanders – particularly Montgomery – were less audacious.

Index

Other Greenhill books on World War II include:

RED STAR AGAINST THE SWASTIKA
The Story of a Soviet Pilot over the Eastern Front
Vasily B. Emelianenko
ISBN 1-85367-649-7

AT THE HEART OF THE REICH
The Secret Diary of Hitler's Army Adjutant
Major Gerhard Engel
ISBN 1-85367-655-1

TANK RIDER
Into the Reich with the Red Army
Evgeni Bessonov
ISBN 1-85367-671-3

BLOOD RED SNOW
The Memoirs of a German Soldier on the Eastern Front
Günter K. Koschorrek
ISBN 1-85367-639-X

LUFTWAFFE OVER AMERICA
The Secret Plans to Bomb the United States in World War II
Manfred Griehl
ISBN 1-86267-608-X

THE RECONSTRUCTION OF WARRIORS
Archibald McIndoe, the Royal Air Force and the Guinea Pig Club
E. R. Mayhew
ISBN 1-85367-610-1

Greenhill offers selected discounts and special offers on books ordered directly from us.
For more information on our books please visit www.greenhillbooks.com. You can also
write to us at Park House, 1 Russell Gardens, London, NW11 9NN, England.